Y0-BSL-001

Culture and Dignity

Nader, Laura,
Culture and dignity :
dialogues between the Mi
2013.
33305228176644
cu   08/14/13

Culture and Dignity
Dialogues between the Middle East and the West

Laura Nader

WILEY-BLACKWELL

A John Wiley & Sons, Ltd., Publication

This edition first published 2013
© 2013 John Wiley & Sons, Inc

Wiley-Blackwell is an imprint of John Wiley & Sons, formed by the merger of Wiley's global
Scientific, Technical and Medical business with Blackwell Publishing.

Registered Office
John Wiley & Sons, Ltd, The Atrium, Southern Gate, Chichester, West Sussex, PO19 8SQ, UK

Editorial Offices
350 Main Street, Malden, MA 02148-5020, USA
9600 Garsington Road, Oxford, OX4 2DQ, UK
The Atrium, Southern Gate, Chichester, West Sussex, PO19 8SQ, UK

For details of our global editorial offices, for customer services, and for information about
how to apply for permission to reuse the copyright material in this book please see our
website at www.wiley.com/wiley-blackwell.

The right of Laura Nader to be identified as the author of this work has been asserted
in accordance with the UK Copyright, Designs and Patents Act 1988.

All rights reserved. No part of this publication may be reproduced, stored in a retrieval
system, or transmitted, in any form or by any means, electronic, mechanical, photocopying,
recording or otherwise, except as permitted by the UK Copyright, Designs and Patents Act
1988, without the prior permission of the publisher.

Wiley also publishes its books in a variety of electronic formats. Some content that appears
in print may not be available in electronic books.

Designations used by companies to distinguish their products are often claimed as
trademarks. All brand names and product names used in this book are trade names, service
marks, trademarks or registered trademarks of their respective owners. The publisher is not
associated with any product or vendor mentioned in this book. This publication is designed
to provide accurate and authoritative information in regard to the subject matter covered.
It is sold on the understanding that the publisher is not engaged in rendering professional
services. If professional advice or other expert assistance is required, the services
of a competent professional should be sought.

Library of Congress Cataloging-in-Publication Data

Nader, Laura, author.
Culture and dignity : dialogues between the Middle East and the West / Laura Nader.
     pages   cm
   Includes index.
   ISBN 978-1-118-31900-0 (cloth) – 978-1-118-31901-7 (pbk.)
1. Civilization, Arab.   2. Ethnology–Arab countries.   3. Arabs–Ethnic identity.
4. East and West.   5. Western countries–Relations–Arab countries.   6. Arab countries–
Relations–Western countries.   I. Title.
   DS36.8.N324 2013
   303.48′25601821–dc23
                                                  2012015890
A catalogue record for this book is available from the British Library.

Cover image: Detail of mosaic, Umayyad mosque, Damascus, Syria, AD 705-715.
© DEA / C. SAPPA / Getty Images.
Cover design by Cyan Design.

Set in 10.5/13.5pt Palatino by SPi Publisher Services, Pondicherry, India
Printed in Singapore by Ho Printing Singapore Pte Ltd

1   2013

In recognition of Donald Cole and Soraya Altorki,
ethnographers of the Arab East par excellence

In memory of Anthony Shadid,
journalist with an ethnographer's eye

Contents

Contents

Acknowledgments

It is not possible to acknowledge all the colleagues, students, family members and others who over the years have enriched my understanding of a world without boundaries, the context for my work. First and foremost were the invitations from the American University of Cairo to deliver lectures that form the core of this book. Soraya Altorki, Donald Cole, Nicholas Hopkins, and Nawal Hassan were warm and generous hosts. The people of Egypt whom I met outside of the university community – the Minister of Energy, as well as Mrs. Mubarak who had studied anthropology at the American University, journalist Gamal Nkruma and others – enriched and broadened my understandings of political happenings in modern-day Egypt.

Support for preparing the manuscript came from the Middle East Center at UC Berkeley and the Committee on Research. The Rothko Chapel hosted my talk on human rights, which was later welcomed for publication in Brazil. My colleague Rik Pinxton of Cultural Dynamics saw my article "Orientalism, Occidentalism, and the Concept of Women" (reissued as Chapter 4 of this book) through to publication in Belgium, a piece that was then considered "controversial" in the United States. Mohammed Hamdouni Alami provided the photograph of the Great Umayyad Mosque in Damascus, taken in 2007, for the cover of this book.

With regard to Chapter 4, I have also to thank Andrée Sursock, Seteney Shami, JoAnn Martin, and Saddeka Arebi, who were of enormous help in searching out and arguing with me about the comparative materials. The need to explore the idea of occidentalism first crystallized in a conversation with Professor Ashraf Ghani of Johns Hopkins University. Comments from Drs Mondher Kilani, Soheir Morsy, and Guita Debert were most helpful, as were the audiences at UC Davis, UC Berkeley, the University of Auckland, Harvard University, Claremont Colleges and other academic institutions where I presented those ideas.

Over the years at Berkeley I was primary thesis advisor to more than a dozen students working in the Middle East: Golamareza Fazel (Iran), Donald Cole, Soraya Altorki, and Saddeka Arebi (Saudi Arabia), John Rothenberger, Cathy Witty, and Osama Doumani (Lebanon), Seteney Shami (Jordan), June Starr and Ayfer Bartu (Turkey), Andrée Sursock (France), Rochelle Shain (Israel), Nell Gabian (Syria), Monica Eppinger (Ukraine) – I learned from every one of them.

My colleagues Elizabeth Colson, Roberto Gonzalez, and Salwa Mikdadi, as well as former students Saddeka Arebi, Seteney Shami, Ayfer Bartu, Andrée Sursock, Maysunn Succarie, Alberto Sanchez, Roberto Gonzalez, Monica Eppinger, Chris Hebdon, and others read, researched, and provided critical comments on this book. Claire Nader, Ralph Nader, and Tarek Milleron were the toughest of critics, forcing simplicity of style and intolerant of facile generalizations. Suzanne Calpestri and David MacFarland of the Mary and George Foster Library were ready to help in myriad ways. Gratitude is due to Shirley Taylor, Tarek Milleron, and Stephen Curtis for editorial help, to Kathleen Van Sickle for patience in typing and retyping various versions, to Chris Hebdon for hanging in to the end, to Rosalie Robertson my editor, always supportive and cheerful, and to the three anonymous readers for their encouraging comments.

Preface

Cultural anthropologists set their discipline apart a century and a half ago by formalizing a historical tradition of extensive observation carried out among peoples foreign to the observer either by distinct customs and practices or by more subtle differences. Through painstaking examination of another culture might come an ability to grasp and understand its honor and dignity – that is, to understand how shared culture may serve a people and how that culture may continue to do so, or where it may begin to break down thereby exposing its members to indignities small and large. But cultures are never as simple as bounded units changing in isolation. The anthropologist must also trace elements that fire across cultural groups and across geographic areas. In the same vein, the observer runs the risk of using imaginary yardsticks, often idealized from his or her own cultural group, to make comparisons unmoored from the real and very messy world. My work related to the Arab East – through field observations, decades of teaching, lecturing, and writing – covers half a century. During this time, I have observed a level of bounded thinking, sometimes referred to as ethnocentrism, that has only grown more rigid as the United States and Europe have become more embroiled in the Arab World and tried to define the East relative to their own societies. This book is my attempt to provide an anthropological sorting out, a sense of what the quality of our observations means for our own culture and dignity, and how thorough an exploration of culture might have to be in order to reach an understanding of another human dignity in relation to ours.

An overview of my work relevant to the Arab East includes fieldwork in south Lebanon in 1961, fieldwork in Morocco in 1980, teaching the introduction to the Middle East at the University of California at Berkeley for over two decades, book reviews and articles, invited public lectures and media invitations on a broad range of subjects often stimulated by the immediate need to counteract public ignorance among my fellow Americans. The subjects covered the status of women, violence, terrorism, Islamic law, and, more generally, Middle Eastern culture – the geography, language, and place of kinship, settled agriculturalists, nomads, and more. Invitations to deliver the distinguished lecture series at the American University in Cairo brought me to Egypt in early 1985 and again in 2005. Those lectures are the heart of this book. The subject matter for my first four lectures included power and the uses of ideologies as a stabilizing technique, the seeds of nonviolence in the Middle East despite stereotypes of a violent East, energy policies and expert knowledges operating in the United States, and a final lecture on covert control, or what I later called "controlling processes." These lectures all illustrated a framework for analyzing the dynamics of power in the contemporary world, a world long recognized as anything but peaceful by Arabs and Americans. In other words, the lectures cut across themes that could be construed as of interest only to Arabs or the United States. Instead, they were themes of general interest that might enlighten our thinking about culture and dignity.

The lecture on energy grew out of my 1980 National Academy of Sciences report, published as *Energy Choices in a Democratic Society*, and a series of articles that followed on the politics of energy in the United States. The essay on power, the subject of my undergraduate course Controlling Processes, was later revised and published in *Current Anthropology* in 1997 as "Controlling Processes: Tracing the Dynamic Components of Power." Thoughts on the seeds of nonviolence in the Arab East are embedded in several publications, for example, "Naturalizing Difference and Models of Co-existence" in R. Pinxten's and E. Preckler's 2006 book *Racism in Metropolitan Areas of Europe.* Because nonviolence and its opposite are so continual in today's Arab East, I combined this topic with an earlier unpublished paper delivered in Saudi Arabia at a conference on social control under crowd conditions as in pilgrimages or the Haj.

Reactions to the 1985 Cairo lectures were anything but passive. The audience participation indicated immediate curiosity about the seeds of nonviolence in the Arab world, while the lecture on energy brought about an unexpected public confrontation between two Egyptians, an antinuclear scientist and a nuclear engineer who disagreed about nuclear power and the politics of energy. These experiences taught me a good deal about the workings of control in contemporary intellectual culture at an American university abroad, where the graduates – desirous of being modern and more developed – know more about the contemporary globalized world than about their own history and traditions. In this they are not today so different from American universities at home.

Between 1985 and 2005 a new century was born: much of consequence had transpired between the United States and the Arab and Islamic world, principally imperial wars: the first Gulf War of President George H. W. Bush in 1990–1991, the war in Afghanistan in 2001, the American invasion of Iraq in 2003, and ongoing US occupations. A few observers saw these events as a rupture, but many others viewed them as part of a story of holy wars, originating in the Crusades (1096–1270), if not before. Historians also remind us, in turn, that the then governor of Tangiers, Tariq ibn Ziyad, invaded Spain in April 711 AD and that the Ottoman Turks bombarded Vienna in 1529.

The 2005 Cairo lectures had an urgent tone. In 1985 I had emphasized connections between shadow or hidden power and the uses of ideology. By 2005 there was little shadow and many rank exhibitions of immense raw power. We had witnessed Saddam Hussein's invasion of Kuwait and the US Gulf War of 1990–1991 followed by the 9/11 attacks on the United States and the Shock and Awe of the invasion of Iraq in 2003. A flood of stereotypes of Arabs and Muslims as either al Qaeda terrorists, insurgents, or suicide bombers flooded the West, while in the East the West was seen as imperialist, lawless, and hypocritical.

Few were, or are, examining the history of nonviolence among Arabs, the subject of my lecture in Cairo. Few in the Western main-stream media were writing about the absence of nuclear warheads in Arab countries and their now long-time threatening presence in Israel. Few reporting on the Israeli destructions in Lebanon in the summer of 2006 noted that the government of Lebanon had no effec-tive military defense. The silences were and still are deafening. Once again, Western hegemonic ideas describe Islamic ideals as emotional and irrational and incompatible with Western democratic ideas. They highlight descriptions of Arab dictatorships (often supported by the United States) rather than report on the Arab masses whose opinion is often more democratic than views we find in some cosmopolitan centers elsewhere in the world. The 2005 lectures were an attempt to put imperialism – both cultural and military – on the front burner, the consequences of which might not be obvious to most concerned peo-ple and which commonly went unnoticed by social scientists.

The 2005 lecture topics involve a critical examination of two con-cepts often taken for granted. One concerns the use of area concepts (whether geographic or linguistic) used in organizing knowledge; the other takes up the importance of comparison, implicit as well as explicit comparison. Relevant to critiques of both area concepts and comparison is the question of who sponsors scholarship – government, the military, or philanthropists – because the interests of sponsors often constrain professional scholarship. Geographic organization of cultures may be a convenient form of ordering for some purposes, as in a focus on the "cultural areas" of Europe or the Middle East, although, at the same time, we know the falsity of such ordering because the borders of geographic areas are not clean, not precise. Area categories ignore the effects on Europe or the Middle East of contact with each other and with Asia and Africa. We know that culture spreads by continuous contact of peoples whether by population movements or through other channels. Thus, the idea of a *bounded* area, geographic or not, is illusory, and it often causes bad histories, bad ethnography, and bad politics. But such area concerns are deeply embedded, even in the marketing of books such as this one, a book that aims to cross borders in our thinking. The Middle East, while structured for the convenience of museums or the military, is a deceptive concept. Just as the concept of bounded communities is no longer acceptable for any scientific ethnography, so area specialties cut against acceptable and competent academic endeavors. The long-term alternative to area studies is world history, or some model that takes into account interconnections – opening us to the possibilities of a human history devoid of present parochialisms. But, for the moment, crossing area borders may give an untidy impression. We realize that air pollution stemming from New York State does not stop at the Canadian border, so why should culture? Why do we think there are clean boundaries between Islamic science and European science? Similarly, although colonial powers drew the borders of the Arab world, separating "Lebanon" from "Syria," the Levant as a whole remains a cultural composite of extensively overlapping traditions.

Comparison is central for better understanding of mutual involvement over time by traveling back in time to gain perspective on how cultural difference and misunderstandings may be perceived. It is true that our earliest ethnographers may be found among the ancient voyagers. As early as the 1600s Arab travelers to Europe were varied and numerous: merchants, ambassadors, missionaries, spies, and more. They traveled to Spain, France, England, Italy, Holland, Russia, and wrote about the lands of the Christians, as is documented in Nabil Matar's 2003 book *In the Land of the Christians: Arabic Travel Writing in the Seventeenth Century*. Seventeenth-century travelers came to Europe from highly developed civilizations, quite the equal of those of the Europeans they met. They wrote down just about everything – what they observed, measured, or learned from interviews and their evaluations of their experiences. The time period and events of the moment of travel were reflected in what they reported. Because few Arab travel accounts have been translated, Western scholars often explain the paucity as due to lack of curiosity, yet some of this Arab travel writing, though not exactly ethnographic, is in some ways startlingly modern.

With the development of the discipline of anthropology and ethnography in the nineteenth and twentieth centuries, writers became more self-conscious about writing about others and in the process developed some rules, some overt guidance, and some unstated recipes one might say, that limited the manner of writing. Free of disciplinary authority, these early Arab travel writers were not governed by such mannerisms as the need for scientific objectivity. Well ahead of their time, their subjective accounts now resonate with our own.

In 1963 anthropologist Jules Henry published *Culture against Man*, a book he called "a passionate ethnography." His opening statement gives an idea of his views on the United States: "This book is about contemporary American culture – its economic structure and values, and the relation of these to national character, parent–child relations, teenage problems and concerns, the schools, and to the emotional breakdown, old age and war" (Henry, 1963: 3). Henry describes a materialistic society that may be dying emotionally. He reports on the state of nursing homes, elementary and secondary schools, advertising, and families suffering from psychosis. He mentions big and small businesses, and uses the words "giant corporations" sparingly. But his focus is on American culture writ large as if undifferentiated from corporate culture. Henry's work was an admirable attempt to define a culture "dying emotionally," yet his conceptual frame was that of national character. Similarly motivated but more broad-gauged work today, stemming from historical research in the 1970s, has zeroed in on the central institution of our time – corporate capitalism and the second industrial revolution. In the social sciences we have made some headway on Jules Henry's courageous start.

At the present, parental powerlessness is felt worldwide, but such powerlessness needs to be better contextualized. In 2005 I called for an expansion of what Christopher Lasch did in *Haven in a Heartless World* (1977) for contemporary families in the United States. Lasch argued that the family has been supplanted by the state and the helping professions in the context of consumer capitalism, that the much criticized nuclear family did provide a haven in a heartless world, and that the family's demise has left children exposed to a heartless world without a haven. I suggested there should be follow-up in the Arab world, in Korea, China, Peru, and over the planet more generally, to understand the effects on families of the externalities of corporate capitalism in this runaway world. Multiple experiences shaped my understanding: the raising of children, service on the Carnegie Council on Children, having grandchildren and, of course, thousands of students, many of whom were the young and socially abandoned. The question being, who is raising our American children? And what are the domino effects that connect the United States and the Arab world?

Business is implicated, but business is not one big thing. Corporate capitalism, as distinct from penny capitalism or regional capitalism, has wide-ranging consequences, whether these impacts be in the form of captive legislatures and agencies, digitalized technologies, factory farming, or the life experience of our children. If we are to make business socially responsive, assessments of consequences must reach the business world where CEOs might worry about business ethics.

It has been repeated *ad nauseam* that the history of the last 200 years has been one of the dominant influence of Euro–American expansion worldwide. Plentiful histories have been written about the foundations of American and European dominance and the assertion that no peoples have escaped from European influences – economic, religious, commercial, and more. Euro–American expansion has also been called a *success* by some, presumably because of an assumed exceptionalism inherent in this dominant expansion. But there is something incomplete in this spectacle of European and now American worldwide power. The words we use are defining. Expansion is a word that makes people think it has been one-way. The idea that there are boundaries between Europe and the rest is sharpened with the advent of nation-states, when in fact there have been no cultural boundaries that have held out against new ideas and cultural patterns across the board. There is selection. The essential point is that when one reads expansion *in reverse* we see a human history characterized by continuous chains of borrowings and interaction. Look at the spread of yoga, or sushi, or acupuncture from East to West in the twentieth century! The same historians may even speak about the expansion of other empires – Chinese, Islamic, Mongol, Indian, Aztec, or Inca – and in all these tales we hear narratives of rivalries, as, for example, between western or eastern Christianity and Islam. But stories about dominance, difference, conquest, contempt, and rivalries, could also be about barbarisms, fusions, borrowings, or co-existence, as Janet Abu-Lughod writes in her 1989 volume *Before European Hegemony: The World System AD 1250–1350*, a world characterized by multiple hegemonies. Amin Maalouf recounts in his 1984 history of *The Crusades through Arab Eyes* a different story than the one that appears in Western accounts. Or, in the case of the contemporary account of expansion, Victoria de Grazia's 2005 book *An Irresistible Empire: America's Advance through Twentieth–Century Europe*, is about how American industries sought to change European culture in less than one century so as to make Europeans more amenable to purchasing American products. The local and diverse gave way to mass standards of consumption in Europe and globally.

While one can hardly challenge the main thread of stories of expansion and influence, parochial descriptions distort our knowledge because they omit the exchanges, the spread of ideas. Agriculture has had an enormous expansionist success radiating out from the Tigris–Euphrates valley through Europe, East Asia, South Asia, and Africa. Technologies and discoveries, such as the uses of metals and building materials (well documented by archeologists) have spread throughout the world, independently of nation-states. Along with Christianity, Arab Islam has had an enormous expansionist success, with the largest number of believers today residing outside the Arab world and is, if the numbers are correct, currently the fastest-growing religion worldwide. All these developments have made and remade both Europe and the West.

These frames of reference inform my scholarship. They outline a twenty-first-century anthropology that focuses on the connections between peoples – what we are like, what you are like, what we have in common, our humanity, our survival, our children, our fears, our solutions to everyday problems – in the context of unequal power and corruption. The planet is a rich place because of diversity in plants and animals and culture. The diversity has enriched the human trajectory. Erecting bounded categories only makes social transformation in an old globalized world one of disconnectedness – a mirage. As many are beginning to recognize, notions of exceptionalism and hubris pose both short and long-run obstacles to survival for our shrinking planet. The Arab Spring and the Occupy movements are indications of a widespread rethinking of future directions.

References

Abu-Lughod, Janet (1989) *Before European Hegemony: The World System AD 1250–1350*. New York: Oxford University Press.

De Grazia, Victoria (2005) *An Irresistible Empire: America's Advance through Twentieth–Century Europe*. Cambridge, MA: Belknap Press.

Henry, Jules (1963) *Culture against Man*. New York: Random House.

Lasch, Christopher (1977) *Haven in a Heartless World: The Family Besieged*. New York: Basic Books.

Maalouf, Amin (1984) *The Crusades through Arab Eyes*. New York: Schocken Books.

Matar, Nabil (2003) *In the Land of the Christians: Arabic Travel Writing in the Seventeenth Century*. New York: Routledge.

Pinxten, R. and E. Preckler (eds) (2006) *Racism in Metropolitan Areas*. New York: Berghahn Publishers.

1

Introduction

The work in this book has an origin that long predates my formal training. Blessed as a first-generation American, I am the daughter of parents who came from the Levant, known by some as Syria, just as or just after Greater Syria was partitioned into Lebanon and Syria and as plans for partitioning Palestine were being invented. To be raised bilingual and bicultural offered a wonderful opportunity to be privy to multiple dialogues about the meanings of Arab and American cultures. Being culturally in-between sensitized me to the sufferings of peoples I might not have heard about in American schools. I grew up knowing about the starving Armenians, the British and French colonizers, the corruption of both Arab and Western leaders, and poetic expression in both English and Arabic. I learned about the yearnings of the Pan-Arabists to model their dream after the United States of America, along with their idealization of Americans, and especially their idealization of American democracy. The indignities faced by colonized and diasporic communities, the

Culture and Dignity: Dialogues between the Middle East and the West,
First Edition. Laura Nader.
© 2013 John Wiley & Sons, Inc. Published 2013 by John Wiley & Sons, Inc.

famous Arab leaders, especially the poets gunned down by colonialists who labeled them insurgents rather than recognizing them as nationalists, the divide and conquer tactics that pitted one religious sect against another – all of this, along with discussion of how to build a sewer system in our New England mill town, was daily conversation at our dinner table, and it instilled in me the importance of mutual respect in everyday life.

Later on, as an anthropologist, I learned about the lives of the disempowered everywhere: disinherited Native Americans, Pacific Islanders, and Africans, those dwelling in urban ghettos, Latin American peasants, inhabitants of refugee camps in the Middle East and elsewhere. My first dissertation fieldwork began in 1957, to study a region yet unexplored by anthropologists, the Rincon Zapotec of the Sierra Juarez in Oaxaca, Mexico. It was an initiation rite of the first order (Nader, 1970). In 1961, after completion of my dissertation, I set out from Berkeley to conduct summer fieldwork in Lebanon and begin preliminary research on Muslim village law. As I explored the question of how to find a good village, as I balanced whether it should be Shia or Sunni Muslim, I was deluged with warnings from Lebanese families and friends: I would get sick; if I worked in a Muslim village, there was no telling what they would do to me; I would not be safe, some told me, because Muslims "don't like Christians"; others said that this was nonsense and the difference in perspective coincided with individuals' political positions. The many and lengthy conversations and admonitions about the dangers of doing fieldwork did not stop. What seemed like acute paranoia was undoubtedly related to the 1958 crisis. Certainly, the fact that I was based in the Christian town of Zahle explained the reluctance of any driver to take me into the villages.

My interest in knowing to what degree formal Muslim law, a law that originated in urban centers, dominates village procedures for conflict settlement augmented my determination to work in a Muslim village. It took about two weeks of talking to people and taxiing to various villages to realize that one of the most successful ways of locating an appropriate village in Lebanon was through politicians or lawyer-politicians rather than through Lebanese social scientists, who did not concentrate their interest in the rural areas of Lebanon. Whereas in Oaxaca the link between the cosmopolitan centers and predominantly Zapotec villages was easily made through a development commission, in Lebanon the link was best made through politicians, who often function like ward heelers and come to know the villages in the process of electioneering. Politicians and lawyer-politicians were the most knowledgeable people, for my purposes at any rate, in dealing with the village scene in Lebanon. Since I had the unusual advantage of having family living in the country, a politician who was a relative finally helped me locate a Shia Muslim village, among the poorest in Lebanon. Unlike Mexico, where my frustrations were mainly connected with the place of actual fieldwork, my difficulties in Lebanon stemmed from my inability to locate a university student who might have been able to assist me; from the ostensibly trivial problem of finding a car and driver; from the fact that there was a lawyers' strike and no court cases could be heard; and, in particular, from the problem of gathering any sort of "objective" information on a good village in which to work. Nevertheless, I found a location.

The village, Libaya, is located near Marjayoun: it was not to be found on most maps of Lebanon because the road had only recently been completed. Its population was about 1400. There were eight large families in town and some 400 houses – a homogeneous population of Shia Muslims. I collected mainly cases of *wasta* making, or the search for remedies in conflicts. Unlike the Zapotec, the Shias readily admitted to conflict and were not at all hesitant to talk about the subject. Consequently, I felt that I was moving with the stream here rather than against it. I became fascinated with the number and class of person with whom a Shia Muslim villager comes into contact when he is in trouble and has to look for a *wasta*. To whom he goes depends in part on the kind of trouble he is in and on the man who is to judge him in the civil court. Among the political elite of Lebanon there is a most incredible knowledge of interpersonal relations, so that it's a rather knowledgeable game to play – to see who can get the best connections the fastest.

Unlike my first experience among the Zapotec, the personal, managerial, and intellectual problems of fieldwork were minimal once I got to the village. I did not have the hindrance of working with a bilingual interpreter, for I could understand spoken Arabic. The fear of being rejected because of my religion proved an empty one. I was at first asked by the family with whom I stayed about my religion; when I said I was a Christian, they advised me to say that I was Muslim if asked by the other villagers. I answered simply that I was not in the habit of lying. When that story circulated about the village, I was treated with an openness and respect that I had not expected.

I was investigating a subject matter that these Shias themselves liked to talk about, and thus probably accomplished as much in those few weeks as I would have in Zapotec country in about four months. The ubiquitous use of proverbs in the Near East is often helpful in guiding the anthropologist to choose what values are important: "As you treat me so I will treat you" (usually referring to bad treatment); "As you are dressed so you are judged"; "You have to be flexible in life, or else you break"; "If you wish to move a man, send a woman after him, and if you wish to move a woman send a child after her"; "In my presence, face like a mirror, in my absence, like a shoe." If I were advising young anthropologists preparing for fieldwork in the Arab Middle East, I would strongly recommend that they become familiar with and memorize a selection of proverbs.

The negative aspects of being a woman fieldworker in the Middle East had been highly exaggerated. In my short time in the village I felt no threats; none, certainly, associated with my being a woman. Perhaps this was because I lived with a family instead of separately; this residence made me a "daughter" of the village. Or perhaps it was because the Arabs have a category of woman called "sister of men" – a natural role that a woman anthropologist could walk into, should she wish. I did exactly that.

In recent years anthropologists have focused on the empowered – government officials, the military, scientists, colonizers, marketing companies, surgeons, and others – connecting the lives of the empowered with the peasants, workers in factories, the poor, the imprisoned, and the soldiers, and thereby clarifying how hierarchy embodies dominance. How the powerful rule is often remembered for centuries – or forgotten and then remembered again.

The Armenians who fled their genocide after World War I were taken in by Lebanon, among other countries, and remember being treated with dignity. The Ottoman Turks in Lebanon featured in well-known stories – humiliations and the taking of Lebanese harvests and other incidents are still remembered by Lebanese 90 years later. Yet today the Turkish government rallies behind the humanitarian attempts to free Gaza. That will be remembered by people of the area. Recalling the experience in Germany after World War I, anthropologists urged General MacArthur in Japan not to repeat the mistakes that were made then: "Do not humiliate the enemy," they cautioned. Human beings, probably everywhere, are sensitive to experiences of culture and dignity and easily note absences of respect. Minor humiliations add up over time, if not softened by mutual respect at other times.

Indignities

Recently I was in Brussels attending a conference on state management of diversity in Europe, a euphemism for how to deal with Islam in Europe. Distinguished lawyers representing most of the countries that make up the European Union were present. In addition, there were a few scholars from North Africa and the Levant and a handful of anthropologists of different nationalities. The subjects discussed mostly dealt with Islamic migrants from North Africa, the Middle East, and places as far away as Pakistan. This was a professional conference about a heated topic that had a passive agenda of flattening diversity. This intolerance of diversity erupted in emotional outbursts. The Spanish jurist heatedly declared, "We will not tolerate polygyny in Spain!" The anthropologist thinks, "Now what was that about?" Countries that tolerate mistresses (as with France's Mitterrand), multiple lovers (as with Italy's Berlusconi), and whatever else will not tolerate legal Islamic plural marriage that comes with legal responsibilities? Numbers are of immediate interest. What percentage of Muslim migrants have more than one wife anyway, or could even afford the responsibilities that come with legal plural marriage? How many of these jurists understand the original logic behind the Muslim allowance of plural marriage in the context of a higher ratio of women to men because of male deaths in war, feuds, and the like? In 1961 the Shia village where I worked in south Lebanon had one case of plural marriage in a population of 1400 people – a man who had married his brother's wife after his brother died. The more the discussions continued, the more the conference began to function like a degradation ceremony for the visiting jurists from Lebanon and North Africa, as well as a reminder of European exceptionalism.

A Dutch anthropologist who had studied cultural diversity and state management issues in Peru broke down at the end of her talk, noting that a Dutch-born boy of Moroccan parents had no future in Holland. A heated discussion ensued when she was challenged by a Dutch legal colleague who had less sympathy for migrants, though they provided cheap labor in his country. I recall that the minister of immigration in Holland in the 1990s developed certain requirements for visa petitioners that included forcing them to view what some regarded as pornographic footage to determine whether they could blend in and be part of Dutch culture. The conference organizer was disturbed that I, as the chair, had allowed an argument about the pros and cons of managing migration to Holland. It was expected to be a harmonious conference. Conference discussions continued to be emotion-ridden when the question of the Muslim scarf in the context of French law surfaced. I have never understood the threat presented by covering the head with the "Muslim scarf." I recalled my field trip to Morocco in the summer of 1980. While staying in a tourist hotel with my two daughters, I watched French women in next-to-nude bathing suits, some even topless, who were totally oblivious of the incongruity of their mode of dresslessness, made the more blatant since it was in the middle of Ramadan. I heard waiters commenting in Arabic, but there were apparently no headlines in Moroccan newspapers about French nudity nor any laws in existence forbidding it, although undoubtedly opinions were registered about shame.

It slowly occurred to me that this beautifully organized and well-funded Brussels conference, concerned with important issues regarding culture and immigration, had an unspoken agenda – the "civilizing process." It *was*, in fact, a degradation ceremony, the unstated idea being that immigrants should act like Europeans in order to be civilized. When I asked a Moroccan participant why he did not object, he responded, "Laura, we have to modernize." The other Arab guests were also polite participants, although not so acquiescent when speaking privately. However, when asked, an Egyptian judge quietly noted that legal education in Egypt entailed knowing about different legal cultures – village law, Bedouin law, customary law, religious law, along with state law – a tolerance for difference, or the importance of cultural context critical for deciding a case. His comment seemed to fall on deaf ears; it was anathema in the context of European state notions of the "rule of law." Representative legal professionals from countries who were insistent that one could not be European and Muslim at the same time were mainly from Spain, France, Belgium, Holland, and Denmark; the German and Italian jurists may have learned something from World War II about intolerance, bigotry, and genocide. Mind you, these conversations were among cosmopolitan participants, cosmopolitans who should have been sensitive to ideas of exceptionalism and the meaning of "the civilizing process." Ironically, these conversations were being conducted while Abu Ghraib and Guantanamo and bombings were ongoing background examples of humiliations emanating from the "civilized."

In the United States there was public outrage at the Abu Ghraib torture revelations at surface level, but little change followed the initial outrage. For the world-famous Colombian painter Botero it went further. He was traveling to Paris when the Abu Ghraib news appeared on the front page of the *New York Times*, and he could not shake himself of the horror in the photographs. He spent months in his Paris studio painting the horrors of Abu Ghraib. Upon completion, he could not find a single art museum in the United States that would exhibit these works, and when, finally, the University of California at Berkeley accepted his offer, the exhibit was held not in the art museum but in the main library and solely thanks to the advocacy of two faculty members, two donors, and a head librarian who understood the importance of public viewing of torture horrors in order to diminish future possibilities for torture. Is there something about Euro–American ideas of culture and dignity that might help us understand such occurrences, or does it go beyond cultural niceties, being explicable only by ideas of cultural superiority? Is the refusal of a Botero exhibit about American denial, or about censorship, or both? Thousands of viewers came to see the exhibit and some reported that the paintings were even more powerful than the photos since Americans have become inured to violence in photographs. Perhaps the powers that be in the university art museum may have rationalized their refusal to exhibit by simply arguing that Botero's paintings were not real art.

In 2011 the United Nations authorized a no-fly zone in Libya, the American-led war in Afghanistan was in a quagmire, and the Iraq war seemed to be moving in the direction of permanent occupation with American bases and private mercenary security forces replacing American military. Meanwhile the drumbeat for war in Iran once again unleashed the old and tired words about Islamic peoples, myth-laden generalizations that have endured for centuries.

When in 2007 Columbia University president Lee C. Bollinger was faced with a speaking invitation to President Ahmadinejad of Iran (an invitation not of his making but for which he would have to account), he introduced him in a manner that violated the most basic expectations of civility – let alone dignity. Indeed, the introduction was not an introduction but an attack, a ten-minute verbal assault (Cooper, 2007). Bollinger called Ahmadinejad a petty and cruel dictator and, by the time he finished, could be seen as having contributed one more drumbeat for war in Iran. Bollinger missed an opportunity as an educator, let alone as a host. He failed to recognize injustice. He might have provided some history of the reasons Iran has had grievances against the United States, at least since the removal of Mohammad Mossadegh in 1953. He might have

8

mentioned the Iran–Contra affair and the taking of American hostages. He might have mentioned the American support of Iraq's war on Iran that cost the country over a million lives, and the constant threats and embargos by the United States government, often with the urgings of the Israel lobby, as any scholar, much less the president of a great university, should have done. It was political bigotry of the worst sort justified by Bollinger's support of free speech. Although Bollinger publicly upbraided the President of Iran, he had not upbraided his own warring President Bush in the name of freedom of speech and open debate. Ahmadinejad's response to these verbal attacks was dignified: in his country guests are customarily not treated in such an insulting manner by the host. "In Iran, tradition requires when we invite a person to be a speaker, we actually respect our students enough to allow them to make their own judgment, and don't think it necessary, before the speech is given even, to come in with a series of complaints to provide vaccination to the students and faculty" (Cooper, 2007). The civilized and the barbarian as public presentations.

The same year brought Islamo-Fascism Awareness Week, a nationwide event designated by the US conservative Freedom Center to "break through the barrier of politically correct doublespeak that prevails on American campuses, if you want to help our brave troops, who are fighting the Islamo-Fascists abroad" (Dowd, 2007). As part of the events, one quoted commentator upbraided feminists and Democrats: "The fact of Islamo-Fascism is indisputable; I find it tedious to detail the savagery of the enemy. . . . I want to kill them." The same commentator also said that Jews need to be "perfected" and that the country would be better off if everyone were Christian. There were also campus protests about the "demonization of Muslims," and one peace activist called the term Islamo-Fascism "beyond demagoguery," an agenda of "anti-Islamic hatred," while still others fanned the flames about the "gathering storm" of Islamic extremism and the ideology that motivates terrorist groups. By 2010 President Barack Obama was being criticized in the mainstream press for not conforming linguistically, for not using terms like Islamic Terrorism.

The year 2010 brought yet another American public outcry in the controversy over the construction of an Islamic center and mosque near Ground Zero. Echoes of "freedom of religion" were shouted down by politicians and by those who lost relatives in the 9/11 attacks (in which Muslim lives were also lost). Republican ideologues like Newt Gingrich and Sarah Palin contributed to the bigotry. Even the academy was not immune. Harvard instructor Marty Peretz implied that Muslims were unworthy of the privileges of the First Amendment (Peretz, 2010). Hate words reappeared in populist and patriotic rhetoric. For some ground zero is a symbol of liberty – Islamophobia. Support for the proposed Islamic Center came from the Mayor of New York. In a speech on Governor's Island Michael Bloomberg called the project "as important a test of separation of church and state as any we may see in our lifetime, and it is critically important that we get it right" (Bloomberg, 2010) – a volatile situation once again indicating the ambivalence of Americans regarding our cherished ideals of diversity, tolerance, and equality.

The origin of the term Islamo-Facism is still unclear, but the most general meaning refers to the use of the faith of Islam as a cover for totalitarian ideology (Ali *et al.*, 2011). But wasn't it President George W. Bush who said in 2006 that "this nation is at war with Islamo-fascists who will use any means to destroy those of us who love freedom" (Bush, 2006)? Mind you, overthrow and imperialist invasions are in practice part of American foreign policy. Hatred is often driven by fear, real or imagined. Although this introduction is not the place to argue for any specific history of the different positions, I will mention that at least one history of the Middle East, by Robert Fisk (2007), concludes by observing that, given what the Middle East has endured from European and now Euro–American imperialism, it is astonishing just how much patience the Muslim world has had with the West.

In an astute commentary on "Colonialism East and West," Elizabeth and Robert Fernea (1997: 88–95) note differences: "Given our pride in our own colonial past, it is often difficult to relate to the Arab world's reactions to *their* colonial past: rage, shame, anger, the kinds of anger that erupted into protest marches, peasant revolts, strikes, terrorism, and guerilla warfare, which culminated in conflicts far more violent than the struggle of colonial America in its revolution against the British." The colonialists – Ottoman, French, British, Italian, and Spanish – spoke different languages and, with the exception of the Ottomans, practiced a different religion. European missionary schools devalued indigenous institutions – law, religion, art, agriculture, and irrigation. Arabic became a liability for the upwardly mobile. Protest against the European presence continued after independence, only to increase with the American support of Israel and then wars in Afghanistan and Iraq in which religious tradition, pride in the arts and literature, and historical traditions became hallmarks in the search for dignity.

Thus, public hatred is often driven by fear, real or imagined, along with ideas of military and commercial dominance as engines of imperial wars. Some knowledge of the culture of the Other might help reduce the fear factor. Even a public intellectual like Barbara Ehrenreich in her critique of the Islamo-Fascists does not understand enough about Islamic women to be able to make her case about the status of women in Islamic countries, and writes as if no differences existed from one locale to another. Nor do such public intellectuals know much about the real place of women in the United States: just compare domestic violence statistics in the Arab world and the United States and differences evaporate. If 26% of Syrian husbands beat their wives (according to Amnesty International), it turns out that about 26% of American husbands also beat their partners (Tjaden and Thoennes, 2000).

It has always interested me that comparisons with Others made by Americans, right or left, work with the assumption that conditions for American women are across the board better than in, say, the Arab world or almost anywhere else! In "Orientalism, Occidentalism, and the Control of Women" (Nader, 1989) I tried to clarify the assertions and counterassertions that have been part of East–West discourses at least since 1095 when Pope Urban II called for the crusades to liberate Jerusalem. Misleading cultural comparisons divert attention from the processes of control in both the East and West. I wanted to identify how images of women in other societies can be prejudicial to women in one's own society. "If you think it's bad here just look at women *there*" can work in both directions. In the 1970s the US women's movement wanted at least equal pay, equal opportunity, and federally mandated maternity leave. We still don't have equal pay, although there may have been some improvement. And the same goes for the rest of our agenda. We did get sex, bare breasts, fake breasts, and bare legs along with the high rape rates in college dormitories. Or, put another way, women opted for personal and sexual rights rather than political, legal, or economic rights. Yet they are confident that American women are freer in every respect than women elsewhere, even though counterparts in the Middle East have had maternity leave and equal pay by law that I have never enjoyed.

"Orientalism, Occidentalism, and the Control of Women" extended Edward Said's observation that the Muslim world exists "for" the West to include the notion that the West also exists "for" the Islamic world, as comparing rape rates, absence of family supports, and more can serve to suggest that Islamic women are better off than their Western sisters. The contrast either way serves as an important means to restrict and control women's resistance. My conclusion noted that gender ideologies emerge not only as a product of internal debate over inequalities between males and females in a particular society, but also out of debates between the prevailing ideologies of different societies and different geographic areas. In other words, gender arrangements are complex wholes that can be related to macro-level distinctions between "us and them," often used to justify the horrors of war. The Afghan burqa was used by some pundits as "evidence" of the need to liberate Afghanistan in the buildup to the 2001 invasion.

In the West both government and business corporations have created and consolidated a cultural hegemony and disseminated it to their own population and to the Arab world by means of media, educational, and developmental organizations. During the George W. Bush era it was referred to as "winning the hearts and minds" of

Muslims, in the main through educational and job training efforts (Succarie, 2008). In the East, nationalisms and religious forces have been powerful agents in the construction of gender hegemony as well as in counterhegemonic efforts, often making things worse for women, as is presently happening in Saudi Arabia. By not discussing hegemonic systems as part of an interactive process between world areas, the Islamic world (as if it were one thing) is discriminated against by a more technologically dominant West because of the way we construct and stereotype their treatment of women. At the same time, a self-satisfied, incremental view of progress is perpetuated in the West that serves to divert attention from the varied mechanisms of gender control in Western Europe and the United States. Simply put, images of women in other societies reinforce norms of subordination of women in one's own society, as in "if you think it's bad here, look at the rape rate in the United States," or "look at honor killings in Syria" (compare those figures with husbands in the United States who kill their wives!). To understand the processes at work in acts of subordination, think about the assertions of commentators on Islamo-Fascism within this broader context. Both East and West are patriarchal; in both societies women are subordinated in different ways, irrespective of recent feminist waves that boast of progress. Some things get better (as in more women professors, doctors, lawyers) while qualitative issues may worsen (as in the high rate of rape for women on college campuses). According to Huang (2011: 1366), in 1974 the salary disparity between female and male scientists was as great as 32%, with women earning less. In 2009, statistical data from the Equal Opportunity Employment Commission showed that different minority groups and women in industry face a glass ceiling. In 2010 the UN World Bank gender index placed the United States eighty-fourth compared to other countries in a number of indices. At the recent 2011 Montreal American Anthropology meetings, Mondher Kilani (2011) pointed out that "whether uncovered in Tunisia or veiled in Bahrain, they [women] are present in the demonstrations that have shaken the Arab states from the Atlantic to the Gulf." He concluded: "All the Arab myths are in the process of collapsing."

Naturalizing Difference and the Great Transformation

One has only to think about the racial-problems and racial-solutions industries to recognize that difference is a major preoccupation of our time. Do-gooders have deeply invested in difference as a "problem." Such insistence forces me to ask, why? And when are differences not so overpowering? Some attribute the problem of difference to the development of nation-states, which also creates boundaries often defined by difference (see Norbert Elias, 1978). Along the same lines, others argue that while movement (migration) is nothing new, migration is considered a problem because of national obsessions with homogeneity; Latinos, for example, many of whom speak Spanish primarily not English, are now the largest ethnic group in California. What happens on the ground when nationals and migrants come together, especially given that European and American nationalists see themselves as by nature "tolerant"? Being "tolerant" implies that the problems must be of the migrants' making. People don't understand that industrial CEOs want these migrants because they provide cheap labor and, unlike European and US unionized workers, are comparatively acquiescent and are often hired to do work the Europeans or Americans do not want to do (*New York Times*, September 21, 2010). Furthermore, Mexican and Central Americans often migrate as the result of despotic conditions in their countries, often reinforced by US military and foreign policy.

With all this talk about difference, similarities between locals and migrants are not noticed. Both Europeans and foreigners in Europe share consumerist habits: they probably drink Coca-Cola or other soft drinks, use computers, watch TV, and follow corporate fashions. And we fail to recall that cosmopolitan centers like London have been multicultural since medieval times, before the arrival of Islam, and so have Paris, Madrid, Brussels, and other similar cities (Asad, 1990; especially notes 4–7).

Contrast Europe's contemporary problems with Islamic immigrants with the situation in the Islamic East where co-existence has been constructed as an ideal, probably to ensure the survival of the whole (Nader, 2006). Medieval Spain is touted as a time and place where Muslims, Christians, and Jews traded and made extraordinary contributions to art and literature (Menocal, 2002; Lowney, 2005). Today, the Damascus market is divided into three sections: Muslim, Jewish, and Christian. In such contexts segregation works. Ethnic communities can and do co-exist. In the cities they co-existed in quarters designated by sect although not by class. The Ottoman Empire, which lasted 500 years, had minority self-government in areas of law and religion.

When relations get difficult, it is important to recognize the assets that migrants and intermingling bring, in aesthetic taste, culinary traditions, ideas in science and engineering. And it is useful to remember that centuries of reverse-immigration, from Europe to the Middle East, were inspired by wars, trade, colonialism, or pilgrim traffic. North African seaports had heterogeneous populations owing to the immigration of hundreds of thousands of Frenchmen, Spaniards, Italians, and Greeks. In 1907, 25% of the population of Alexandria and 28% of Port Said were foreign citizens (Issawi, 1969: 108–109). Difference became the norm.

And so it is that most Europeans, because their knowledge of such history is limited, have no sense of payback when North Africans move to European cities. And most immigrants, because *their* knowledge is limited, do not understand that Europeans themselves are coping with the European Union's erasure of differences within Europe itself. But European CEOs understand full well that "normative blindness" is congenial for the bottom line. The two conversations about difference and cultural intermingling should be intertwined in a world filled with social engineering of a neo-liberal sort – the movement of capital investment and labor across national boundaries and the concomitant creation of a pool of high youth unemployment and other issues that go beyond cultural or religious differences.

My essays are also an attempt to put on the front burner what might not be obvious, as in institutions created by corporate capitalism and religious fundamentalisms, both in the United States and in the Arab world, where children and their parents often need-lessly suffer ruptures. We call them generation gaps. Increasingly and urgently the challenge is to assess the externalities, the hidden consequences, social and environmental, of corporate capitalism, to understand what is happening in this runaway world. Corporate capitalism is a different kind of capitalism with critical and immediate impact for the intimate environment of families and children. President Wilson saw it as diplomacy. There is no such agreement by the people impacted. Assessments are needed that will reach the business world. Making connections is not just for the victims of untrammeled actions; it is for leaders as well, leaders who may rec-ognize that they suffer from a "normative blindness" that promotes a culture of denial of the social consequences of business practices.

There is too much hubris in the world; we need more eye-to-eye exchange. Sometimes it is useful to travel back in time, to look in the mirror and see ourselves. Chapter 2 of this book, "From Rifa' ah al-Tahtawi to Edward Said: Lessons in Culture and Dignity," indi-cates what can be learned by adopting a frame of mutual respect. In this regard, both al-Tahtawi and Said, and other Arab thinkers that I include, reject a lens embedded in hierarchy, in positional superiority. After all, they might say, we are all humans, are we not? Both Said and al-Tahtawi rejected the idea that *ipso facto* one culture or people is better than another. Their writings challenge what was (and still is) so prevalent: nineteenth-century European unilineal evolution that ordered a staging of humankind into savagery, barbarism, and civilization, with European culture as the top stage – "civilization." No people or culture has a monopoly on wisdom, or greed, or vio-lence, although at any one point in time some people have more *might* than others. But might need not be equated with superior or worldly possibilities, even though the uses of power, especially power backed by technological destructions, could determine the possibilities for human survival.

Although understanding difference is important, when difference is not set within overall frames of humanness it can be fraught with prejudice of a dangerous kind. Raphael Patai's book *The Arab Mind* (1973) is of particular contemporary relevance because it eschews variation in favor of homogenous and stereotypic generalizations – a means of dehumanizing Arabs. Thus, devoid of nuance and subtlety, stereotypes about privacy and sexuality were used by the American military in training soldiers for combat in Iraq as well as for torture inside the walls of prisons like Abu Ghraib. Anthropologists like Patai have no monopoly on what amounts to racist generalizations (Gonzalez, 2010: 95–96). Historians adopt the same postures. Even *Arabs*, by Anthony Nutting (1963), as good a history as it may be, ends the story with tired words like "emotional," "irrational," and "violent," to characterize a whole people – though it notes that the Irish have similar characteristics! It does not help that Nutting adds that both peoples have charm, a sense of humor, and so forth. In times of crises like wars those adjectives go by the wayside. He could have mentioned, for example, that both Arabs and the Irish have endured colonialism, or that the Europeans managed a 100-year war from 1336 to 1453, perennially fighting with one another.

Comparison, Ethnography, and History

Comparison can become not only an overt method but also an issue to face, depending on whether it is explicit or implicit (Nader, 1994). In Chapter 2 a famous traveler is front and center of my presentation. He is Rifa' ah al-Tahtawi, a man of the first third of the nineteenth century, whose stay in Paris followed Napoleon's conquest of Egypt in the late eighteenth and early nineteenth centuries. The French stay in Egypt was short, but of enormous consequence for Egyptians, who were vulnerable to the greater military might of the Europeans. As the writings of al-Tahtawi and others of his period indicate, these travelers wrote about Europe in the same way they wrote about their own and nearby Asian peoples, open to the wonders before them. The purpose of their writings was to describe what they were observing. Al-Tahtawi's book was first published in 1836, but did not appear in an English translation until 2004.

Al-Tahtawi, who spent over half a decade living with the French in Paris, tries to differentiate one French habit from another; he comments on French cleanliness or the handling of dead bodies, noting the variations within the culture while also comparing the French with the Egyptians. But what he speaks to is the human condition – going beyond the French and the Egyptians as people to note their military organization and their developments in science as well. If we say that Arabs don't treat their women well, there is the implicit assumption that we do better, an assumption that is being challenged by both Western and Eastern scholars (Nader, 1989). If we say that Arabs are violent people, we seem to deny that the military-industrial complex in the United States is an indicator of violence, not nonviolence. For simple comparison we should encourage the "as compared to what?" question: emotional and irrational as compared with whom, or what, and under what conditions? For mutual understanding the implicit should be made explicit. This activist stance is not the same as relativism, nor does it imply that anything goes. It is simply giving recognition to the eye that sees.

Chapter 3 focuses on "Ethnography as Theory: On the Roots of Controversy in Anthropology," on the unstated rules both of the profession and of the wider society that sponsors anthropological research. The ethnographic examples selected are those of creative ethnographic works that violate one or another of the unstated consensuses that define the role of ethnography sometimes with consequences for the ethnographer. "Work within the system," "don't step on any toes," or "don't ask a novel question," and consideration of "historical realities" are among the issues oppressing those concerned with scientific creativity. What happens when unstated rules are stated and how does this affect the knowledge the readers have of other peoples? In such cases representations become a political act whether or not this is the intention of the writer. "Ethnography as Theory" addresses ethnography as something beyond "just description" or "my opinion," an anthropological method that makes possible a more or less adequate understanding of others and ourselves. Its influence on the sister disciplines of sociology, history, geography, and psychology has been stunning. Ethnography is a special kind of description and embedded in ethnographic activity is a theory of description itself. Ethnographies are composed of more than one method, which is partly the point – we observe, we count, we analyze documents, we embed in history, we compare anything that is useful in composing an adequate theory of how the lives of people work. There has been an enormous lack of understanding about what ethnography is, both in and out of anthropology, which has been partly responsible for its fashionable and widespread acceptance not only in the social sciences but also in literary exploration. But a weekend retreat or just hanging out is not what makes an adequate ethnography, nor is just a qualitative bias, nor is counting or analyzing law cases, nor is embedding with the military. Eclecticism is at the core of ethnographic method and theory, but so is an ethical stance – to do no harm. This is the crucial question now. Do we tell it like it is, warts and all, with respect to both the weak and the empowered? To do no harm has been the basis for debate on the role of anthropologists embedded with the US military in Iraq and Afghanistan (Gonzalez, 2009). Who does the anthropologist represent? In addition, there is the unstated consensus on what constitutes harm.

In anthropology there have been varieties of ethnographies, and no one country or political context has produced a single model. Studying a people at war is not the same as studying people in a peaceful paradise or in some kind of transitional situation. However, in this period of self-consciousness, or what some call navel-gazing anthropology, there has been some recognition of the influence of colonialisms on the anthropologist in the past and present, and the same would be true for neocolonialism or neoliberalism as well. The eye that sees has come under scrutiny – the self-trained ethnographer, the museum-trained or academic university-trained ethnographer, and the British, Brazilian, American, or Japanese ethnographer all reflect a combination of personal, societal, cultural, and theoretical influences. Ethnographic theory enters in precisely because, although ethnography is the central product of the work of the sociocultural anthropologists, anthropologists themselves realize how tainted any of our methodologies will be and so the results are subject to criticism. This is a recognition that knowledge is not neutral – neither in anthropology, nor in physics or biology. Humility must be our contribution to a world filled with hubris. Our knowledge, precious as it might be, is always partial, never complete.

Chapter 4, on the control of women in Islamic and Western patriarchies, introduces the uses that can be made of a comparative consciousness (Nader, 1994), an awareness of asking "as compared to what?" thereby expanding the context of an assertion such as "Islamic women are badly treated." The motivating question "as compared to what?" led to "Orientalism, Occidentalism and the Control of Women," which, incidentally, was accepted immediately for publication in Belgium after agonizing critiques in the United States. It was my best effort to explain the controlling dynamics of power over women in two patriarchal societies. For those who thought Islamic patriarchy's control of women was total, the Arab Spring of 2011 challenged the usual stereotypes of downtrodden Islamic women better than any academic work has been able to do.

In Chapter 5, I address "Corporate Fundamentalism: Constructing Childhood in America and Elsewhere," for what can be of greater concern to all of us than the fate of our children? I highlight connections that are seemingly hidden from public view, both in the United States, where corporate consumerist movements had their origins, and in the Arab world. In an earlier piece (Nader, 1980), I reiterated what others have said: parents who in earlier periods had both power over and responsibility for their children find themselves in a double bind with increasing responsibility and decreasing power to raise their own children.

Chapter 6, "Culture and the Seeds of Nonviolence in the Middle East," examines the various violent contexts that erupted and the techniques of conflict resolution that were invented over centuries prior to Western colonialism to deal with differences within and between religious sects, between tribes and settled people, or between urban and rural peoples. The dynamics are such that facile stereotyping is of little help in governing secular or religious states, or in predicting behavior.

Chapter 7, "Normative Blindness and Unresolved Human Rights Issues: The Hypocrisy of Our Age," and Chapter 8, "Breaking the

Silence: Politics and Professional Autonomy," on unresolved human rights issues, highlight the need for less ethnocentric dimensions in the definition of what human rights violations are. Like Chapter 4 on "Orientalism, Occidentalism, and the Control of Women," "Normative Blindness and Unresolved Human Rights Issues" was first published in Brazil owing to the very ethnocentric problem described in it. The "Breaking the Silence" chapter, written a week before the 2003 invasion of Iraq, is a continuation of the theme: what is an acceptable anthropology in a world of dominant hegemonies in the academy? The final chapter, "Lessons," indicates what might be learned about the Arab world and ourselves from applying the methods of comparison, ethnography, and history in the craft of anthropology, and suggests strategies for new directions.

References

Ali, Wajahat, Eli Clifton, Matthew Duss, Lee Fang, Scott Keyes, and Faiz Shakir (2011) *Fear Inc.: The Roots of the Islamophobia Network in America*. Center for American Progress. Available at http://www.american progress.org/issues/2011/08/pdf/islamophobia.pdf (accessed April 16, 2012).

Asad, Talal (1990) Multiculturalism and British Identity in the Wake of the Rushdie Affair. *Politics and Society*, 18, no. 4, 455–480.

Bloomberg, Michael (2010) Mike Bloomberg on the Proposed Mosque in Lower Manhattan. *Mikebloomberg.com*, August 4. Available at http://www.mikebloomberg.com/index.cfm?objectid=38F02174-C29C-7CA2-FB24F2BA115AF739 (accessed April 20, 2012).

Bush, George W. (2006) President Bush Discusses Terror Plot Upon Arrival in Wisconsin. Office of the Press Secretary, August 10. Available at http://georgewbush-whitehouse.archives.gov/news/releases/2006/08/20060810-3.html (accessed April 3, 2012).

Cooper, Helene (2007) Ahmadinejad, at Columbia, Parries and Puzzles. *New York Times*, September 25. Available at http://www.nytimes.com/2007/09/25/world/middleeast/25iran.html (accessed April 20, 2012).

Dowd, Maureen (2007) Rudy Roughs Up Arabs. *New York Times*, October 17. Available at http://query.nytimes.com/gst/fullpage.html?res=9C06E1DB1E3CF934A25753C1A9619C8B63 (accessed April 20, 2012).

Elias, Norbert (1978) *The Civilizing Process: Sociogenetic and Psychogenetic Investigations*. New York: Urizen Books.

Elliott, Justin (2010) Michael Bloomberg Delivers Stirring Defense of Mosque. *Salon*, August 3. Available at http://www.salon.com/2010/08/03/mayor_bloomberg_on_mosque/ (accessed April 3, 2012).

Fernea, Elizabeth Warnock and Robert A. Fernea (1997) *The Arab World: Forty Years of Change*. New York: Doubleday.

Fisk, Robert (2007) *The Great War for Civilization: The Conquest of the Middle East*. New York: Vintage.

Gonzalez, Roberto (2009) *American Counterinsurgency: Human Science and the Human Terrain*. Chicago: Prickly Paradigm Press.

Gonzalez, Roberto (2010) *Militarizing Culture – Essays on the Warfare State*. Walnut Creek, CA: Left Coast Press.

Huang, Alice S. (2011) Passions. Presidential Address. *Science*, 334, pp. 1362–1366.

Issawi, Charles (1969) *An Economic History of the Middle East and North Africa*. New York: Columbia University Press.

Kilani, Mondher (2011) What Are "Arab Revolutions" Expressions Of? An Anthropological Perspective. Unpublished paper presented at the American Anthropological Association Annual Meeting, Montreal, November 19, 2011.

Lowney, Christopher (2005) *A Vanished World: Medieval Spain's Golden Age of Enlightenment*. New York: Free Press.

Mattei, Ugo and Laura Nader (2008) *Plunder: When the Rule of Law Is Illegal*. Malden, MA: Blackwell.

Menocal, Maria Rosa (2002) *The Ornament of the World: How Muslims, Jews, and Christians Created a Culture of Tolerance in Medieval Spain*. Boston: Little, Brown and Company.

Nader, Laura (1969) Up the Anthropologist: Perspectives Gained from Studying Up. In *Reinventing Anthropology*. Dell Hymes, ed. New York: Pantheon Books, pp. 284–311.

Nader, Laura (1970) From Anguish to Exultation in Mexico and Lebanon. In *Women in the Field*, P. Golde, ed. Chicago: Aldine Press, pp. 96–116.

Nader, Laura (1980) The Vertical Slice: Hierarchies and Children. In *Hierarchy and Society: Anthropological Perspectives on Bureaucracy*, G. Britan and R. Cohen, eds. Philadelphia: ISHI Press, pp. 31–43

Nader, Laura (1989) Orientalism, Occidentalism, and the Control of Women. *Cultural Dynamics*, 2, no. 3, pp. 323–355.

Nader, Laura (1994) Comparative Consciousness. In *Assessing Cultural Anthropology*, Bob Borofsky, ed. New York: McGraw Hill, pp. 84–96.

Nader, Laura (2006) Naturalizing Difference and Models of Co-Existence: Concluding Comments. In *Racism in Metropolitan Areas*, R. Pinxten and E. Preckler, eds. New York: Berghahn Publishers, pp. 173–182.

Nutting, Anthony (1963) *The Arabs*. New York: Penguin.

Patai, Raphael (1973) *The Arab Mind*. New York: Scribner.

Peretz, Martin (2010) The New York Times Laments "A Sadly Wary Misunderstanding of Muslim-Americans." But Really Is It "Sadly Wary" Or A "Misunderstanding" At All? *The New Republic*, September 4. Available at http://www.tnr.com/blog/77475/the-new-york-times-laments-sadly-wary-misunderstanding-muslim-americans-really-it-sadly-w (accessed 20 April, 2012).

Succarie, Mayssun (2008) Winning Hearts and Minds: Education, Culture, and Control. Ph.D. dissertation, University of California, Berkeley.

Tjaden, Patricia and Nancy Thoennes (2000) *Extent, Nature, and Consequences of Intimate Partner Violence: Findings from the National Violence against Women Survey*. US Department of Justice, NCJ 181867. Available at http://www.ojp.usdoj.gov/nij/pubs-sum/181867.htm (accessed April, 3 2012).

Further Reading

Aziz, Barbara Nimri (2007) *Swimming up the Tigris: Real Life Encounters with Iraq*. Gainesville: University of Florida Press.

Doukas, Dimitra (2003) *Worked Over: The Corporate Sabotage of an American Community*. Ithaca, NY: Cornell University Press.

Khan, Mirza Abu Taleb (2008 [1814]) *The Travels of Mirza Abu Taleb Khan*. Ontario, Canada: Broadview Press.

Nader, Laura (1996) *Naked Science: Anthropological Inquiry into Boundaries, Power, and Knowledge*. New York: Routledge.

Nader, Laura (1997) The Phantom Factor: Impact of the Cold War on Anthropology. In *The Cold War and the University*. Noam Chomsky, ed. New York: New Press, pp. 107–146.

Nader, Laura (2005) Law and the Theory of Lack. *Hastings International and Comparative Law Review*, 28, no. 2, pp. 191–204.

Price, David (2008) *Anthropological Intelligence: The Deployment and Neglect of American Anthropology in the Second World War*. Durham: Duke University Press.

2

From Rifa' ah al-Tahtawi to Edward Said

Lessons in Culture and Dignity

[E]thnocentricity [is] one of the great perverters of truth ... [T]o see and appraise humanity ... free from the distortions of ethnocentricity ... , to contribute to such an attitude is perhaps the largest contribution of anthropology.

(A. L. Kroeber, 1948: 849)

Introduction

It is important, especially today, to realize that Western practices of empire are not a given, that is, they are not inevitable. There are other possibilities (past, present, future), new cultural forms can and do emerge, and there are multiple fruitful ways of conceiving global relationships. Ethnocentrism is a disease, one that breeds hubris no matter what its origin. A knowledge of the history of our whole world can help reduce its pernicious consequences. Such a world history enriches

Culture and Dignity: Dialogues between the Middle East and the West,
First Edition. Laura Nader.
© 2013 John Wiley & Sons, Inc. Published 2013 by John Wiley & Sons, Inc.

Western-centric stories and disrupts ideologically laden European or Euro–American narratives of exceptionalism that travel imperialist routes far beyond Euro–American borders and often undermine democratic possibilities. There was a time *When Asia Was the World* (Gordon, 2008). This essay is part of a larger work on how travelers from other extant civilizations – Japanese, Chinese, Indian, and Islamic (ethnocentric or not) – see "the West," whatever that word might mean to the missionaries, diplomats, scholars, traders, and adversaries who came into first-hand contact with Europe or the New World.

Although I wish to concentrate on commentaries from the nineteenth and twentieth centuries, with specific reference to the work of Rifa' ah al-Tahtawi and Edward Said, it is useful to know that others came before. Humans have been walking the earth since the beginning, commenting on and borrowing from other peoples whom they encountered. But it is only recently that we have written records of these travels. Hiuen-Tsiang (Beal, 1911), a Chinese Buddhist missionary, went west in the seventh century AD. For him the West was India. He wrote his impressions of Indian civilization, detailing their caste system, their forms of politeness, how they cultivated their land, the climate. In Hiuen-Tsiang's day, the predominant faith of India was Buddhism, which since has been replaced by the reemergence of Hinduism, with large minorities adopting Islam, Sikhism, and Janism. Times change; religions migrate.

In 922 AD Ibn Fadlan, an Arab missionary (Frye, 2005), was sent by his caliph from Baghdad to Russia to convert the Tartars to Islam. On his way up the Volga he encountered the spectacle of Scandinavian traders in beads and shoes, beads then being the currency found from the Congo to China. Ibn Fadlan's is the earliest known text describing in detail the Scandinavian traders who traveled to the Volga to reap the rich overland trade from India and China. The missionary for Islam met merchants whose manners and customs deeply impressed him. They were barbarians in need of civilizing – he thought they were the dirtiest creatures of God in body and in manner. Of particular importance to Ibn Fadlan were washing, bathing, and sexual practices.

A similar critique appears in the records of Arab historians and chroniclers contemporary with the Crusades in the eleventh, twelfth,

25

and thirteenth centuries, as narrated by Amin Maalouf (1984). These Arab historians saw the confrontation as one between the culturally superior East and the technologically superior "wild beasts" of the West, who knew mainly blood, torture, and cannibalism. The rationality of the Arab who values books is compared with the Westerner who destroys books. Similar deprecatory observations are made in relation to judicial behavior, the lack of tolerance for diversity, and the religious fanaticism attributed to Crusaders. But it was in medicine that the gap between East and West was greatest. The methods used by the Franj (the name that Arabs gave to the Europeans) in medical practices failed to heal – in contrast to those of Arab physicians.

As works by Janet Abu-Lughod (1989) and Edward Said (1978) indicate, when we sample such chronicles in both directions, the Arab historians on Westerners and the reverse, we find a mirrored image of the East in the West. Each thinks of the other as barbarian. Such contrasts between the civilized and the technologically superior continue today in the heart of other civilizations from Gibraltar to Japan. Indeed, as a Moroccan governor recently said to me while arguing about the wisdom of placing French light-water nuclear reactors in Morocco, "The French, they have no culture, they have no civilization, but they do have technology." Superior technology does not necessarily equal civilization. Some observers paint the world in black and white. Others suffer illusions of cultural invulnerability. In Saudi Arabia the motto was modernization without Westernization. When questioned as to the validity of such beliefs, a Saudi pointed to the Safeway sign in Jeddah which read "Open 24 hours, except during prayer." As we shall see, Rifa' ah al-Tahtawi was more subtle in his observations of European, primarily French, culture.

Rifa' ah al-Tahtawi and France

The Napoleonic invasion of Egypt in 1798 inaugurated a new set of encounters between the Arabs and the West, the first of such intensity since the Crusades, and what Sandra Naddaf (1986) refers to as the enforced contact of two radically different cultures. It was an all too abbreviated piece by Naddaf, "Mirrored Images: Rafa'ah al-Tahtawi and the West," that first introduced me to the work of al-Tahtawi. Napoleon's venture resulted in a new European interest in the Orient, producing the great age of European scholarship known as orientalism. At about the same time, the Orient began to rediscover the West, although English translations of written accounts of early travelers to Europe are few and far between (Matar, 2003). Nabil Matar describes these early writings as belonging to a tradition. The travelers were not harbingers of an Islamic imperialism compelled to make changes. "Rather they wrote empirical accounts about Europe with the same precision that many of their co-religionists used to describe their journeys within the world of Islam. . . . They went with an open mind and a clean slate" (Matar, 2003: xxxii); "The writers viewed travel as a means of experiencing rather than denouncing that which was culturally and socially different" (2003: xxxi); especially if they were writing to governmental or religious superiors, they described what they saw, the lands, customs, religion, and social organization. There was no true "occidentalism" (writing the West) to oppose to "orientalism" (writing the East).

Al-Tahtawi was part of the first scientific mission sent to the West by ambitious modernizer Muhammad 'Ali (1770–1849). Al-Tahtawi spent five years in France, mostly in Paris, and in 1834 published a book on his observations between 1826 and 1831 – *Takhlis al-Ibriz fi Takhlis Bariz*, or *Extracting Pure Gold to Render Paris Briefly Told* (transl.). *Al-Rihlah, The Journey* (the Arabic title), is his account of the manners and customs of the French written about the same time as Britisher Edward Lane's book on Cairo, *The Manners and Customs of the Modern Egyptians* (1836).

When al-Tahtawi published the first Arab ethnographic study of "a strange land with strange customs" in Europe, he included in his description the social, political, and intellectual achievements of the French, and much more. In Naddaf's nuanced commentary:

> The west does not finally stand, for al-Tahtawi, in a relation of absolute difference to the east. It presides not as a presence to be observed, to be reflected, to be described for its differential value. Rather it provides a

locus of exchange, invites mutual reflection, of interactive relationships between two seemingly oppositional forces. The representation of another culture does not become finally a means of distancing oneself from the other; it becomes instead a means of integration, of investigating the possibility of mirrored images between east and west (Naddaf, 1986: 76).

Earlier in her essay, Naddaf had compared al-Tahtawi with Lane, Cairo with Paris. Lane, in his description of the cafés of Cairo, maintains his stance as an objective, detached observer; as Naddaf notes, he "deliberately hides himself." He does not even suggest the possibility of a comparison with their Western counterparts. Al-Tahtawi, on the other hand, remarks on the French use of mirrors as a device that enlarges and aggrandizes: "The first time I visited this coffee shop, I thought it was a bustling city because there were so many people there . . . their reflections appeared on each of the mirrored walls . . . their numbers seemed to increase . . . until I saw my own reflection in the mirror" (Newman, 2004: 153). By distinguishing his own image, seeing that the mirror can reflect both subject and object, al-Tahtawi indicates the presence of his own tradition in a work about Western traditions.

The Orient discovered, or more accurately rediscovered, the West, in "an ethnographic study of a strange land with strange customs" (Naddaf, 1986: 74). Naddaf focuses on a play of oppositions. The sense of difference between the two cultures – between secular and religious, between intellectual supremacy and spiritual integrity – remains intact while she addresses his admiration of the ways of a land that is radically different from his own – with the exception of the café, an institution the East shares with the West. Edward Lane's description, on the other hand, establishes the café as an institution specific to Cairo.

Naddaf is correct. The West does not finally stand, for al-Tahtawi, in a relation of absolute difference to the East. Rather, he references a locus of exchange, of mutual reflection, points to and encourages interactive relationships between two seemingly oppositional forces. Upon returning to Cairo, al-Tahtawi assumed the role of director of the School of Translation. As an intellectual he distinguished himself in being able to find the common points of reference between Arab and European cultural traditions. It helped that he was being trained as a specialist in translation. But once back in Egypt his reform efforts aimed at modernizing European-style were controversial, endangering his status and livelihood.

Works like al-Tahtawi's can be read in multiple ways, indeed translated with multiple meanings. Daniel Newman's (2004) English translation of al-Tahtawi's work was reviewed by Francis Robinson (2004) under the title, "How clean they are." The review quotes al-Tahtawi's observations about the Franks' love of external cleanliness. Al-Tahtawi compared French Christians to Coptic Christians, but then he also noted that the Dutch were cleaner than the French. Picking out the flattering and scandalous, Robinson fails to capture the subtlety of al-Tahtawi's multi-leveled and nuanced comparisons. Al-Tahtawi's concept of comparison, which goes unnoticed by Robinson, can be seen even in how he includes in his book the reviews of his French mentors and friends, thereby allowing his informants their own critiques side by side with his own interpretations (Newman, 2004: 249, 278–287, 298–302). What comes through in the overall picture (perhaps in spite of his mentors' critiques) is a highly intelligent scholar, a reflexive scholar, educated both at al-Azhar university in Cairo and then in Paris, self-confident but not arrogant. As it turns out, he is not always overly impressed by what he sees in Paris (contrary to Robinson's review of Newman's translation). Rather, al-Tahtawi strives for, and succeeds in giving, an erudite and multi-dimensional view of Paris to his countrymen.

Now to my own reading of Newman's translation. As an imam for 44 students sent to France under the directeur d'études E. F. Jomard, al-Tahtawi at age 26 was singled out for translation training, a training that became pivotal for this young man. From the outset al-Tahtawi, influenced by Hasan al-Attar (his polymath professor at al-Azhar in Cairo), had the zeal for and an overwhelming commitment to learning from the West, while standing firmly within his own Arab-Islamic tradition, maintaining in that way his cultural dignity. Al-Tahtawi has been considered the pioneer of al-Nahda, a progressive Arab movement centered principally in Cairo, consciously advocating the adoption and adaptation of some Western forms to Arab settings. Working with knowledge of Ibn Khaldoun's sociology, which was pivotal to Émile Durkheim's work later in the century, he highlights positionality and links higher development to both knowledge and belief. At the beginning of his book al-Tahtawi posits his work as based on eyewitness accounts, not on exaggeration or hyperbole, although it is not "free from faults related to indulgence or prejudice" (Newman, 2004: 99).

Al-Tahtawi was "in the field" for five years, more field time than 99.9% of contemporary anthropologists, albeit as a formal student. As one who delved deeply, his immersion must have taken its toll on him. He became an apostle of development, wishing "to rouse all Islamic nations from the sleep of indifference" (Newman, 2004: 100), but the road he traveled was complex, full of equivalences and ambiguities, delight and disgust. Given that his French teachers wanted to convert him to their notion of what it is to be civilized, the dialogue with himself that *Takhlis al-Ibriz fi Takhlis Bariz* recorded for the Egyptian public, does not reflect total mind colonization. Parts of the work are straightforward reporting – the way the French eat, what they eat, utensils used, food preparation, the beds they use, women and chastity, the climate and its effect on people, the language, or the French form of government, concepts of justice, and the museums that he called warehouses. But there were other parts that were not straight description, parts where he did not leave comparison implied or silent as most modern Euro–American descriptions of the East or others do. He *made* comparisons explicit, gave his opinions, or challenged the arrogance and the positional superiority assumed by those around him. For example, he notes that Arabs had taught the Europeans in math, science, law, and politics. And certainly "credit goes to the precursor." He goes on: "Islamic countries . . . distinguish themselves in legal sciences but they still can accept from the West what they do not know" (Newman, 2004: 105). As an Egyptian scholar he knows a great deal about his own cultural traditions and history. He is forthright in his admiration of French notions of freedom, justice, and equity

(Newman, 2004: 194, 196), but he also notices that the French are Christians in name only and thinks the prohibition on marriage for the clergy dreadful because of the shameful acts it engenders. How observant! He compares French private baths, which are cleaner, to Egyptian steam baths which, though not as clean, are more "beneficial, more perfected and generally better." In France people do not sweat since the steam heat is restricted to the bathtub (Newman, 2004: 233–234). As he himself notes, his reaction includes both praise and rebuke (Newman, 2004: 252). He has no pretense of the "scientific objectivity" that Edward Lane presented in his work on Cairo.

His examples, especially in relation to commerce, charity, and language, are also enlightening. On charity, al-Tahtawi, not the only Arab or Muslim observer to so comment, writes that "The French show charity only in words and deeds, not when it involves their money and possessions . . . They never give things away, except if they are certain of obtaining some form of recompense. In truth, they are avaricious rather than generous" (Newman, 2004: 175). In reaching for an explanation he concludes that "generosity is peculiar to the Arabs." On the next page (Newman, 2004: 176), he states "Rich or poor, none of them tires from working." In a later section on charitable institutions in Paris (Newman, 2004: 237–39), he reports, "So, hostels with a charitable aim have been set up so that people would not have to hold out their hands to others. . . Admittedly, generosity is quite rare in civilized countries. They believe that giving something to somebody who is capable of working induces him not to concern himself with earning a living" (Newman, 2004: 239). Writing at about the same time as de Tocqueville (*Democracy in America* was published 1835, two years after al-Tahtawi's book), al-Tahtawi's comments are a preview to de Tocqueville's comments on public welfare institutions, and a precursor to the twentieth-century studies of Michel Foucault.

Later al-Tahtawi concedes that "while in Paris more is done for [public] charitable works than anywhere else, it is primarily aimed at the collective [that is, society as a whole], at the kingdom. The situation is quite different when it concerns individual people," about whom some might say, "There is never an excuse for begging" (Newman, 2004: 89, 241). This statement is followed by a section on earnings and the "love of profit and the passionate craving for it . . . as in the single-minded drive towards it . . . and the condemnation of laziness and slowness . . . terms of abuse." And later, "They are highly ingenious in finding ways of acquiring wealth," even by "not clinging to things that entail expenditure." For example, in Egypt, even "a simple soldier has several servants" (Newman, 2004: 248), thereby entailing expenses that a soldier in France would never have. But al-Tahtawi also criticizes the European capitalist ethic as something strange in that it does not serve to affiliate people, nor to connect people (Newman, 2004: 237–248). The French *distribution* system is different from Egypt's: it is public, not private (or religious) or personal, effected by institutions that create distinctions; it atomizes people (Newman, 2004: 241).

In matters of language his insights, which may be read as a precursor to Walter Benjamin's, are brilliant, aided by his translation training that made him sensitive to the subtleties involved. He began to pose questions about language in relation to culture before there was such a field of study. He enumerates how the French language has been enriched with an abundance of nonsynonymous words by borrowing from both Greek and Latin, but he also observes that the converse is true: "When it comes to word plays, expressions, and the multiple usage of them, ornate rhetorical figures based on pronunciation, French is devoid of all this. What in Arabic is seen as embellishment, the French sometimes perceive as weakness." In sum, "all of the elegance of an Arabic text disappears once it has been translated" (Newman, 2004: 182). He recognizes only too well that each language has its own particular conventions of usage, which do not always translate.

By the time one completes a reading of *An Imam in Paris*, one comes to feel intimacy rather than distance between Egypt and France, possibilities of exchange between two different yet comparable cultures. What shines through the text is the mind as a starting point for constructing the common humanity we all share. Yet, al-Tahtawi does not shun or cover up differences; rather, he uses them to engage possibilities of co-existence. Still to come were the Muslim migrations to Europe of the late twentieth and twenty-first century engendering an intolerance of co-existence on European soil, as seen in the contemporary European debates about *the veil* or the scarf.

Three further incidents can serve to demonstrate some of al-Tahtawi's insights on the difference between French and Arab conceptions of what it means to be human. The first occured when al-Tahtawi was walking along a street in Paris and a drunk shouted, "Hey, you Turk!" and grabbed at his clothes. Al-Tahtawi took him into a nearby confectionery shop and said jokingly to the shop-keeper, "Would you like to buy this man for some sweets?" To which the shopkeeper replied, "Here things are not like in your country where you can dispose of the human species at your will" (Newman, 2004: 222). Al-Tahtawi says that, in his current state, the drunk is not part of the human race and goes on his way. Al-Tahtawi's point here can be better understood by contrasting it to a second reflection that follows a number of observations on what he sees as the French obsession with animals. The body of an Egyptian, who had mar-tyred himself by assassinating a French general of the occupying forces in Egypt, was brought to Paris and put on display in a room at the Jardin des Plantes, the Salle d'Anatomie. Al-Tahtawi is horri-fied and disgusted. The French could fuss over their animals, treat them humanely, but yet strip a man, a real human, of all dignity. Not only did they deny the Egyptian a proper burial, they put his corpse on display as merely that of another curious organism. Whereas al-Tahtawi, as a good and upright Muslim, might be inclined to con-sider the man who allowed himself to fall into a state of drunkenness as a lesser being, he could not understand how the French could consider a whole segment of the human species as not meriting due respect. Did not the proprietor of the confectionery shop, after all, express the highest ideals of human respect and equality, values that al-Tahtawi himself admired? Yet the French seemed incapable of extending such respect to most Egyptians. A third reflection provides a conclusion to this point. After the occupation of Egypt, the French transported two obelisks to France. Al-Tahtawi notes,

"The fact of stripping [this heritage] away piece by piece is . . . like taking away the jewels and fineries of others in order to adorn oneself. . . . It is, in fact, tantamount to robbery!" (Newman, 2004: 359). For al-Tahtawi, while the Egyptian is inclined to consider a priori the entire human race as human and thus deserving of dignity, for the French, the Arab, "Turk," or Egyptian must first prove his humanness by adopting French values and abandoning his own cultural dignity.

A Hundred Years Later: Edward Said

About 100 years after the Arabic version of al-Tahtawi's book was published, Edward Said was born in Palestine. He was schooled in Egypt, lived in Lebanon, and received his higher education in the United States. Then, for many years, until his death in 2003, Said was a professor of comparative literature at Columbia University in New York. Probably the most distinguished Arab intellectual of the twentieth century, he was a prolific writer and critic. His book *Orientalism* (1978) caused an intellectual storm and perhaps forever changed the orientalist industry that he criticized. His was an extraordinary and creative scholarship that touched people and groups worldwide. He was no parochial soul.

Although much has been written about Said's work and about Said himself, it was only in writing this essay that I came across an article on Said comparable to Sandra Naddaf's article on al-Tahtawi, a short piece by Ferial J. Ghazoul, "The Resonance of the Arab-Islamic Heritage in the Work of Edward Said." Published as part of the book *Edward Said: A Critical Reader* (1992), Ghazoul's article is unpretentious and a rare attempt to further consolidate the notion of an intellectual tradition found among Arab and Islamic thinkers. I first began to capture a glimpse of this tradition in al-Tahtawi's work. In her description and evaluation, Ghazoul (1992: 158) uses words such as "critic," "comparativist," "neither universal in concentrating on idealist essences, nor cosmopolitan in covering up differences under a common veneer." She writes,

"Said finds himself between two civilizational modes . . . expanding the cultural space of the other in the dominant Eurocentric discourse." She saw his contribution as linking Arab–Islamic and Western cultures, providing "a model for breaking down normative and artificial barriers, to dismantle accepted fallacies and entrenched views by attacking its scholarship in *Orientalism*" (1992: 159). Said, she says, is feeling his way toward:

> ushering in a more global comparative approach that goes beyond the cosmopolitan essentially European approach, to undo the binary opposition of East/West and Self/Other to show how they co-exist in a cross-fertilizing heterogeneous global whole thereby delivering the marginalized culture from the isolation of the ghetto. He wants Arab–Islamic culture readmitted to the discourse of nations by introducing and establishing hitherto unnoticed parallelisms and affinities to its Western counterpart (1992: 160–161).

Ghazoul emphasizes the sophisticated manner in which Said accomplishes a change in intellectual discourse. He discusses the Irish poet William Butler Yeats in the same article with the Palestinian poet Mahmoud Darwish, Michael Foucault with Ibn Khaldun. The significance is that "Foucault had a precursor – and an Arab at that." Said reminds us that Ibn Khaldun, the great fourteenth-century Arab historiographer and philosopher, saw "the historian's task as work taking place between rhetoric, on the one hand, and civil politics, on the other. This," says Said, "describes Foucault's analytical attitude uncannily well. . . . The difference between Ibn Khaldun and Foucault . . . is no less instructive" (Ghazoul, 1992: 162). Ibn Khaldun sees power, "not as extensive and tight, but as fragile and subject to decline. This view undermines and challenges the logic of power as defined by Foucault. It offers fresh ways of looking at the phenomenon of power" (Ghazoul, 1992: 162). In other words, Ghazoul says Edward Said sought to revise distortions in Western discourse in order to arrive at a more representative perspective, a perspective resembling al-Tahtawi's. Both authors strive to produce a new perspective that can overcome tribalism and parochialism of the Western sort.

Remembering Edward Said after his death, his partner in music, Daniel Barenboim (2004), said the following:

> His fierce anti-specialization led him to criticize very strongly and very fairly the fact that musical education was becoming increasingly poor . . . Said was interested in detail . . . The genius attends to detail as if it were the most important thing. And in doing so, he does not lose sight of the big picture, rather he manages to trace out that big picture. He also knew how to distinguish clearly between power and force. He knew quite well that, in music, force is not power, something that many of the world's political leaders do not perceive.

Barenboim also spoke of Said's idea of interconnection and the impossibility of separating elements, the "perception that everything is connected, the need to always unite logical thought and intuitive emotion. . . His concept of inclusion."

What is of particular interest to me is how Said's commentary on the West connects the West and the rest of the world. Al-Tahtawi confined himself to the manners, customs, and institutions of France in Paris; Edward Said focused on Western scholarship about the East after more than a century of colonialism and imperialism. They both were members of the Arab elite, as I once put it, "studying up, down, and sideways" (Nader, 1969). Said focused primarily on the uses of scholarly representation in the context of dominant powers that were meant to "manage and even produce the Orient politically, sociologically, militarily, ideologically, scientifically, and imaginatively during the post Enlightenment period" (Said, 1978: 3). While al-Tahtawi, like Foucault later, was interested in France's internal process of control, Said's analysis extends such processes of control externally. Said's *Orientalism*, as some have described it, is a catalogue of Western prejudices about Arabs and Muslims "produced again and again through literary works, travelogues, scholarly texts and more – a filtering of the Orient in Western consciousness" (Said, 1978: 2). Said's purpose was to dismantle the discourse, expose it as an oppressive system, to clear the deck of prejudice. What are the techniques by which he intended to do this?

In a 1975 article called "Shattered Myths," which he wrote after the Arab–Israeli war of 1973, Said explains how myths work. He mentions a number of scholars and enumerates a set of myths – a prelude to his 1978 book *Orientalism*. The myths are many and extensive: Arabs are incapable of peace, they have a bent for vengeance, they are tied to a concept of justice that in actuality is anything-but-justice, they are not to be trusted, all notions that he calls "naked racism." Arabs are said to stress conformity, inhabit a shame culture, only understand how to function in conflict situations. Objectivity is not a value in the Arab system, according to the scholars he cites. Only Westerners are capable of holding real values, able to be rational, peaceful, logical, while Arabs are passive, fixed, stable, and so forth. I would not call these myths; rather, they are examples of raw propaganda and double talk, examples of the pot calling the kettle black. According to world historian William McNeill, Western Europe during the so-called age of faith was the most warlike civilization on earth (Lazare, 2004: 33), incapable of peace.

Said quotes a passage from Israeli anthropologist Raphael Patai's (1962) *Golden River to Golden Road: Society, Culture, and Change in the Middle East* about how to untie the Gordian knot of resistance to Westernization in the Middle East. He also mentions Patai's *The Arab Mind* (1973: 83), in which Patai (who, unfortunately, is an anthropologist) addresses what he sees as an Arab inability to reason and the failure of the Arab family. He belittles Arab character and Arab rhetoric and makes exaggerations about sexual matters. Said is not speaking here only of a school of thought and the institutions that support such thought, but of the social, political, and economic significance of such prejudice.

Patai does what master propagandists do – mixes truths with lies, quotes both insiders and outsiders, plays on prejudice both inside the Arab world and outside, and writes with such assurance and confidence that the reader is ready to believe that he knows what he is talking about. Early on, he quotes Ibn Khalhun on Arab Bedouins and Khaldun's student Taqi al Din Ahmad al-Mougrizi of the fourteenth and fifteenth centuries who in their analysis use words like cowardice, indecision, inconstancy. He uses Arab proverbs, and even quotes Hourani on the Arabic language to evince "the flawed mirror in which [the Arabs] see the world." He describes Egyptian national character as cunning, deceitful, given to a love of pleasure, all the while building his case that (Patai, 1973: 142) ultimately the Arab mind will have no choice but to accept Western mores, apparently unaware that Arab culture has been penetrating the West for centuries.

In the section under language we see headings such as: exaggeration, over-assertion, repetition. Patai concedes that Bedouin values include that of hospitality, but notes that they have an aversion to physical work. He generalizes (1973: 156) about the "Arab tendency to take a polarized view of man and the world, to see everywhere stark contrasts rather than gradations, to note opposites rather than transitions, to perceive extremes and be oblivious to nuances." Again and again, he portrays the Arab mind as lacking in self-control; Arabs are artists who choose to express their creativity in the decorative fields in repetition as found in music, in repetitive literary styles. But even here Patai predicts (1973: 186) that Arabs will have to concede, "the days of Arabic music are numbered since aspiring Arab musicians study in Western-style musical academies." And since conflict-proneness is an outstanding characteristic of the Arab mind, Arabs must unlearn the old values and accept new and contrary values in their stead (1973: 179). Patai's inattention to historical accuracy is extraordinary. If any of this sort of stuff were published about Jews or Blacks as serious scholarship, there would be an uproar.

Even so, Patai's 1983 edition of *The Arab Mind* was used in 2004 to train the US marines who were sent to fight the war in Iraq! Goebbels of Nazi notoriety could not have written better propaganda. Why, I ask, is this work referred to as scholarship? Why is it being used by the American military? If the pen is stronger than the sword, why is Patai, in particular, being read by American marines?

For Said (1978), the racist affirmations of orientalist literature are not simply a Western construct: Arab Muslims themselves are complicit in supporting such stereotypes – the Oriental was a participant. Said looks in the mirror as he quotes Franz Fanon: "It is the white man who creates the Negro. But it is the Negro who creates negritude." To replace white officers and bureaucrats with colored equivalents, or to imitate "Western" political behavior, does nothing to address the issue. Instead, what is needed is the creation of new and imaginative reconceptions of society and culture to mobilize resistance into something other than the replication of injustices. All of this requires a large understanding of world history: "Cultures are not impermeable; just as Western science borrowed from the Arabs, Arabs had borrowed from India and Greece. Culture is never just a matter of ownership, of borrowing and lending with absolute debtors and creditors, but rather of appropriations, common experiences, and interdependencies of all kinds. . . . Who has yet determined how much the domination of others contributed to the enormous wealth of the English and French states?" (Said 1978: 217).

Said's vision was wide-angled, neither traditionalist nor modernist. He was a man who had a sense of world history and saw the possibilities for globalization to be a good thing: "Partly because of empire, all cultures are involved in one another; none is single and pure, all are hybrid, heterogeneous, extraordinarily differentiate and unmonolithic. This is, I believe, as true of the contemporary United States as it is of the modern Arab world" (1994: xxv).

Since *Orientalism*, books and articles have been written to correct the record. Yet, Minou Reeves, recent author of *Muhammad in Europe: A Thousand Years of Western Myth Making*, notes in her preface "more often than not these more balanced views have been thrust aside by the revival of old calumnies. It was as if the clichés and prejudices had been planted so deep in the Western mind that nothing could displace them" (Reeves, 2001: xi). Who benefits? European exceptionalism was, and continues to be, functional; it is a myth, but a myth that serves imperial and colonial purposes. It was and continues to be well organized, simply observe the justifications for the US invasion of Iraq in 2003, the Israeli invasion of Lebanon in 2006, and the Israeli destruction in Gaza 2008–2009.

Geographer-engineer Edme François Jomard (1836), al-Tahtawi's French mentor, was not embarrassed to publish the Napoleon-inspired project for colonizing the Egyptian mind, a project that was designed to function through the creation of awe and education (much like President George W. Bush's project for winning the hearts and minds of Muslims (see Succarie, 2008). Like Patai, Jomard issued his racist propaganda:

> It is by instruction . . . that Egypt had to march. It was in the natives themselves, on European soil, that we had to inculcate the principles of the arts and sciences. And as Oriental languages are strangers to scientific terms, just as the lands of the Orient are to the sciences themselves, there was no other certain path to take . . . the obstacle of religion wavered and the old barriers between the Orient and the Occident fell. If, as early as 1813 . . . the viceroy of Egypt could have sent one or two hundred Egyptians to study here, the work of regeneration and of civilization would be still more advanced than it is today (Tageldin, 2011: 112).

Curiously, numbers of Egyptians accepted the unveiled arrogance and superiority attributed to nineteenth- and twentieth-century European arts and sciences – as al-Tahtawi notes "as if there were no precursors." Al-Tahtawi did point out a French ability to misrepresent (or distort) beliefs that transgress the law of reason by fortifying them philosophically so that they appear to be truthful and accurate. But perhaps orientalism was never meant to be accurate; rather, it was meant to awe, to dazzle, and to seduce, as earlier pointed out by al-Jabarti in his seminal history of the French invasion of Egypt in 1798 (Al-Jabarti, 2003 [1798]). Al-Tahtawi himself noted that it would be by means of language that the French would seduce Egypt. French texts were translated into Arabic, and Arabs were taught to read Arab history within European time. What was and is at stake is culture and dignity. Thus Egyptians came to accept as their own these narratives of European exceptionalism, and lost a sense of their true history and belonging in the world (see Tageldin, 2002). That the pen is mightier than the sword is a lesson that may be applicable to Iraq and to projects like General Petraeus's counterinsurgency efforts in the first decade of the twenty-first century.

A more recent work, *Winning Hearts and Minds: Education, Culture, and Control* by Mayssun Succarie (2008), zeroes in on the war of ideas, specifically, the process of idea construction during a neo-colonial encounter, when culture is altered and used so that certain identities can be maintained, or to transform the cultural environment among "Middle Eastern" youth. What she describes is part of a public diplomacy project, associated with US military actions, a multi-pronged effort to reshape the cultural environment in the Arab world. She argues that young minds are being colonized by teaching youth to be neoliberal subjects. The training involves entrepreneurship, leadership, school to work (as opposed to liberal education), and decentralization as well as community education.

As early as 2002, Paul Wolfowitz, then Deputy Secretary of Defense, declared, "this is a battle of ideas and a battle for minds . . . to win the war on terror, we must win a war of ideas . . . in order to do that we need to place a greater emphasis on non-military tools" (Succarie, 2008: 4). This became the Bush mantra. Succarie explores the public relations/marketing emphasis that included exhibitions, publications, exchange visits (especially for opinion managers such as journalists, professors, teachers, lawyers (ABA), political leaders, and NGO heads) – attempts to improve the image of America to a young Arab audience, a kind of cultural imperialism similar to cultural imperialisms of earlier periods. In the political science literature this is often referred to as "soft" power.

In Iraq the study of national culture was replaced with a new human rights and democracy book, not to teach democracy but to promote individualism and free market ideology. As the former Dean of Engineering at the University of Baghdad declared, "They need to individuate us, divide us and this is why they cancelled the story of the lion and the three bulls from the third grade. Unity is not allowed at the level of the country or the Arab world, or between generations" (Succarie, 2008: 263). The war Succarie describes is one of divide and conquer, a separation of Arab nationality into nation-state nationalities and then into ethnic as well as sectarian identities within the same nation-states – contemporary cultural imperialisms that are indeed not so different from those recommended by al-Tahtawi's mentor, Jomard, in 1836.

We live in a time and a world permeated by ideology and propaganda, so it behooves us all to be skeptical of accepted wisdoms, especially in the academy. Janet Abu-Lughod put this nicely in her challenge and contribution to so-called modern world systems theory. In *Before European Hegemony: The World System AD 1250–1350* (1989), she reminds us that Western knowledge changes by three means: through cross-fertilization among disciplines (in her case between economics, politics, sociology, and history), by incorporating work done by scholars originating from outside the Western world such as the Subaltern Group in Indian historiography, or by changing the distance from which "facts" are observed, the level of abstraction.

Abu-Lughod's work on the history of Cairo convinced her of the Eurocentrism of Max Weber's (1958) *The City*. In her reading of Gernet's study of thirteenth-century Hangchow, China, she found the largest and most advanced city in the world. Immanuel Wallerstein's *The Modern World-System* (1974) heightened her realization that, along with others, Wallerstein tended to treat the European-dominated world systems that formed in the sixteenth century as if they had appeared out of nowhere. All of these intellectual encounters led Abu-Lughod to write about the world system *before* European hegemony, which involved a vast region between northwest Europe and China, an "impressive set of interlinked subsystems in Asia, the Middle East, and parts of Europe, a world system in which [there was] a wide variety of economic systems from near private capitalism to near state production" (Abu-Lughod, 1989: 353). Her work expands the mind and shows us the number of historical possibilities that are available. World systems can be organized in different ways, and such systems are dynamic and undergo periodic restructuring, old systems and elements sometimes being incorporated into new ones. It is not as simple as the Rise of the West and the Fall of the East. By learning about what came before, we come to suspect that there just might be something after European hegemony, as observers of China and Asia more generally are intimating. No system has been eternal. No civilization remains in place; civilizations rise and fall. Such a realization encourages humility as we explore possible paths for human survival and fulfillment.

This kind of "studying back" in order to "study up" is superbly illustrated in the work of Columbia University Professor George Saliba, specifically his research on *Islamic Science and the Making of the European Renaissance* (2007). Saliba studied astronomy texts produced in the Islamic world between the ninth and the thirteenth centuries (such as the work of Ibn al Shatir of Damascus) that were later incorporated in the works of Renaissance scientists in Europe (such as Copernicus), and ultimately became part of our own Western scientific legacy. The schools of translation and European publishing houses were producing works also in Arabic, and Italians were collectors of Arabic texts up until the sixteenth century. Saliba's work relates to the debate over whether "modern" scientific tradition made its first appearance in this very ambiguous "West." Research is ongoing to determine why this phenomenon supposedly took place in Europe and nowhere else, a question addressed by the likes of Joseph Needham (1969) who notes that when modern science was supposed to have been born in the West – namely, during the European Renaissance of the sixteenth century – both the Chinese and Islamic civilizations had already acquired a superior level of scientific knowledge, especially in natural science. And yet it is said that modern science was born in the West and not in those other civilizations.

One needs to demonstrate the independence of Western science, but, as Saliba and others have shown, "the most innovative mathematical and astronomical ideas that were employed during the European Renaissance were themselves borrowed from Islamic/ Arabic or Chinese civilizations through many circuitous routes that are now being investigated" (Saliba, 2002: 1). During the nineteenth century, which Saliba labels as a time of ignorance of history, people could speak openly of modern science and its roots in the genius of Greek civilization, conceiving it as purely a Western enterprise – pseudo-history. Given the contemporary achievements in the history of science such ignorance is no longer tolerable. Saliba (2002: 2) quotes the sinologist A. C. Graham: "Indeed if we wish to find the best historical perspective for looking forward toward the Scientific Revolution, there is much to be said for choosing a viewpoint not in Greece but in the Islamic culture that from AD 750 reached from Spain to Turkestan."

There are dangers implicit in assigning national, linguistic, or cultural markers to science production. Increasingly those of us who work in the area of "other sciences" (see Nader, 1996) understand that the very processes of sciences themselves respect no such boundaries. Saliba calls on his colleagues to drop such adjectives as Arabic, Greek, or Western science from the discourse because they are not useful analytical categories, and instead serve to distort studies of the history of science.

In a review article on Toby Huff's 1993 book *The Rise of Early Modern Science: Islam, China, and the West*, Saliba (1999) addressed three myths that he thought needed correcting: namely, that Arab science is merely a preservation of Greek science, that the translations of Arab science in Europe ended with the thirteenth century instead of the sixteenth century, and that the Renaissance was a purely independent European phenomenon. The review generated a reply from Huff (1999) and a further reply from Saliba (2002) and is interesting because one can see the orientalist mechanisms at work in Huff's reply, the inability to think beyond borders that, ironically, are so antithetical to the workings of science itself. Ideas do not stop at borders. We need a diffusionist vision of cultures that transcends the narrow focus of area studies rooted in a post–world war geopolitical dynamic, the cold war.

Finally, the framework for Islamic scientists according to Saliba was the *Shukūk* tradition – a tradition that served as a framework for doubting previous scientific work by examining the assumptions undergirding findings. More specifically, Saliba described a tradition of critique that "disqualifies falsehood by expanding proof" (2007: 96), dubbing his Islamic scientists "doubters." Problems or doubts revealed contradictions that can be explained 2007: 97). In example after example of Islamic scientists from Muhammad ibn al-Wazzan (Leo Africanus) to Abu Bakn Razi and Ibn al-Itaitham, Saliba uncovers a critical tradition of alternative construction and shows how this critical spirit questioned the reliability of the very foundations of the classic Greek science, thereby correcting errors. Although the thirteenth century was an age of Islamic scientific discovery, the texts were poorly read, if read at all, in the West and even though discoveries of Islamic scientists continued on into the sixteenth century, European scholars chose to ignore further debts. Saliba was describing a new genre of science writing – books on doubts (2007: 235). "This is the accepted opinion, but according to us it is false," the Islamic scientists would write, and their rejection would be based on observation (2007: 246). European historians had prejudged Islamic scientists and the novel ideas that followed after critique. Other native observers have referred to the Levantine area as having a tradition of skeptics lasting until the present, as illustrated by the work of Nassim Taleb in *The Black Swan* (2007).

Concluding Comments

Culture is powerful. The minds of human beings everywhere are caught in processes that constrain what is thinkable. And yet there are those who push these limits of thinkable thought everywhere, in the East as well as the West, whatever those terms actually mean. I think of leading world historians like William McNeill and other world historians like Joseph Needham. And then I think of al-Tahtawi struggling with mechanisms of control or Edward Said over a century later, a specialist in comparative literature, analyzing the very cage that often houses closed thinking in scholarship. But prejudices often precede scholarship. It takes an idea of mind, one that is grand, to view the whole of human endeavors. We have all been munching on each other since the beginning, from the first globe-walker to the present. As Said (1994: xxv) put it, "Partly because of empire, all cultures are involved in one another, none is single and pure, all are hybrid, heterogeneous, extraordinarily differentiated, and unmonolithic," a very anthropological stance. Remember the precursor as well as the innovator: lessons in culture and dignity involve both.

The tradition that I have been describing for al-Tahtawi, Edward Said, George Saliba, and others is not only Arab–Islamic or any number of other possibilities such as good science or ecological science; it is also anthropological. It consists of taking what appear to be isolated events or ideas and placing them in a larger context, to make connections between seemingly disparate events and ideas. Indeed, this is what world historians like William McNeill have been doing. In this manner, one can discover underlying frameworks such as European exceptionalism or cultural racism (Arab or European) – uncovering building blocks of what Said refers to as "the agreed upon codes of understanding," basically the edifices of positional superiority (Said, 1978: 79). Anthropologists, at least the best among us, know better than most because we have studied the human condition going far back over the past 200 000 years or so, far enough back to know that boundaries created through culture are mostly ignored in the diffusion of ideas and peoples.

At one point in time, in the twelfth and thirteenth centuries, Genghis Khan built an empire, the first world system stretching from China to the Danube, linking through trade the Chinese, Indian, and Islamic civilizations. Europe benefited. A recent work by anthropologist Jack Weatherford (2004: xxiv) notes that, as a result of Mongol influence, every aspect of European life – warfare, technology, map reading, commerce, food, art, literature, clothing – changed. In addition to new forms of fighting, new machines, new foods, European daily life was dramatically affected. Europeans switched to Mongol fabrics, adopted pants and jackets instead of tunics and robes, played their musical instruments with the steppe bow rather than plucking them with fingers, and painted their pictures in a new style. And yet by the end of the eighteenth century, Genghis Khan, so admired earlier by Roger Bacon and by Geoffrey Chaucer in the *Canterbury Tales*, became the stereotype of the barbarian, the uniquely ruthless conqueror who enjoyed destruction for its own sake. The Mongols did not make any technological breakthroughs all their own, but they passed numerous skills from one civilization to another.

They moved products and commodities around, combined them to produce entirely novel products and unprecedented inventions. They created unusual hybrids. And the Khans also adapted – they were flexible. Kubelai Khan understood that to rule China he had to adapt to it.

With an army of no more than 100 000 warriors, Genghis Khan conquered more than twice as much territory, in numbers of people and area occupied, as any other man in history. Yet today his accomplishments are pressed into oblivion, as his violence and that of his sons and grandsons is remembered as their sole legacy. Who remembers his global order based on free trade, international law, and a universal alphabet? We all should, because it is part of human history and because in due course the Mongols became the scapegoats for other nations' failures – Russia, Japan, Persia, China, India, the Arabs. And so history has condemned Genghis Khan. Although conquerors such as Caesar, Alexander the Great, and Napoleon may have been treated more kindly, Genghis Khan was a historical victim.

As representatives of the older civilizations commonly point out, older configurations have much to teach the younger civilizations. For starters, we can accept the fact that we are all derivatives. This suggests that our choices are not binary, as between modernism and traditionalism. There are a plethora of possibilities that stem from individual dignity, mutual respect and its corollary, a profound respect for coexistence. Another possibility of course is cultural stagnation and annihilation, but one of the wonderful aspects of historical knowledge is the realization that new possibilities may come from unexpected directions: creativity in the arts, in film, in banking, in healing, in food, in movements of human empathy. None of this can be imagined when history is considered to be bunk, when lessons in history are short-term lessons, what one might read in the *New York Times* on a Monday morning. The one certainty that anthropologists have understood by using a long time frame is that civilizations rise, but they also fall, decline. Yet, as history has also shown, the human spirit moves on. How it moves on is up to each one of us, inhabitants of one planet.

References

Abu-Lughod, Janet (1989) *Before European Hegemony: The World System AD 1250–1350*. New York: Oxford University Press.

Al-Jabarti, Abd Al-Rahman (2003 [1798]) Al-Jabarti's Chronicle of the First Seven Months of the French Occupation of Egypt, June–December, 1798. In *Napoleon in Egypt: Al-Jabarti's Chonicle of the French Occupation*. Shmuel Moreh, ed. Princeton: Markus Wiener Publishers, pp. 33–123.

Barenboim, Daniel (2004) Sound and Vision: Edward Said Was a Great Thinker, and It Was Music That Made Him Tick. *The Guardian* , October, 25. Available at http://www.guardian.co.uk/music/2004/oct/25/classicalmusicandopera1 (accessed April 4, 2012).

Beal, Samuel (trans.) (1911) *The Life of Hiuen-Tsiang* by the Shaman Hwui Li. London: Kegan Paul, Trench Trübner.

Frye, Richard (2005) *Ibn Fadlan's Journey to Russia: A Tenth-Century Traveler from Baghdad to the Volga River*. Princeton, NJ: Markus Wiener Publishers.

Ghazoul, Ferial J. (1992) The Resonance of the Arab-Islamic Heritage in the Work of Edward Said. In *Edward Said: A Critical Reader*. Michael Sprinker, ed. Oxford: Blackwell, pp. 157–172.

Gordon, Stuart (2008) *When Asia Was the World: Traveling Merchants, Scholars, Warriors, and Monks who Created the "Riches of the East."* Philadelphia: Da Capo Press.

Huff, Toby (1993) *The Rise of Early Modern Science: Islam, China, and the West*. Cambridge: Cambridge University Press.

Huff, Toby (1999) The Rise of Early Modern Science: A Reply to George Saliba. *Bulletin of the Royal Institute for Inter-Faith Studies*, 4, no. 2, pp. 115–128.

Jomard, Edme François (1836) Coup d'oeil impartial sur l'état présent de l'Égypte, comparé à la situation antérieure. Paris: Béthune & Plon.

Kroeber, Alfred (1948) *Anthropology: Race, Language, Culture, Psychology, Prehistory*, second edition. New York: Harcourt, Brace and Company.

Lane, Edward William (1836) *An Account of the Manners and Customs of the Modern Egyptians: Written in Egypt During the Years 1833,–34, and –35, Partly From Notes Made During a Previous Visit to That Country in the Years 1825,–26,–27, and –28*. London: Charles Knight and Co.

Lazare, Daniel (2004) The Gods Must Be Crazy. *The Nation*, 279 (16), pp. 29–36. Available at http://www.thenation.com/article/gods-must-be-crazy (accessed April 5, 2012).

Maalouf, Amin (1984) *The Crusades Through Arab Eyes*. New York: Schocken Books.

Matar, Nabil (2003) *In the Lands of the Christians: Arabic Travel Writing in the Seventeenth Century*. New York: Routledge.

Naddaf, Sandra (1986) Mirrored Images: Rifa'ah al-Tahtawi and the West. *Alif: Journal of Comparative Poetics* 6, pp. 73–83.

Nader, Laura (1969) Up the Anthropologist: Perspectives Gained from Studying Up. In *Reinventing Anthropology*. Dell Hymes, ed. New York: Pantheon Books, pp. 284–311.

Nader, Laura (1996) *Naked Science: Anthropological Inquiry into Boundaries, Power, and Knowledge*. New York: Routledge.

Needham, Joseph (1969) *The Grand Titration*. London: Allen and Unwin.

Newman, Daniel L. (trans. and ed.) (2004) *An Imam in Paris: Al-Tahtawi's Visit to France (1826–31)*. London: Saqi.

Patai, Raphael (1962) *Golden River to Golden Road: Society, Culture, and Change in the Middle East*. Philadelphia: University of Pennsylvania Press.

Patai, Raphael (1973) *The Arab Mind*. New York: Scribner.

Reeves, Minou (2001) *Muhammad in Europe: A Thousand Years of Western Myth-Making*. New York: New York University Press.

Robinson, Francis (2004) How clean they are. *Times Literary Supplement*, No. 5283. July 2, p. 24.

Said, Edward (1975) Shattered Myths. In *Middle East Crucible*. Naseer H. Aruri, ed. Wilmette, IL.: Medina University Press, pp. 410–427.

Said, Edward (1978) *Orientalism*. New York: Pantheon Books.

Said, Edward (1994) *Culture and Imperialism*. New York: Vintage.

Saliba, George (1999) Seeking the Origins of Modern Science? *Bulletin of the Royal Institute for Inter-Faith Studies*, 1, no. 2, pp. 139–152.

Saliba, George (2002) Flying Goats and Other Obsessions: A Response to Toby Huff's "Reply." *Bulletin of the Royal Institute for Inter-Faith Studies*, 4, no. 2, pp. 129–141.

Saliba, George (2007) *Islamic Science and the Making of the European Renaissance*. Cambridge, MA: MIT Press.

Succarie, Mayssun (2008) *Winning Hearts and Minds: Education, Culture, and Control*. Ph.D. Dissertation, University of California, Berkeley.

Tageldin, Shaden M. (2002) The Sword and the Pen: Egyptian Musings on European Penetration, Persuasion, and Power. *Kroeber Anthropological Society Papers*, no. 87, pp. 196–218.

Tageldin, Shaden M. (2011) *Disarming Words: Empire and the Seductions of Translation in Egypt*. Berkeley, CA: University of California Press.

Taleb, Nassim (2007) *The Black Swan: The Impact of the Highly Improbable*. New York: Random House.

Wallerstein, Immanuel (1974) *The Modern World-System: Mercantilism and the Consolidation of the European World-Economy, 1600–1750*. New York: Academic Press.

Weatherford, Jack (2004) *Genghis Khan and the Making of the Modern World*. New York: Crown.

Weber, Max (1958) *The City*. Glencoe, IL: Free Press.

3

Ethnography as Theory
On the Roots of Controversy
in Anthropology

As I see it, the advances in scientific thought come from a combination of loose and strict thinking, and this combination is the most precious tool of science.

Gregory Bateson, *Steps to an Ecology of Mind* (1971: 75)

Introduction

Ethnography has commonly been summarized as description, albeit description in context, but not exactly theory. Yet theory is defined as the analysis of a set of facts in their relation to one another, or the general or abstract principles of any body of facts. This, to my mind, makes ethnography most definitely a theoretical endeavor – one that has had, and still has, worldly significance as description and explanation. Thus, ethnography itself as well as its explanatory use is a theoretical endeavor.

Culture and Dignity: Dialogues between the Middle East and the West,
First Edition. Laura Nader.
© 2013 John Wiley & Sons, Inc. Published 2013 by John Wiley & Sons, Inc.

Historically, doing ethnography has involved living and talking with people, "being there" and "participant observing," an attempt to understand how the people studied see and account for their world, which includes the anthropologist. Ethnography has also been commonly connected to the idea of holism. Cultures are interconnected, not fragmented; they are whole systems, and therefore any description of them, to be complete, must tackle the whole. The reality of doing and writing ethnography has always been more complicated than simply assuming and even arguing the interrelatedness of cultural elements. Are we recording what people say they do, how we see them living, or how they want the anthropologist observer to know them? Ethnography, whatever it is, has never been *mere* description. It is also theoretical in its mode of description; *ethnography is a theory of description*, if you will. The whole of a culture cannot be assumed, and there has never been a total consensus on how whole is whole enough, especially when dealing with questions of boundaries. Nor has there been agreement on what makes ethnographic reporting "factual," a problem in mainstream scientific work as well. The absence of agreement or total consensus has been the strength of anthropology's ethnography, inspiring a dynamic process of "doing ethnography" that resonates with changing worlds in and out of academia.

Thus, from the beginnings of anthropology there was controversy, a simultaneous romanticizing of "being there" among isolated, exotic people and doubts about the limitations of a methodology that, at times, has sought to answer all the essential questions regarding the human condition. At the same time, discussions of the many possibilities of ethnography have been cause for discomfort, or at least uneasiness, about the stability of our field endeavors and the continuous need for revitalization. With James Mooney (1896), we had the nineteenth-century beginnings of a critically engaged ethnography and ethnography as critique of Western thought. With W. H. R. Rivers (1906), and to a lesser extent Bronislaw Malinowski (1984 [1922]), the ethnographer proceeded as if conducting a laboratory-bounded natural-science experiment. With Gregory Bateson (1958 [1936]), and to some extent Sir Edmund Leach (1965 [1954]), the ethnographer proceeded much more like an ecologist. The ecological model of ethnography, whatever that is, is *not* the laboratory model, nor the model proving a linear cause-to-effect hypothesis sometimes associated with the theoretical work of A. R. Radcliffe-Brown.

These forerunners were not governed by any one doctrine, did not adhere to a single model, yet they were all doing ethnography by most people's standards: they went, they observed, they stayed, they returned home and wrote ethnography. They were methodologically eclectic (including quantitative techniques) and were not afraid to innovate and create those techniques that they found to be necessary for pushing forward their work – which was often described as urgent anthropology, salvaging the cultures of non-Western peoples before they were erased by Euro–American colonizing adventures.

Although ethnographic standards above the radar *were* debated, there were unstated rules or consensuses about how to do ethnography that were not debated openly, although there were some brief hints of debate in the 1960s, especially with the publication of *Reinventing Anthropology* (Hymes, 1969). As a graduate student at Harvard University in the 1950s, I understood that an unstated consensus had already been long established concerning what ethnographic work should be. Although Bateson's highly original *Naven* (1936), reissued in 1958 (to the distress of the more scientistic Harvard faculty) with an additional methodological epilogue, and Edmund Leach's solid *Political Systems of Highland Burma* (1954), which had a deliberate focus on power and its uses, the unstated rules were clear: we were to work in non-Western societies, write about them as if they were bounded entities, ignore power politics which included colonial and imperial presence, ignore similarities between "us and them," deplore nineteenth-century unilineal evolutionism and exceptionalism but still practice it. Perhaps the only sign of the philosophically inspired questioning that was to develop further in subsequent decades was the fact that Wittgenstein, Cassirer, and Langer (not Marxian philosophers) were being read widely by graduate students, whether or not they were interested in linguistics.

What I should like to do in this chapter is to describe what may be the components of the *still unstated consensus* in elite quarters regarding ethnography in Anglo–American anthropology. I shall sample the critiques that have erupted at different levels, comment on the spread and fashionable acceptance, or marginalization, of different parts of ethnography as practiced by anthropologists, indicate the dissatisfaction of some anthropologists with ethnography as done by those outside the discipline, and, finally, conclude with comments on how ethnography is continuing to be renewed by calls for the liberation of anthropology from a professionalization that, though so often unstated, is powerful in silencing colleagues, more often than not under the radar.

Unstated Consensus

At the outset in Anglo–American anthropology, participant observation in a non-Western society was justified as a practice in defamiliarization. According to this scenario, anthropologists move to a place removed from their own culture with the idea that the newness and unfamiliarity they confront will allow them to discover or figure out something about the people they visit that would be a contribution to anthropology as "the science of man." Participant observation was the key operational phrase. Places such as an island in the Pacific, a tribal village in Africa, or a pueblo in the American Southwest were common research sites. The goal, for the anthropologist, was to figure out the pieces of the social system and discover how they fit together in a *bounded* sense that was sometimes modeled after Radcliffe-Brown's organic metaphor of society. Multisided interpretations at times served to widen the scope of intellectual possibilities, but such instances were rare. More commonly, interpretations were closed. An example is Clifford Geertz's (1973) essay on the cock fight in Indonesia, which found no ethnographic space for the half-million people killed by Indonesian government forces at the same place and time. The massacre was included only as a footnote, a not unfamiliar example of elision in the history of anthropology. As I noted in my 1999 review of

Geertz's later work *After the Fact: Two Countries, Four Decades, One Anthropologist* (1995), Geertz rejected positivism, borrowed from the philosophers named above, and was unable to deal with political and economic power. For him the 1966 massacres in Pare were "hardly . . . a memory at all" (1995: 10), indeed hardly knowledge that is humanistic, reflexive, or situated – suitable for a literary ethnography.

Throughout more than 100 years of Anglo–American ethnography, participant observation has always been combined with theory, whether functionalist, structural functionalist, interpretive, Marxist, progressivist, evolutionary, symbolic, feminist, or just plain critical. Given shifting theoretical and methodological frameworks, anthropology and ethnography, as a discipline and research practice, have remained open to innovation. In ethnography itself the theory was in the writing, and throughout the twentieth century, anthropological theory did not proceed in a linear fashion (although historians of anthropology often depict it as having done so) – from functional, to structural functional, to structuralism, to interpretive, reflexive, critical, and so forth. Today, all of those theories are in use to some extent or other. I do not mean to suggest that there are no paradigm shifts over time, that is, no shifts in an implicit body of intertwined theoretical and methodological presuppositions, rather that anthropology has always appeared to be theoretically heterodox. While there appear to be competing schools, anthropologists who take one side or another in theoretical debates, what defines anthropology and ethnography as such are not these divisions but rather what is shared, held in common, which includes the unstated. I shall refer to specific ethnographic works as a means of indicating how evaluations of the work of one's contemporaries often proceed.

Defining Ethnographic Worth: 1896–2000

In James Mooney's 1896 multi-reservation project, fieldwork was carried out in the eastern and southwestern parts of the United States with Cherokees, Kiowas, and Cheyenne, focusing on religion and the ceremonial use of peyote. In *The Ghost-Dance Religion and the Sioux Outbreak of 1890*, the book for which he is most remembered, Mooney was concerned with what today could be termed control and resistance, with social movements, with the political use of religion, and with the civil and human rights of Indians. He compared the nativistic movements with the deeds of white Europeans as a way of provoking a sympathetic understanding of Indian deprivations in land and livelihood, and cited the tragic implications of wrongs done to them as reasons to protect them further from the demands of white society. However, perhaps because he explicitly wrote whites into his ethnography of Indian peoples (and perhaps because his book was well received by the reading public), he invited the ire of missionaries, the US government, educators, and anthropologists who sought to turn the people they called savages toward so-called progress and civilization, in some cases using humanitarian rationales, such as being the only way to save Native Americans. By writing white people into his ethnography, equating them to Native Americans, Mooney, who was the son of Irish immigrants and a self-trained anthropologist, violated what was already in the late nineteenth century an unwritten rule: ethnography is about the other, *not* the other intertwined with their conquerors, not about us and them. He was dismissed as an amateur by academics like Franz Boas, or a lover of Indians by government officials and the Indian Bureau, and was subsequently barred from fieldwork on American reservations (Moses, 1984: 222–235).

At the time of Mooney's death, prevailing views of professionalization narrowed the boundaries of what constituted a real as versus an amateur anthropologist; a kind of "specialized competence" was coming to the fore. On many fronts Mooney was ahead of his time. He included the colonizers as well as the colonized, and on an equal footing, and by doing so already defined an ethics of research decades ahead of the American Anthropological Association's Code of Ethics.

Some decades later, in 1922, Malinowski, in his work with the Pacific Trobriand Islanders, underscored the scientificity of ethnography by outlining three methodological tenets of research: statistical documentation, attention to the imponderabilia of actual life and observed behavior, and the recording of spoken statements indicating the mentality of native thought. Before becoming an anthropologist Malinowski had studied philosophy, mathematics, and physics in Poland. His methodologies were meant to allow the ethnographer to "grasp the native's point of view, his relation to life, to realize his vision of the world" (Malinowski, 1984: 25). Yet if we read reviews of *Coral Gardens and Their Magic* (1935) by Malinowski's contemporaries, we glimpse what he was up against:

> The use of magic, which is analogous to the delusions of grandeur and the fear constructs of the individual neurotic, may be the invariable result of man's limited ability to control his environment. But to extol it thus as the 'very foundation of culture,' as Malinowski does, is not justified on scientific grounds (Stern, 1936: 1018).

Malinowski broke ground with what today would be called multi-sited fieldwork, and scientific rigor. He described the Kula ring of reciprocal trade and friendship that connected a series of island societies. The Kula exchange was fundamental to social relationships because partners are connected for life through mutual obligation and support. In Malinowski's description, Trobriand life appears to the readers as reasonable. Writing culture as reasonable was a conscious strategy for Malinowski and his editors, specifically because he was refuting notions of primitives who only act in terms of self-interest: "The real native of flesh and bone differs from the shadowy Primitive Economic Man, on whose imaginary behavior many of the scholastic deductions of abstract economics are based" (1984: 61–62). He was not a comparativist; he let his ethnography speak about Us, with more or less *implicit* observations, whether he wrote about law and order, about magic, science, and religion, or about sexuality.

A decade later, New Zealander Reo Fortune published *Sorcerers of Dobu* (1932) in which he recounts the irritation of Australian colonial administrators because he as the ethnographer was relativizing sorcery as a form of social control that makes conformity strategically wise in societies without well-developed legal mechanisms. Sorcery, for these Melanesian Dobuans, had a function, and Fortune gave it standing. He violated the rule, the normative frame imposed by

colonial administrators, that degraded sorcery and those who practiced it to the level of barbarism. Although the normative frame of
the ethnography did not fit colonial and imperialist objectives
or even native preferences, Fortune used the threat of government
or mission to secure information about sorcery. Colonial control
enabled him to carry out his work, but he opposed the social turmoil brought on by colonial administration. Anthropologists did
not always share the goal of "civilizing" and developing the natives.
After 1930 independent anthropologists were banned from fieldwork in Papua, and Fortune was not appointed to government posts
following World War II. But by then he was at Cambridge University.

In the same and following decades Max Gluckman, E. Epstein,
and Peter Worsley were accused of being left to communist and
their access to field sites was denied outright, as with James Mooney
in the previous century. Gluckman's 1936–1938 fieldwork was
conducted in South Africa. His 1940–1942 publication "Analysis
of a Social Situation in Modern Zuzuland" was an assault on
the concept of the bounded tribe. It was a cross-section study
demonstrating the impossibility of conceptual segregation. For
him, South Africa was a single society "composed of heterogeneous
culture groups . . . overlapping, interpenetrating, and cross-cutting"
(MacMillan, 1995: 64). He was criticized for living like the natives,
eating their food, "bringing himself down to their level," accused
of being pro-Russian and a communist, and then banned from
further fieldwork in the area by the Secretary for Native Affairs.
Although many anthropologists cooperated with colonial officials,
anthropology as a discipline has consistently disturbed received
knowledge and challenged many imposed norms of colonial
administration. The same was true with E. E. Evans-Pritchard's
ethnography, *Witchcraft, Oracles, and Magic Among the Azande* (1937),
in which he describes the role that witchcraft plays in the life of
the Azande, something that appeared irrational to British colonial
administrators, as we saw in the Dobuan sorcery example. Evans-
Pritchard went further than Fortune in crediting the Azande with
having a rationality of their own: "Witchcraft participates in all
misfortunes, and is the idiom in which Azande speak about them

and in which they explain them" (1937: 19). He provided examples of the ways in which the Azande understand misfortune with witchcraft supplying the reason "why," his best example being a granary collapse. The Azande understand that termites eat the supports but the why – witchcraft. In this ethnography Evans-Pritchard drew an explicit comparison to "us" in Western culture: "It may have occurred to many readers that there is an analogy between the Zande concept of witchcraft and our own concept of luck. When, in spite of human knowledge . . . a man suffers a mishap, we say that it is his bad luck, whereas the Azande say he has been bewitched" (1937: 65). He shakes the notion of "primitive mentality" when he writes of Azande medicines, classifying their specific use of trees and plants, mode of use, and type of activity. Many years later (1996), I edited *Naked Science: Anthropological Inquiry into Boundaries, Power, and Knowledge* and encountered publishing problems over arguments I had with my associates relating to the same issues with respect to rationalities as Evans-Pritchard. Primitive mentality as a concept is alive and well, although misplaced in application.

In spite of the exceptions, anthropologists' complicity with Euro–American colonialism can be perceived by the use of colonialist terms; anthropologists historically called those being studied "primitives"; the ethnographer conceived of his or her world as civilized. This much they shared with the colonial official. Evolutionary and comparative approaches, where so-called primitive societies were believed to be located at an earlier stage of development through which modern societies had already passed, encouraged researchers to use their own categories unselfconsciously – categories such as law, religion, politics – to describe others as if they were "natural" categories. But then there were those who continued to upset the apple cart.

Gregory Bateson, with his book *Naven* (1958 [1936]), violated many of the accepted rules of doing and writing ethnography. His work on the Iatmul of the Sepik River region of New Guinea was not holistic, at least not by any traditional definition of the term. In his ethnography he described only one ceremony, not the whole of Iatmul society. At the start he writes, "I shall first present the ceremonial behavior, torn from its context so that it appears bizarre and nonsensical; and I shall describe the various aspects of its cultural setting and indicate how the ceremonial can be related to the various aspects of the culture" (1958: 3). Each chapter of the book is an experiment in explaining the ceremony using a different lens. In the functionalist chapter, he attempted to show that such an explanation implied that change would be blocked, innovation would be stifled, and conflict would be seen as pathological. Bateson's work is a criticism of standard classic ethnography, written long before Marcus and Fischer's 1986 work on cultural critique. *Naven* was a study of the nature of explanation, an examination of "the scientists'" way of putting the jigsaw puzzle together (Bateson, 1958: 280). Theoretical concepts, he argues, are "really descriptions of processes of knowing adopted by scientists . . . and no more than that" (1958: 281).

In my reading of the history of anthropology, the two figures who are central to the critique of ethnocentrism were Gregory Bateson and Edmund Leach. Of the two, Leach was probably the less abstract and the most radically explicit. A good example of his clear and incisive vision can be seen in a letter he wrote to his father when he was beginning his studies at Cambridge University shortly after the end of the World War I:

> Ours is the *first* generation to have grown up wholly since the war, my education began with the peace. It being so, it is inevitable that we should have a wholly different standard of values to all those who preceded us. The war marked the death bed of a great age, and gave birth to a new one altogether without standards or stability. Consider, only for a moment, civilisation as it is today. On the one hand we have the vast and terrible tyranny that is typified by American business, that is but the logical succession to the more sober commerce of the last century; so vast and unmanageable has this huge monster become that it has utterly lost control of itself, so that of its own mechanism it is *bound* to operate in alternate cycles of prosperity and depression bringing misery and destruction with every downward swoop of the pendulum. Against this you have arrayed the deadly efficient machine that is aimed at by the Russian Soviet . . . in cruelty there is little to choose between the machine world of the Soviet and financial tyranny of Western big business.

Thirdly apart from these two lies the whole realm of science. The early achievements can little have realized what a Pandora's box they were unloosing when they delved into the mysteries of the elements. Today absolutely nothing short of universal annihilation can stop the progress of science. If man does not destroy himself in the process, a wholly mechanical world is *bound* to evolve during the course of the next two centuries; the machine is the symbol of the age. . . .

And so there is gradually being taken out of life all that made it possible for man to be something higher than the beast. Culture is being killed by the speed at which we are forced to live, and we are compelled to struggle where our forbears were at ease to contemplate (quoted in Tambiah, 2002: 28–29).

For Leach, as was true with Mooney earlier, anthropology was just as much about *us* as about *them* (Leach, 1989: 13).[1]

There is no modern as opposed to primitive society, no static versus dynamic. We are all rational. Others have to solve problems of existence, build boats, cure their sicknesses, just as we do. Social systems are open, not bounded and never to be found in equilibrium. The other is interesting because what we see in them is directly relevant to understanding ourselves.

He spoke of a long tradition of attributing ignorance to native people, attributing to them a kind of childishness, superstition, an incapacity for rational thought. He believed, as Malinowski wrote in his *Magic, Science and Religion* (1948), that Western scholars should assume that people are as rational and credible in so-called primitive societies as they are in their own, and in that way discover the rational explanations for what might seem to be strange behavior. For Leach, double standards were not defensible. You should not apply one standard to primitive man and quite a different one to so-called civilized man. Nor is it tenable, he argued, to use racist ideologies that ascribe intellectual inferiority to natives. He disapproved of the preservationist ethic of romantics, but neither did he approve of applied or development anthropology, which he thought to be neocolonialist.

Leach understood the anthropologist and the people they studied to be co-temporal (Tambiah, 2002: 259–263, 429–455). One is no more contemporary than the other. He developed the idea of positioned or situated knowledge. The anthropologist and their informants are differentially situated and thereby cannot be, in the strict sense, objective. He also had little sympathy for the narcissism of contemporary critics and their style of writing critiques – all aspects that, in my view, highly recommend his thought. But the way out of the unstated consensuses is not as easy as Leach believed or makes it seem. Anthropologists continue to be blind to assumptions that he challenged. This is because, as Eric Wolf stated in 1969, anthropology is not autonomous; it is a reflection of the society of which it is a part. Ethnographers are caught in their culture much as the people they study. Thus, we are all complicit, although to different degrees. Wolf's observation relates directly to the matter of how we treat our ethnographic innovators, both past and present. Anglo–American culture is not culturally motivated to analyze the power elite or to educate ourselves in the realities of power – an observation that motivated me to write "Up the Anthropologist" (Nader, 1969), in which I analyzed the obstacles and objections to studying up, down, and sideways.

If the classic ethnographies were all rooted in place and ethnic communities – the Todas, the Andaman Islanders, the Trobrianders, the Azande, the Dobu, and so forth – and if it is true that what ethnographers do is in part dependent on their culture of origin, then what kind of ethnographies have begun to appear in a context of rapid globalization, the rise of new imperialisms, and a desire to reinvent anthropology? After all, changing industrial and technological means have transformed the world and us with it. June Nash (1993 [1979]) studied Bolivian Indians working in mines that are embedded in a world system of which her country of origin is also a part. Hugh Gusterson (1996) studied nuclear weapons workers in a US National Laboratory, a place that produced weapons of mass destruction that potentially could affect all the peoples of the planet. As a critical medical anthropologist, Margaret Lock (1993) studied the differential construction of menopause in

Japan and North America, indicating the role of pharmaceuticals in defining "change of life." And Ted Swedenburg (1995) studied *Memories of Revolt* in Palestine, a place that today reverberates politically around the world, though not necessarily in ethnography. Ethnographic localities are now embedded in larger political and economic circuits, connected increasingly by global exchange. Even community-based ethnographies, such as my own *Harmony Ideology: Law and Justice in a Mountain Zapotec Village* (Nader, 1990), have worldwide significance because dispute resolution tools established through Spanish colonial control that I identified at the community level are also to be found as techniques of pacification operating in the arenas of international law, trade agreements, and the like. Robert Borofsky (1987) in his *Making History: Pukapukan and Anthropological Constructions of Knowledge* speaks of different ways of constructing knowledge about the past, something that by now is hardly controversial, but in some thought still is. Continually changing their theoretical constructions and the traditions they subscribe to, anthropologists often overdetermine their positions, emphasizing uniformity at the expense of diversity, stasis at the expense of change, something that Leach cautioned against. At the same time, as Bateson points out, loose and strict thinking can be conducive to creative findings.

Although the above-mentioned ethnographers have their adherents, opposition to innovative, eclectic, and open-ended loose and strict works have been dismissed by judgments that use words like "journalistic," "political," "nonanalytic," or "unscientific," – expressions of outrage that the ethnographers, by placing themselves, their societies, and those that they study all on equal footing, have crossed a line, violated an unspoken consensus. It is still easy to denigrate or to mark the boundaries of acceptable ethnography, even though it has been clear for a good long time now that science is not, and cannot be, politically neutral. As in past times, people still argue in the present for scientific objectivity, but it is a concept that often does little else than conceal the scientist's highly subjective position.

Ethnographic Audiences

It would perhaps be impossible to use the ethnographies I have mentioned to govern natives by standardized procedures. Or would it? By now the benefits of ethnography to marginal people have come under question. What does it mean to speak to the benefit of another? What good does ethnography do anyone, and if it does do some good, have some utility, then for whom? Ethnography, like any other scientific research practice, can be, and has been, used over time for all kinds of moral and political ends, both good and bad. Witness the US military's Human Terrain Project in Iraq and Afghanistan (Gonzalez, 2009), in which cooperation between anthropologists working for the military and occupied peoples is presumed to be saving lives – though no significant evidence supports such a presumption.

There are no sequential paradigm changes as yet universally observable in modern ethnographic works. There is, however, controversy whether one looks backward or forward. When Malinowski said of the Trobriander, "He is in it [the kula], and cannot see the whole from the outside" (1984: 83), he may not have imagined that his statement would also be applied to the ethnographer himself. Clifford Geertz said as much in the 1990s while lecturing and answering questions at Berkeley: "They [native peoples] don't know how to do this kind of work." When Leach (1965: x) notes that he fully appreciates that a great deal of sociological analysis of the very highest quality makes it appear that social systems are naturally endowed with an equilibrium which is a demonstrable fact and referred to such analyses as having the appearance of an illusion, he was criticized for replacing equilibrium with power analysis as the keystone of social dynamics. June Nash (1993 [1979]), by enlarging her scope to include bosses as well as workers, challenged the attitude taken by others toward the miners and more generally the working class in less industrialized societies:

> The opposition between "traditional" and "modern" or "rational," of "heteronomy" and "autonomy," deny the possibility for reinterpreting and growing within a cultural idiom different from that of the

developed centers of the world but nonetheless capable of generating new understandings and alternative adaptations, sometimes far in advance of the models we have from industrial societies. (1993: 310)

Her statement questions what constitutes rational behavior for a marginal labor force in a dependent economy. Yet, ethnographers (with Leach as a salient exception) still speak regularly about modernity or development as if it were something different from unilineal cultural evolution or cultural colonialism. When Margaret Lock (1993) asks whether the contradictions over menopause are there because menopause is a culturally constructed psycho-physical reality, she calls into question the received knowledge regarding menopause that is generally uncontested in North American medicine. Lock was determined to "carry the results of this project beyond a simple interpretation of the Japanese materials that left a comparison with North America largely implicit" (1993: xix). I write more about implicit comparisons in my concluding remarks, but for the moment I call attention to Lock's method of juxtaposition that seems to build on Leach's early call for ethnographers to examine Western rationalities as well.

Some of the themes that have been introduced thus far are elaborated in Roberto Gonzalez's prize-winning book *Zapotec Science* (2001). Gonzalez joins other anthropologists who break with the fiction of ethno-science versus techno-science, or the "they have knowledge/we-have-science" binary. Gonzalez argues that Zapotec farming practices cannot be categorized into "traditional" versus "modern," because they reflect a plurality of influences that cross over from traditional-indigenous to conventional-industrial. For example, Zapotecs cultivate native maize varieties, but have incorporated European and Middle Eastern techniques (plowing) and tools (such as steel blades). They have adopted foreign crops like coffee or sugar cane, but farm these crops in accordance with local practices such as intercropping and cooperative working arrangements. In this way Gonzalez unbinds the us/them notion of knowledge production, opening alternative possibilities to the dominant paradigm Leach and others have been alluding to.

Zapotec Science, like Rob Borofsky's earlier work on *Making History* (1987), is a reconsideration of knowledge production within the discipline of anthropology, a discipline that from the beginning has been implicated in European expansion and domination as critics often noted. For Gonzalez, the division between local or ethnic and cosmopolitan sciences is inadequate for thinking about science. The intellectual challenge is now to disentangle dominant norms and the inequalities entailed in what Edward Said (1978) labeled orientalism, the biasing of the cultural field in such a way that Europe and the United States gain and maintain positional superiority. In *Zapotec Science* Gonzalez extends Nash's observation that "European categories as to what constitutes rational behavior . . . have little meaning for a marginal labor force" (Nash, 1993: 251). Like Evans-Pritchard (1976) when he explains how Azande witchcraft was compatible with empirical knowledge of cause and effect, Gonzalez also describes the rational and scientific basis for the practices of family farmers. Such efforts are part of an anthropological tradition – to liberate other modes of thought from those who would apply different criteria to "modern" than they would to "traditional people," to us as compared to them, and thus fall into contradictions. Indeed, the same sorts of contradictions appear in ethnography itself.

As late as 1964, Leach regarded his Burma book "as a piece publicizing a relatively novel way of looking at things." Given the context in which he was writing, readers could take his work as giving support to a more holistic, less positivistic approach. By 1977, however, Leach remarked that the pendulum had swung so far over in the opposite direction that "I am obliged to present [my book] as a defense of empirical observation" perhaps because anthropology had swung into interpretive anthropology (Leach's second reprinting, xvi–xvii). In order for one to extend a project such as Leach's, one would need to know about the differences or similarities between many knowledge-making practices around the world. Again, I am arguing that implicit comparison needs to be made explicit if we are to have any hope of learning from the experiences of others. Importantly, the internal view and the external view appear and reappear in several of the more current ethnographies, but we anthropologists have barely made a dent in "the ethnocentrism problem."

To return to Gonzalez for a moment, it is worth examining some of the reviews of this young author's work. In one reviewer's estimation, "few agricultural scientists will seriously consider the idea that the earth is a living being that feels pain or that maize has a soul. These are spiritual beliefs worthy of our respect, but they are not science" (Bentley, 2003: 358). The reviewer, however, does not go far enough. Instead of presupposing the opinions that others might have of Gonzalez's work, we should continue Gonzalez's project by also studying those school-trained agricultural scientists themselves. We cannot know that agricultural scientists do not have functionally equivalent beliefs unless there is direct comparison. Interestingly enough, other reviewers properly called for such a comparison, though a further reviewer was again to ask, "should these practices be called science?" That such a question is even posed, points to the fact that Gonzalez, by putting Zapotec practices on a par with the practices of Western science, has transgressed a consensus still held dear by many social scientists. They have knowledge; we have science, by which is often meant "we have science institutions."

In his controversial-from-the-start ethnography *Nuclear Rites* (1996), Hugh Gusterson examined the internal logic of laboratory life by examining its "central axiom." Gusterson conducted his work in California at the Livermore National Laboratory. The central axiom, according to Gusterson, was that scientists at the laboratory design nuclear weapons to ensure that nuclear weapons will never be used. Gusterson describes the numerous socializing processes, endemic to the laboratory, that give form to this way of reasoning; the belief that guides and justifies for these scientists their involvement in building the most powerful weapons on earth. Through Gusterson's description, the reasoning of scientists never seems quite consistent. One scientist corrected Gusterson's use of the term "vaporized" instead of "carbonized" to describe the effects on victims of the nuclear bomb dropped on Hiroshima. The scientist commented, "The problem with [you] non-scientists, [is that] you are so sloppy with detail" (Gusterson, 1996: 110). And so we have scientists who can distinguish between vaporization and carbonization, but do not question whether or not the logic behind building extremely destructive weapons for deterrence might today be a faulty or obsolete strategy. Perhaps professionalization, in this case of nuclear scientists, the extreme specializing in certain details, precludes being able to take into consideration the bigger picture and to ask for or demand coherence on a larger scale.

Nancy Chen, in her ethnography *Breathing Spaces* (2003: xii), notes that critical medical anthropology has "helped to reframe the divide between biomedicine and other forms of medicine to understanding biomedicine itself as a form of ethno-medicine." Her study of Qigong practices is embedded in China's recent history of reengagement with global capitalism and its shift from state-subsidized medical care to for-profit medicine. Qigong reconnects its practitioners on a national and at times an international scale, an example of unbounded ethnography.

Many of the ethnographies mentioned here are experimental departures from the consensual model that Leach was so explicit about, but experimental ethnographies can constitute a model in themselves. In Bateson's case, his self-conscious engagement with forms of explanation allowed him to critique his own approach. His is an example of an ethnography that was "not primarily an ethnographic study, a retelling of data for later synthesis by other scientists." Rather, it was "a study of the ways in which data can fit together, and the fitting together of data is what I mean by 'explanation'" (Bateson, 1958: 280–281). Starting with the Naven ceremony of the Iatmul, Bateson constructed a cybernetic model for understanding the system of ritual as indoctrination, one that may also be applied to the nuclear weapon scientists studied by Gusterson. And Leach was able to construct a model of the Kachin political system that illuminates its inherent contradictions as part of a functioning system, an idea that has been useful to Nash and Nader. But Gusterson's comparison of a laboratory institution with the movement of antinuclear activists was as powerful as the comparison made by Lock between North American and Japanese constructions of menopause, even though his institutional units of comparison, the institutions of a military industrial unit and democratic networks of citizen activists, were not made comparable in a controlled manner. Ethnography, as theory, recognizes the importance of ethnographers reconstructing their categories as a contribution to theory. But it took a long time to arrive at such an understanding. Paradigms are powerful tools for maintenance of the normal. But so are reviews.

In a review of Donald Cole and Soraya Altorki's ethnography *Bedouin Settlers and Holiday-Makers: Egypt's Changing Northwest Coast* (1998), Dinero (2000: 197) concludes by chastising the authors for their lack of space:

> stepping out of the role of traditional anthropologists and into the roles of advocate and policy analysis, they question, "the relative benefits to the region of investing huge amounts of capital to construct [these tourist villages]." Their desire to advocate for Bedouin interests in opposition to Western forces is both a strength and a weakness. Cole and Altorki are strongest when explaining the intricacies of Matruh social life and weakest when they lose academic distance to go off on politically charged tangents. For example, a diatribe on the Israeli occupation of the Sinai is minor, but unnecessary and distracting (Cole and Atorki, 1998: 23). In another instance, an off-hand reference to a Matruh Bedouin boy being injured by a mine "planted by the '*civilized*' British, Germans, or Italians" 50 years ago (1998: 88, emphasis added) seems pointless and petty.

An Outsider Looking In on Anthropology's Ethnography

As anyone familiar with the current literature on ethnography knows, the genre is popular today, maybe even a fad. In sociology some write that the ethnographer is a worker, a professional like any other, unattached to any particular discipline: ethnography is a technique. Students in education, geography, political science, and psychology all want to learn how to do ethnography and may even think ethnography is historically intrinsic to their discipline. What ethnography is, however, changes as it is adopted and appropriated. In the corporate world, ethnography is now an accepted market research technique, and there is an all-time high in the demand for ethnographers to do market research. Furthermore, some of the components of ethnographic work have been borrowed and adapted for varied purposes. *Participant observation* has become *participatory research*, particularly as conducted in World Bank projects or by the ethnographer who poses as the voice of the Other. Or ethnography gets equated with "hanging out," qualitative as opposed to quantitative research. Some people even believe that you can do an ethnography in, say, six weeks or less. In applied anthropology "rapid assessment" is all the rage right now. What follows from this diffusion of ethnography across disciplines and out into the marketplace are the inevitable criticisms of, or compliments paid to, its discipline of origin. One such critique was a seminar paper by Mayssun Succarie (2004), at that time a UC Berkeley graduate student in the School of Education, originally from Lebanon. She called her essay "Controlling/Liberating Ethnography."

Succarie first encountered ethnographers and anthropologists in 1993 as a student at the American University in Beirut, while working at the nearby Palestinian camp of Shatila. At Shatila, she witnessed many waves of ethnographers, some of whom conducted their research on the third generation of Palestinian youth living there. (As we shall see, she came to resent ethnographers and their activities.) Shatila is one of twelve Palestinian refugee camps in Lebanon. Over time, Shatila attracted ethnographers from Europe and the United States who researched topics in human rights, conflict resolution, education, public health, and architecture. An early ethnographic project conducted in 1995 by a student from Columbia University dealt with how the memory of the massacre was transmitted to young children between 9 and 18 years old. Succarie (2004) observes: "Besides being painful, the process of interviewing [about the massacre] internalizes in the mind of the children that they are victims to forces they cannot deal with." Summing up the situation, a 14-year-old asks, "What makes researchers so interested in the dead . . . but still abuse the living?"

Succarie, as an outsider to ethnography, makes her first observation – the ethnographers were hurting their subjects in the camp.

An anthropologist from Norway stayed in Shatila eight months in the late 1990s doing ethnography on children's rights. Succarie (2004) remarked: "The children were always asked about what they do not have, what they lacked, and what 'children's rights' they were deprived of." The Norwegian ethnographer used focus groups (a marketing innovation, by the way) to ask the children, for example, if their right to play was being satisfied in the camp. When the children answered in the affirmative and told the ethnographer about the games they had invented, the ethnographer countered with, "[but] do you have playgrounds and green spaces? . . . [If not], then your right to play is violated."

Later, UNICEF funded a child-to-child program in the camp, and Succarie, our critical observer, watched as those very same children now repeated to UNICEF officials what they had learned from the first researchers. They had learned that their life is nothing but a bunch of problems, and that they are nothing but poor and helpless – a victim mentality. They learned that they are children who need someone, somewhere, to solve their problems for them. If they are really going to be able to play and have fun, to be "normal," they need the help of an NGO (nongovernmental organization). The concept of "lack" and "scarcity" induced the children to consider themselves as needy. Inasmuch as humanitarian workers and ethnographers focus on such things as a child's right to play in the refugee camp, important as the problem might be, the political cause of Palestinians and the need to find a resolution to the conflict that is the cause of the situation in the first place are lost sight of. The political problem becomes psychological. Succarie, then, as an outside observer, came to consider these foreign ethnographers as agents of pacification. Instead of children engaged in a dignified struggle for recognition and liberation, refugee camp children, with the help of entrepreneurial NGOs and ethnographic researchers, became victims, poor, needy, helpless, and appropriate pacified objects for palliative "humanitarian" intervention. In this light, Succarie noted, ethnography was operating as a process of government by creating needy people pacified by questioning, projects, and research focused on problems – problems with no solutions. The meaning given to past suffering, and to an intolerable present, is overwhelmed by a new external vision, adopted from the outsider, where the present and the future become nothing but uncertain and hopeless.

Upon arriving at UC Berkeley, Succarie continued critically observing anthropologists and ethnography. She found that anthropologists were embroiled in issues she found strange, given her experience with researchers in Lebanon: for example, the so-called crises of representation, neutrality, and concerns over how to present academic work in a way that avoids politics. Why were anthropologists so afraid to "give voice" to the people they worked with? And how is it that somebody could even ask her – what does politics have to do with education? Can there really be such a thing as an apolitical research method, especially when one deals with real human beings and critical situations?

At Berkeley, "participatory" kept surfacing for Succarie as an important methodological concept. It caused her to recall an event of so-called participatory research on menopause that she observed at Shatila. First, the researcher translated the word menopause into Arabic, inventing a phrase, since no exact equivalent of the English exists. The unfortunate phrase that the researcher chose was "the age of despair." As the researcher explained to the women at Shatila, it usually starts in the late forties and early fifties. "It is '48," one of the older women responded, "The age of despair for all Palestinians started in '48 when we were driven from our homeland." The woman, not knowing what "the age of despair" was, attributed it to the 1948 forced exodus from Palestine. When the researcher tried to explain, she was fiercely attacked by another of the older women who accused her of being a spy trying to distract women in the camps from the issue of Palestine to focus on trivial topics such as women caring about "our own bodies." A great example of how ethnographic research can be devoid of anthropology.

After enrolling in a seminar covering the last 100 years of ethnography at UC Berkeley, Succarie was again shocked to read the first set of monographs covering the period 1896–1960; she found them to be "incontrovertibly meant for small scale, designed to elucidate social processes in bounded communities." However, when she got to the 1990s and specifically to June Nash's work, she noted, "Her analysis of existing power structures and social inequalities that are due not only to local but also to global forces broke [with] the concept of ethnography as confined to [the] local." She found Lock's and Gonzalez's works refreshingly liberating in that they moved beyond the earlier modernist discourse of progress and the Western exceptionalism and superiority that it implies. My own *Harmony Ideology* (1990) and Julia Paley's *Marketing Democracy* (2003) gave her the idea that ethnography could also play a role in a project of liberation. As she later (2004) reflected, "Practices of the present have their roots in a colonial past. The connections and comparisons between history, local knowledge, colonial influences, global hegemony, cultural ideology, actual practice made me reconcile with studying history for understanding today."

In a way, Succarie's classroom experience with anthropology and ethnography is a story with a happy ending. Her former disgust with anthropologists and ethnography, as she observed it practiced in the Palestinian refugee camp of Shatila, was transformed into a critical appreciation of ethnography as a practice that can also be employed in projects aimed at opening up the possibilities of thought and innovative action in the present. Ethnography is not any single practice; practitioners are highly heterodox with respect to the conceptual frames to which they subscribe, and the purposes toward which they implement their research practices. Ethnography is double-edged. But the story of Succarie, as ethnographer, never fully escapes the conditions of time and place. I tell Succarie's story here as a parable of how ethnography came of age. But I also tell her story because, like the anthropologists that I cite, her critical reflections on what it means to know about and act in the world continues to challenge those who would divide the human race, disparaging a part of it, and use the methods of the social sciences not to celebrate human creativity and dignity but rather to participate in making some people the objects of others, even if only the miserable objects of humanitarian aid.

Concluding Comments

If indeed we are co-temporal with the people we seek to study, if we are contemporary with each other, ethnographers can contribute to this shared reality in a number of ways. We can start, for example, by making explicit comparisons that most often have remained implicit. Lock's work on menopause, where she compares not only the experiences of women in the United States and Japan but also how the phenomenon is treated differently by medical scientists in both countries, is a wonderful exception. We can also study the subordination of First World citizens, as June Nash (1989) did with the Pittsfield workers, revealing something that Third World peoples have a hard time fathoming, that First World people are often colonized people as well. Or we can study the propaganda system that feeds the denial of reality. As Chomsky noted (1987: 186), "To this day we cannot face the elementary fact that the U.S. attacked Vietnam." The United States managed to transfer the blame to the Vietnamese, virtually without comment, probably even without awareness. For Chomsky this was a natural feature of a business-run society, "a society based on forms of manipulation and deceit as found in marketing and advertising." He made a direct contrast: "The Russians knew they had invaded Afghanistan and [that] Russia was not the injured party." The United States did not.

A Canadian prize-winning essayist and novelist, John Ralston Saul, argues in his *The Unconscious Civilization* (1997) that the twentieth century was a century of ideologies. Among the ideologies mentioned he includes free-market capitalism, the social sciences, neoconservativism, and psychotherapy – "all based on certainties as rigid and narrow as those doggedly held by the Bolsheviks and Fascists" (Nader, 1997: 732). Thus, "the West [and its institutions such as the World Bank and IMF] is still dispensing 'civilization,' the economy imagined as impersonal, an irresistible force that will benefit private choice free of coercion" (Nader, 1997: 733). The belief in the infallible invisible hand of the market is a belief that contributes to the cause of business and commercialization in the world and the power that it wields over us, not only as members of the general population but also, as I have tried to indicate, as anthropologists.

The study of how the powerless become empowered is not so different from how the powerful got their power. Ethnography, with all its flaws, has been an influential practice, helping us make connections between different people and the experiences that they hold in common at a time when more and more we find ourselves divided and even isolated from one another. However, ethnography cannot serve this purpose if it continues to be practiced in a bounded and closed fashion, if the comparisons that we all make between ourselves and others remain implicit in our rigorous academic work. Today there exists a large potential for contemporary anthropological research which remains untapped because the transforming powers of commerce or unregulated accumulation and plunder are too infrequently configured politically. Leach was quite right: it is time to move beyond the binaries of us and them. In fact, if we do not, our ethnographies will increasingly be used as means of control rather than enlightenment (as in imperial wars) by the allied social sciences, marketers, national security planners, or by anthropologists themselves. And while enlightenment is salient in the stated ethnographic mission, the history of its uses and misuse indicates a close alignment with colonialism, imperialism, unilateral invasions, and other aggressive activities. This is why Leach urges that Western scholars should apply the same standard of rationality and credibility to the thought of their own society as they do to the thought of native and "primitive" people.

If followed, such rigor leads us necessarily, I argue, to practice ethnography as explicit comparison. For example, in my own work I have asked: What do people actually mean when they state that Islamic women are oppressed? To whom exactly are these women being compared? Our own society? The rates of violence against women in the United States might surprise the self-righteous. Making our assumptions explicit often leads to surprising insights and conclusions not only about others but about ourselves. The Yanomani are hostile and aggressive as compared to whom? Are the Yanomani more violent than members of an inner-city gang or then military strategists who would have the United States military actively engaged on multiple fronts in the Middle East? When we speak of torture in Chinese prisons, should we not also consider torture in US prisons or as conducted by US agencies and personnel? Of course there is torture in US prisons. An estimated 80000 Americans are in solitary confinement. Once we forge across the barrier dividing us from them we may find, for example, as with the history of torture, that it implicates agents the world over. Such self-consciousness about comparison as a discovery tool automatically leads to engagement, enlightenment, and humility appropriately befitting a discipline designed to study the human condition writ large.

As quoted in the epigraph at the opening of this essay, Bateson considered "the most precious tool of science" to be a combination of both loose and strict thinking. Anthropology and its research methods are particularly well positioned to push the social sciences forward in this way. Professionalization acts as a regulator, constraining us as to what is considered good, right, or fashionable. Calls for the liberation of anthropology would do well to work for a discipline that is creative rather than repetitive, inclusive rather than exclusive, dynamic rather than static. Instead of fleeing from a research practice that has often been tainted by its involvement with both colonialism and US imperialism, cloaking ourselves with and defending our relevance in purely philosophical terms, and thereby disengaging, we should embrace the power that comparative ethnography still affords us for opening up possibilities for reflection and action in the present. We cannot escape the moral responsibility resting on our shoulders as scientists and citizens by isolating ourselves even further from those we study and the population at large in the name of false objectivities, or by forcing the same disengagement on colleagues. The road to take is the one that would connect humans rather than divide them, increase the circulation of critical perspectives across disciplines and geopolitical regions instead of block them. *Reinventing Anthropology* (Hymes, 1969) was intended to call our most cherished assumptions into question, whether in relation to race, gender, or science. And as if the rewards that I have pointed to are not enough, wouldn't such an engaged anthropology, by making itself relevant to current critical situations and the lives of contemporary humans, also attract to itself a larger readership? Us and Them – in addition to mutual respect for human dignity, better theorizing.

Note

1   See also Tambiah (2002) Chapter 10, pp. 259–90, "The Comparativist Stance: Us and Them and the Translation of Culture," and Chapter 17, pp. 429–555, "Retrospective Assessment and Rethinking Anthropology."

References

Bateson, Gregory (1958 [1936]) *Naven: A Survey of the Problems Suggested by a Composite Picture of the Culture of a New Guinea Tribe Drawn from Three Points of View*. Stanford: Stanford University Press.

Bateson, Gregory (1971) *Steps to an Ecology of Mind*. San Francisco: Chandler Publishing Company.

Bentley, Jeffery W. (2003) Review of *Zapotec Science: Farming and Food in the Northern Sierra of Oaxaca* by Roberto Gonzalez. *Latin American Antiquity*, 14, no. 3, pp. 357–359.

Borofsky, Robert (1987) *Making History: Pukapukan and Anthropological Constructions of Knowledge*. Cambridge: Cambridge University Press.

Chen, Nancy (2003) *Breathing Spaces: Qigong, Psychiatry and Healing in China*. New York: Columbia University Press.

Chomsky, Noam (1987) *The Chomsky Reader*, ed. James Peck. New York: Pantheon Press.

Cole, Donald, and Soraya Altorki (1998) *Bedouin, Settlers, and Holiday-makers: Egypt's Changing Northwest Coast*. Cairo: University of Cairo Press.

Dinero, Steven C. (2000) Review of *Bedouin, Settlers, and Holiday-Makers: Egypt's Changing Northwest Coast* by Donald P. Cole and Soraya Altorki. *American Ethnologist*, 27, no. 3, pp. 756.

Evans-Pritchard, E. E. (1976 [1937]) *Witchcraft, Oracles, and Magic among the Azande*. Oxford: Clarendon Press.

Fortune, Reo (1932) *Sorcerers of Dobu: The Social Anthropology of the Dobu Islanders of the Western Pacific*. London: G. Routledge & Sons.

Geertz, Clifford (1973) *The Interpretation of Cultures*. New York: Basic Books.

Geertz, Clifford (1995) *After the Fact: Two Countries, Four Decades, One Anthropologist*. Cambridge, MA: Harvard University Press.

Gonzalez, Roberto (2001) *Zapotec Science: Farming and Food in the Northern Sierra of Oaxaca*. Austin: University of Texas Press.

Gonzalez, Roberto (2009) *American Counterinsurgency: Human Science and the Human Terrain*. Chicago: Prickly Paradigm Press.

Gusterson, Hugh (1996) *Nuclear Rites: A Weapons Laboratory at the End of the Cold War*. Berkeley, CA: University of California Press.

Hymes, Dell (ed.) (1969) *Reinventing Anthropology*. New York: Pantheon Books.

Leach, Edmund R. (1965 [1954]) *Political Systems of Highland Burma: A Study of Kachin Social Structure*. Boston: Beacon Press.

Leach, Edmund R. (1989 [1987]) Tribal Ethnography: Past, Present, Future. *Cambridge Anthropology*, 11, no. 2, 1–14.

Lock, Margaret (1993) *Encounters with Aging: Mythologies of Menopause in Japan and North America*. Berkeley, CA: University of California Press.

MacMillan, Hugh (1995) Return to the Malungwana Drift – Max Gluckman, the Zulu Nation, and the Common Society. *African Affairs*, 94, 39–65.

Malinowski, Bronislaw (1935) *Coral Gardens and Their Magic: A Study of the Methods of Tilling the Soil and of Agricultural Rites in the Trobriand Islands*. New York: American Book Company.

Malinowski, Bronislaw (1948) *Magic, Science and Religion, and Other Essays*. Boston: Beacon Press.

Malinowski, Bronislaw (1984 [1922]) *Argonauts of the Western Pacific: An Account of Native Enterprise and Adventure in the Archipelagoes of Melanesian New Guinea*. Prospect Heights, IL.: Waveland Press.

Marcus, George, and Michael Fischer (1986) *Anthropology as Cultural Critique: An Experimental Moment in the Human Sciences*. Chicago: University of Chicago Press.

Mooney, James (1896) *The Ghost-Dance Religion and the Sioux Outbreak of 1890*. Washington, DC: US Government Printing Office.

Moses, L. G. (1984) *Indian Man: A Biography of James Mooney*. Urbana, IL: University of Illinois Press.

Nader, Laura (1969) Up the Anthropologist: Perspectives Gained from Studying Up. In *Reinventing Anthropology*. Dell Hymes, (ed.). New York: Pantheon Books, pp. 284–311.

Nader, Laura (1990) *Harmony Ideology: Law and Justice in a Mountain Zapotec Village*. Stanford, CA: Stanford University Press.

Nader, Laura (1996) *Naked Science: Anthropological Inquiry Into Boundaries, Power, and Knowledge*. New York: Routledge.

Nader, Laura (1997) Controlling Processes: Tracing the Dynamic Components of Power. *Current Anthropology*, 28, no. 5, pp. 711–738.

Nader, Laura (1999) Review of Clifford Geertz's *After the Fact: Two Countries, Four Decades, One Anthropologist. Isis*, 90, no. 3, 626–627.

Nash, June (1989) *From Tank Town to High Tech: The Clash of Community and Industrial Cycles*. Albany, NY: State University of New York Press.

Nash, June (1993 [1979]) *We Eat the Mines and the Mines Eat Us: Dependency and Exploitation in Bolivian Tin Mines*. New York: Columbia University Press.

Paley, Julia (2003) *Marketing Democracy: Power and Social Movements in Post-Dictatorship Chile*. Berkeley, CA: University of California Press.

Rivers, W. H. R. (1906) *The Todas*. London: MacMillan.

Said, Edward (1978) *Orientalism*. New York: Pantheon Books.

Saul, John Ralston (1997) *The Unconscious Civilization*. New York: Free Press.

Stern, B. (1936) Review of *Coral Gardens and Their Magic*, by B. Malinowski. *American Sociological Review*, 1, no. 6, pp. 1016–1018.

Succarie, Mayssun (2004) Controlling/Liberating Ethnography. Paper submitted in the seminar "Classic Ethnographies." Department of Anthropology, University of California, Berkeley.

Swedenburg, Ted (1995) *Memories of Revolt: The 1936–1939 Rebellion and the Palestinian National Past*. Minneapolis: University of Minnesota Press.

Tambiah, Stanley J. (2002) *Edmund Leach: An Anthropological Life*. Cambridge: Cambridge University Press.

Wolf, Eric (1969) American Anthropologists and American Society. In *Reinventing Anthropology*. D. Hymes (ed.). New York: Pantheon Books, pp. 251–263.

Further Reading

Chomsky, Noam (1985) The Bounds of Thinkable Thought. *The Progressive*, 28 October, pp. 28–31.

Succarie, Mayssun (2000) For the Sake of Remembrance: A Reader in English for the 9th Graders in the Palestinian Camps in Lebanon. MA Thesis submitted to the American University of Beirut, Beirut.

Succarie, Mayssun (2008) Winning Hearts and Minds: Education, Culture, and Control. A dissertation submitted for Doctor of Philosophy in Education at the University of California, Berkeley.

4

Orientalism, Occidentalism, and the Control of Women

Presently there is a worldwide concern for improving the status of women. Some of this concern has come from the West. However, the implementation of strategies to "improve" women's lives has moved out from national policies to the agenda at the United Nations. A central dogma[1] in both Western and non-Western states is that Western economic development and industrialization will improve the condition of Third-World women. There is also a widespread belief that women in the United States and Western European countries are better off vis-à-vis their menfolk than their sisters in societies that are not "developed." These assumptions are challenged on many levels.

One source of challenge comes from the increasing number of studies conducted by Western and Third-World scholars that question the definition, aims, means, scope, and results of development (see, e.g., Rihani, 1978; Nelson and Olesen, 1977). Another challenge to Western assumptions comes from women who are part of nationalist,

Culture and Dignity: Dialogues between the Middle East and the West,
First Edition. Laura Nader.
© 2013 John Wiley & Sons, Inc. Published 2013 by John Wiley & Sons, Inc.

religious, or ethnic movements in the Third World. These women believe that they are better off than their exploited Western sisters.

Such assertions and counterassertions are important parts of Eastern and Western discourses. They have great implications, some of which will be dealt with here. This chapter is *not* about scaling societies to prove which is better or worse, nor is it geared toward answering questions of improved status for women. In fact, it steers away from such simplistic notions as "progress" and "improvement," so prevalent among Westerners and Eastern elites and yet worthless tools in comparative research. My aim here is to identify how images of women in other societies can be prejudicial to women in one's own society. Although male dogmas are common in contemporary nation-states, the patterns vary. It is this variation that is so important to the maintenance of different patriarchal systems. In other words, misleading cultural comparisons support contentions of positional superiority that divert attention from the processes that are controlling women in both worlds (Hatem, 1989).

An examination of East–West critiques of gender relations forces us to consider the use of comparison in gender construction. Critique of the other may be an instrument of control when the comparison asserts a positional superiority. The questions are twofold: (i) How does critique of the other operate as a key to the process by which civilizations and nation-states control their own women and the women of other cultures?; (ii) How are the dynamics of male dogma controlled by notions that women's place vis-à-vis men improves with the development of civilization, or the contrary view – that the higher the civilization, the increased ascendancy of men? These two questions will combine to address the dynamics of male dogma operating in contemporary and interacting world systems: How could images of women in other cultures act as a control to women in one's own society?

The theoretical framework for this research stems from the concept of hegemony, the notion of "true discourse," and the idea of positional superiority. The notion of hegemony, as developed by Gramsci (1971), implies that systems of thought develop over time and reflect the interests of certain classes and/or groups in society who have managed to universalize their own beliefs and values. These beliefs or dogmas are produced and reproduced through the work of "intellectual elites," and, according to Gramsci, the resultant control is structured in terms of consent rather than force or domination, through "civil society" rather than "state-as-force." Foucault's analysis shifts attention from theorizing about ideology to "a consideration of the relations of truth and power which is constitutive of hegemony" (Smart, 1986: 160–161). His notion of "true discourses" (Gramsci, 1971) refers to the restriction of discourse on alternative conceptions of reality and provides a set of concepts with which to understand the exercise and the operation of power in its different forms. Both Gramsci and Foucault agree that a hegemonic relationship is established "not through force or coercion, nor necessarily through consent, but most effectively by way of practices, techniques, and methods which infiltrate minds and bodies, tastes, desires and needs" (Smart, 1986: 160–161). Edward Said approaches the relation of East and West with these Gramscian–Foucaultian concerns. He questions how, in a specific historical and cultural context, a hegemonic discourse has resulted from a play of "power" and "truth." Posed this way, Said moves the domain into the comparative realm and posits a relationship between the East and the West in which, he asserts, the latter has come to situate itself as "positionally superior" to the former.

This chapter extends Said's observation that the Muslim world exists "for" the West, to include the notion that the West also exists "for" the Islamic world and serves as an important contrastive comparison that restricts and controls women's resistance. The ideas of hegemony, restricted discourse, and positional superiority are used as complementary theoretical devices to illuminate the juxtaposition of dogmas of female subordination in US and Western European writings with those from the Arab Islamic world and will enable us to provide materials with which to understand the dynamics that emanate from homogeneous and formulaic images of the other. The model I am introducing explains gender construction as a result of interactions between two large world regions – the European West and the Arab East.

Feminist strategies are so often part of the controlling male dogmas – not feminist in origin, but directly related to the shape of the male control structure (Reiter, 1975). And, of course, the reverse might also be true, that male forms of control may be associated with patterns of adaptation (or submission) and resistance found among women.

Cultural Hierarchy and Processes of Control

In his 1955 Fawcette Lecture to the women students of Bedford College in London, England, Evans-Pritchard is quoted as saying that:

> primitive societies and barbarous societies and the historical societies of Europe and the East exhibit almost every variety of social institutions, but in all of them, regardless of the form of social structure, men are always in the ascendancy, and this is perhaps the more evident the higher the civilization.

The two editors who quote from Evans-Pritchard's lecture then note that his lecture is full of contradictions because he "does not . . . associate servility with high civilization" (Etienne and Leacock 1980: 1–2). That Evans-Pritchard stopped short of associating servility with high civilization is an example of a comparison redolent with ambivalence and contradiction. What Said calls "positional superiority" is evoked not only on the political level between cultures, but it also works itself into the structure of knowledge. If ambivalence and contradiction characterize the thesis of universal subordination, how do apologists for civilizations East and West deal with those contradictions? They do so by using positional superiority.

As noted in Chapter 2, Edward Said's controversial book, *Orientalism*, was published in 1979 as a critique of Western writings about the Orient. It was perceived by many reviewers as an attack on orientalist scholars. Said had been deeply influenced by the work of Michel Foucault, and his was an analysis of scholarship as cultural control. Orientalism is about the mechanisms through which the West managed its relation to the East. As he himself stated the process:

> Orientalism – a way of coming to terms with the Orient that is based on the Orient's special place in European Western experience. The Orient is not only adjacent to Europe; it is also the place of Europe's greatest and richest and oldest colonies, the source of its civilization and languages, its cultural contestant and one of its deepest and most recurring images of the other. In addition, the Orient has helped to define Europe (or the West) as its contrasting image, idea, personality, experience (Said 1978: 1–2).

Said describes orientalism (1978: 3) as a "Western style for dominating, restructuring, and having authority over the Orient." It is, he says, a form of discourse, a way of dealing with the Orient "by making statements about it, authorizing views of it, describing it, by teaching it, settling it, ruling over it . . . an accepted grid for filtering the Orient into Western consciousness. . . . which puts the Westerner in a series of relationships with the Orient without ever losing him the relative upper hand." For Said, the strategies of orientalist scholars were apparent. Their writings are shot through with various kinds of racism and a dogmatic view of the Orient is portrayed as an ideal and unchanging abstraction.

The concept of an "accepted grid for filtering the Orient into Western consciousness" is a concept akin to thought control. What filters through is all we are allowed to know about the Orient from scholars and experts. Although Said does not have much to say directly about the condition of women either in the Orient (most orientalists are male) or in the Occident, I would like to use his notion of the orientalist grid to show how women are maintained as a subordinate class in both the Eastern and the Western worlds. In addition, I wish to point out that writers of the East also use a grid through which they filter the West and by which they react to the West. The "other" is not mute, in either direction. The Orient's grid, which we might call occidentalism, also operates as a controlling process over Eastern women.

The Specificity of Eastern and Western Grids

Although, as we will see, orientalism and occidentalism both impact women, the two represent quite different processes.[2] Orientalism is a construction that we can deconstruct. Occidentalism is not a historical or ideological category that we know a lot about. Notions about the Occident are not coalesced in a large body of scholarship. There are very few books and articles written by contemporary Arab scholars about the West. A comparable literature to orientalism is nonexistent. There is much spoken about the West, and there is an Islamic fundamentalist view of the West that we can delineate, but this is hardly shared by all Muslims. There are "grids" through which the West is filtered, but how the East filters the West is barely understood. The word "occidentalism" is nonexistent in Arabic, although it can be derived. The derivative – *esteghrab* – is rarely used, and when used has to be contextualized, because the common use of *esteghrab* is in the meaning of wonder and astonishment. Orientalism, on the other hand, is partly defined by the proliferation of books on the Orient. In a century and a half, 1800–1950, it is estimated that 60000 books were published on the Arab Orient alone (Salama, 1981). The fact that these books were one of the most effective mechanisms through which the Orient was filtered into Western consciousness (especially with the higher literacy rate in the West) calls attention to the various means available for "filtering" other cultures: books, newspapers, radio, television.

These means are important to explicate, for they are an expression, and also a consequence, of the nature of the relationship between the Occident and the Orient. Today the West is accessible to the people of the Orient through modern communications technology. The East is not accessible to the West in the same way. The West presents itself by means of soap operas or movies about the Wild West, or by the nightly news. The West also presents its construction of the East through the variety of media that portray Arabs as terrorists whose women are veiled.

While people are fascinated by the technological advances of the West, they are also aware of its social problems. News of scandal, rape, drugs, murder, and molestation in the West occupy considerable space in the major news media of the Arab Middle East. Such problems are rarely commented upon, but are a very effective mechanism by which Eastern conservatism is maintained. Common sense and public oratory lead people to believe that they are spared the social problems of the West because of their religion.

Knowledge about the West has a strong bearing on the position of women, for it is through this knowledge that the grip on women is justified in many countries of the Middle East. Women are no longer treated as Arab women, but as "potential Westerners," posing a severe identity crisis. How Arab women should act and what they should want to achieve are no longer a matter of consensus, and differ within the varied frameworks of Arab political and religious nationalisms. Arab Muslim women resent Western models of aspiration as they encroach on their lives and are used as justification of Muslim "fundamentalism." Some religious leaders have put the entire matter into an internalist perspective. Instead of blaming the West for exporting its ills, they are searching for the agencies that import them. In fact, one factor that helps various religious groups gain legitimacy for their political activities among the populations of many Muslim countries is this tendency to hold their governments responsible, at least partly, for bringing these "ills" home. This adds up to a kind of "siege mentality" in which stripping Arab women of their rights has become well justified, and condoned as a protective act.

The "siege mentality" has theoretically reversed a long-maintained Eastern view of Westerners as "potential Muslims." Muslims adopt religious dichotomies in which peoples of the world are either *Mu'minoon* (believers) or *Kafironon* (nonbelievers). If the orientalists' view of the Orient is redolent with racism, as Said (1978) maintains, for Muslims, at least in theory, nonbelievers are not inherently "bad" or "inferior," they only need the "right" religion. Consequently, Muslim positional superiority is not based on intrinsic qualities specific to a certain race, but on the acceptance of religious ideas that can be shared by all humans.

Positional Superiority, Thought Systems, and Other Cultures

Evoking positional superiority as a method of control between and within civilizations takes different forms and makes use of different mechanisms. In the West, positions of superiority are translated into development programs for transforming the lives of those who are technologically underdeveloped, and the mechanisms used are related to programs of economic development (see Rihani, 1978). Development then becomes a strategy by means of which the West can help promote and spread the idea of progress and the technological society that symbolizes progress.

In the East, evoking positional superiority as a method of control takes a quite different shape in rhetoric claiming to be more philosophical and less materialist. Many modern Islamic movements have concerned themselves with a "theology of universalism, a monolithic religion, a perfect blueprint for a just society" (Stawasser, 1987: 4), a vision which is meant to be a challenge to the West, in particular, and a hope for the large numbers of impoverished Muslims. The intent is messianic in both the Western and Eastern positions. In this context female subordination increasingly comes to be rationalized or maintained in terms of the "other." By taking a position of superiority vis-à-vis the "other," both East and West can rationalize the position of their women and manage their relation to the "other," at least as long as they can keep the fiction of otherness in place. Under conditions of modernization and cultural diffusion of Western forms it becomes increasingly difficult to assume positional superiority. (Although perhaps it is closer to the truth to say that it becomes increasingly difficult to assume the same forms of positional superiority: in reality, the West has long maintained its assumed superiority, at one time or another, through religion, science, technology, political systems, etc.) When the East borrows Western technology, a lifestyle accompanies these new forms and Western gender relations travel with the technology. The crisis that ensues complicates the situation for Eastern cultures and for its women and stimulates some to search for solution in Islam.

The crisis for women arises from the discrepancy between development beliefs and development results. In the West economic development arguments support the belief that, with the spread of Western educational systems, the modernization of the workforce, and by strengthening the individual, women would be free from domination by men governed by traditional patriarchal values. With economic development would come progress and increasingly egalitarian relations between the sexes. Ester Boserup argued to the contrary in her critical book *Women's Role in Economic Development* (1965). Her conclusions – that development was decreasing women's self-sufficiency, that it was increasing dependence on men while adding a double burden to women's workdays – were startling.[3] In the two decades of gender research that followed Boserup's original argument, case studies such as those of the apparel and micro-electronics industries, and studies of the expansion of industrial production to areas of Asia, Africa, Latin America, and the Caribbean, confirmed Boserup's conclusion that women's lives were changed, but not necessarily for the better (Tinker, 1976; Dangler, 1976; Chaney and Schmink, 1976; Boulding, 1976; Rogers, 1980; Nash and Femandez-Kelley, 1983; Ong, 1987). In spite of these findings, the argument that economic development contributes to the emancipation of women in the less developed countries is still popularly believed, and operates as a basic building block in organizations such as the World Bank and the US Agency for International Development. The positional superiority of Western women as symbolic of the positional superiority of the West is a deeply ingrained idea. The contrastive mechanisms by which such beliefs are continually imprinted are interesting in themselves.

Ways of Seeing and Comparing – East and West

The ways in which other cultures are filtered are important to explicate, for they are an expression and a consequence of the nature of the relationship between the Occident and the Orient. As I mentioned in Chapter 2, Sandra Naddaf's (1986) comparison of an Egyptian scholar/translator's description of his travels to Parisian cafés of the 1830s and an English traveler's description of Cairo during the same period suggests that the author may hide his existence in the scene he describes as a detached observer or he may reflect both subject and object. The Egyptian traveler includes his own reflection in the cafe mirror as integral to the scene he describes. His representation of another culture, as Naddaf points out, does not become a means of distancing oneself from the other, rather it becomes a means of integration.[4] The Egyptian assumes the role of translator between the two cultures finding the common points of reference. The English traveler holds the mirror to reflect Egyptian society without being a part of the reflected image.

Naddaf's observations provide a useful analogy to the pattern of keeping feminist literature on the Orient separate from comparison with the literature on Western women "as if Muslim women represented a species apart, one subject to its own unique laws and imperatives" (Rassam, n.d.). Indeed, it is revealing that American conferences on the international status of women usually focus on women in the Third World. Margaret Mead in her 1926 book on *Sex and Temperament* certainly sought to implicitly compare the role of non-Western women vis-à-vis their menfolk with that of women in the United States. The tradition in anthropology since Mead of juxtaposing the position of women in other cultures with women in the West has not been explicit.

In *Women and Colonization* (1980) Mona Etienne and Eleanor Leacock relate gender roles and status to Western colonizing processes, and although they write about the effects on women of Western colonization practices with the spread of industrial capitalism, there is no article dealing with the large literature on the first female victims of Western industrialization – European and American women. The absence of explicit comparison is a controlling process suggestive of the idea that, while it may be bad here, it is really worse in the Middle East or elsewhere. The rigorous comparison of where Western women really stand vis-à-vis their men relative to Third-World men and women has not been made, perhaps because to deconstruct the basic building blocks of Western positional superiority would constitute a threat to our relations with the developing world.

In the Islamic world, the deconstruction of the building blocks of positional superiority was accomplished by an expansionist, colonizing West. Since the beginning of the colonial encounter with the West, the Islamic world has had to face Western standards of modernism that were often foisted upon it from the outside. However, both internal and external efforts to modernize brought increased dependence upon, and domination by, the West. In *The Islamic Impulse*, edited by Barbara Stowasser (1987a), the authors attempt to chronicle the crisis that results when the positional superiority of Islamic civilization is confronted by a secularism that challenges the very core of Islam (see Stowasser, 1987a: 4). Stowasser, however, overstates the degree of challenge Islam faces, for secularism is a two-edged notion, and the assessment has to be made not only in terms of the challenge but also in terms of the response. According to the authors in her volume, Islamic fundamentalism is not a program in the Western sense, like a development program, for example. It can be understood as a mood, a search for an Islamic meaning in the modern world, a movement directed toward self-improvement (inward) not toward changing others (outward) as is the case with development programs.

"Religious Ideology, Women, and the Family: The Islamic Paradigm" (Stowasser, 1987b) introduces a contemporary interpretation of the role, rights, and responsibilities of the Muslim woman. Stowasser studies a popular guide for the Muslim woman by Egyptian author Shaykh I-Sha'rawi, who published it in Cairo in 1982 as the ideal paradigm by which a woman's life may be measured and accounted as truly Islamic. Although the entire article is a fascinating account of strategies of internalist control, I will concentrate my attention on the strategy of positional superiority used by Shaykh I-Sha'rawi. In the selections that Stowasser presents there are recurrent derogatory references to the West. Such references may be designed to present the Islamic paradigm in the most favorable light, to respond to provocative criticisms from the West, or simply to correct the record.[5]

In regard to women's rights Stowasser presents the following comparisons made by Shaykh Sha'rawi:

Islam . . . provided the woman with complete civil rights which do not exist in any other religion. The Jewish woman is subject to the guardianship of her father before marriage and to her husband after marriage. In French positive law, she does not have the right to stipulate individual property for herself against her husband.

If we were to take a good look, we would find that Western civilization deprives the woman of her particular attributes. What are the primary characteristics of the human being? They are shape, characteristic features, and name. When a woman marries in Europe, she calls herself by her husband's name. She does not have the right to retain her name or her father's or mother's name. As a result of the infatuation of the "imitators" with the West at the beginning of the Renaissance, women found themselves compelled to eliminate their fathers' and their families' names and retain only their own. This was difficult to do, although in Europe and America a woman relinquishes her name altogether and is addressed by the name of her husband and his family as a matter of course. What equality exists there for a woman after she has been deprived of her name? In Islam, however, even the wives of the Prophet – what was the noblest of all creation and whose name to carry would have honored every single one of them – were not called Madame Muhammad ibn 'Abd All, or wife of Muhammad, but 'A'isha bint Abi Bakr, Hafsa bint 'Umar. . . . They retained their names and those of their fathers. But the West does not give the woman any rights, neither concerning her name, nor concerning her wealth. Rather, the freedom that women obtained there came about only because of the war, when the males were soldiers and needed the women to replace them in their civilian jobs; so they gave them some rights to benefit from their labor.

Socrates, for instance, has said that the woman is not prepared by her nature to understand rational knowledge . . . but that she is prepared to cook, and raise the children. Plato gave her a share in education, which made him unpopular. The satirist Aristophanes made fun of educated women in his play "The Pedantic Women," and Molière after him wrote a play entitled "The Women's Parliament." Indeed the Prophet has said that "the pursuit of knowledge is a religious duty for every Muslim man and woman" (Stowasser, 1987b: 267–268).

In his discussion of polygyny, Sha'rawi once again defends the Islamic order by comparison with the West:

> Once, I asked some people in America who put this objection to me – that men can have several women but women cannot have several husbands simultaneously – whether prostitution was legal in America and they answered that it was in some states. I asked them how they took precautions so as to ensure public health, and they said that these women are medically examined twice a week to protect them and their customers against venereal diseases. I asked if they had to examine married women . . . and they answered: no, since the married woman is exposed only to the husband's semen . . . and that venereal disease only occurs when the semen of many men come together in one place. I said that, therefore, God was right to permit plurality of wives, but not of husbands.
>
> I also asked them since they had these places for young men to find release for their sexual drives, why did they not have them for young women. Why was there no place staffed with young men that young women could visit to release their sexual tensions? They said that this had never happened and I answered that this was proof that it would bring disgrace upon the woman (Stowasser, 1987b: 280–281).

Sha'rawi continues to note that, as mothers, women find themselves in high regard in Islam while:

> The European thinkers found that the children were forgetting their mothers and failed to protect them, hence they designated one day in the year on which the children should remember their mother. We, however, are celebrating "Mother's Day" as every moment of the year. . . . Hence, we do not need this festival; still we have adopted it, as if it were a glorious feat of the West, while in reality it is a disgrace.
>
> In Europe, the son abandons his mother to live in a home for the aged, while his father lives somewhere else. Islam, however, has given us the principle of mutual support and solidarity, according to the parents' need. The mother is thrice more entitled to a son's companionship and support than the father. . . . This is so because the father is a man who could survive even if he were reduced to begging; not so the mother (Stowasser, 1987b: 281).

Sha'rawi's use of intercultural dialogue from a distance across time is itself worthy of analysis, as is his use of comparison as a method of control. Stowasser comments that Sha'rawi is a highly visible media personality, an example of the contemporary traditionalists who are rearming Islamic women to spearhead the construction of a social order that will counter the impact of the West. The motivation is not necessarily against Western capitalism; rather, it is a reaction to the Western devaluation of Eastern women, which encourages conformity with Western ideas more generally. Stowasser questions the faithfulness of the Islamic paradigm that is being constructed in the popular press, and she is correct in assuming that interpretations of the Koran are constructed and that they change in their interpretation of the place of men and women in Islam – but that is not my main point in presenting these excerpts. What the excerpts show is that the West plays an important part in the construction of Islamic gender paradigms and in holding them in place. Paradigms are legitimated by their contrast with the West, especially a barbaric, materialistic West.

Sha'rawi is not a theologian nor a revolutionary, rather he is a religious man who is popularizing ideas about the role of women in contemporary Egyptian society. The women who listen to him are women who believe that Western women in general, and US women in particular, are not respected as a class. Such women recount that American women are sex objects and cite the multibillion dollar pornography industry as evidence. Women in the West are said to be under daily threat of rape; not so in Cairo. US incest and family violence rates are cited, and we are forever reminded that the portrayal of women in American magazines is disrespectful of women. And we in the West reciprocate. There is much in the American media that is critical of the manner in which Islamic society treats women, and we regularly discredit and discriminate and dehumanize and stereotype Muslims, and with them Muslim women, as backward (see, e.g., Fanon, 1963; 1967).

In large measure, stereotypes of the Muslim woman depict someone who is pitiable and downtrodden. Usually these stereotypes are formed by focusing on selected areas of contrast: Muslim women wear the veil, a symbol of subordination for the Western observer; Islamic society fixates on the cult of virginity and stigmatizes women who are not virgins, thus promoting a double standard; Islamic societies abuse children of the female sex by various techniques such as *Jabr* or forced marriage, or by clitoridectomy, a form of sexual scarification that is said to limit sexual satisfaction for women; polygamy and easy divorce are used in subjugating women psychologically and materially; attention is paid to spirit possession requiring exorcism and the manner in which women's resistance takes form.

There are political implications to such stereotyping.[6] The Middle East is backward and deserving of cultural disrespect, needs to be modernized and in the process civilized. The grid through which we rank the humanity of the area is based on how we perceive their treatment of their womenfolk. The way in which we construct the place of Arab women is one of the keys to the control of others, and the converse is true as well. The West is more civilized by the status and rights of its women. According to Muhsin Mahdi, the former director of the Middle Eastern Studies Center at Harvard:

> Middle Eastern women have been the object of the most malicious campaign of defamation in human history, a campaign that was initiated in early anti-Muslim theological tracts (Mahdi, 1977).

In this context it is interesting to learn that Muslim women describe themselves as proud and active participants in their culture. They entrepreneur in business ventures, many are professionally trained, and others form intellectual and literary groups.[7] The University of Khartoum Law School in the Sudan hired their first woman law professor before Harvard Law School began to hire women professors, and the University of Rabat in Morocco had in 1980 approximately 38% women faculty with maternity rights and equal pay, a condition that did not exist at many American universities including the one in which I teach. An understanding of the veil as a symbol of subjugation misses the observation made by anthropologist Fadwa el Guindi (1981: 465)

94

after studying veiling in contemporary Islamic movements in Egypt, when she notices that

> a new Egyptian woman is emerging – educated, professional, non-elitist and veiled. The veil is part of an assertive movement with a powerful message symbolizing the beginning of a synthesis between modernity and authenticity.

Identity becomes relevant to the plight of women for it offers the possibility for women to be related to and judged by their own history and culture, not by Western women's standards.

The evolution and perpetuation of female subordination are evident in both East and West. Both are under patriarchal systems of control. Both are publicly male-dominated societies and, more specifically, both have male-dominated governments. In both East and West women work longer hours than men as a class, and in both cultures women and children constitute the majority of the poor and impoverished.[8] Although in both areas there are ideologies that glorify the status of women, in both places the lower status of women is explained as due to the inherent inferiority of women. In both the East and the West, women's subordination is institutionally structured, culturally rationalized, and leads to situations of deference, dependency, powerlessness, and poverty. Yet, in both cultures the manner of gender construction – whereby the inside culture is idealized in comparison to the outside culture – allows members of both East and West to feel superior to the other, while ignoring common traits. Comparison requires comparative consciousness (Nader, 1994), which steers away from comparisons that are only of a dichotomous nature, comparisons that draw on the differences between us and them as evidenced in Eastern as well as Western discourses. We must also compare to find points of convergence and commonality. Dichotomies tend to stress the unique features of each in which the West not only appears to possess the highest standards of technological apparatus but is also made to seem morally and spiritually superior. Jack Goody's (1983) analysis of historian Pierre Guichard's characterization (Guichard, 1977) of the contrast between Western and Eastern structures is pertinent.

Goody describes a method of comparison in which the compared features are looked at not only from the standpoint of the East or the West, but also from a third angle, such as Africa south of the Sahara. Seen from this vantage point, not only do the differences that Guichard asserts seem rather slight (Goody, 1983: 10–12), but also our sensitivities are raised as to the nature and purpose of comparison (Marcus and Fischer, 1986).

The Controlling Role of Ideas

Ideas have played an important role in the persistence of female subordination. The control of women in the West depends heavily on the concept of progress; the idea of progress also plays a central role in the diffusion of Western female subordination patterns. The key notion that comprises the concept of progress is the idea of change as incremental while, in fact, evidence to the contrary is both overpowering and denied.

In 1970 a report of the subcommittee on the status of academic women on the University of California, Berkeley campus was published. In this most thoughtful and detailed study, the authors observed that the figures for female faculty appointments are not incremental although they are for male faculty.

> The percentage of women in ladder positions (Senate members) rose during the twenties and thirties, especially for assistant and associate professors, but has declined during the last twenty years. The percentage of women professors has gone back down to 2%, the same as it was in the twenties, although it was more than 4% during the fifties. The percentage of women associate professors has decreased to 5%, comparable to the late twenties. The decrease in women assistant professors is the most striking – now only 5% are women, which is half the figure of the early twenties and less that one-third the percentage for the period 1925–1945. Indeed, the number of women assistant professors is now only 16, about the same as it was in the twenties, while the number of men assistant professors is 305, more than three times its early value (Scott, Ervin-Tripp and Colson, 1970).

Many of us who read this report on the status of academic women on the Berkeley campus had our assumptions shattered. The idea that progress operates on an incremental model is deep: somehow things always improved.[9]

But what significance did the idea of an incremental progress have? As long as one believed that things were better than they had been before (the incremental model), one could feel relieved and anxiety would be reduced. In addition, political apathy was to be expected. The incremental model functions as control. Those who perceive the status of women as sometimes one of gaining ground and at other times one of losing ground are closer to reality. In the United States today, political apathy describes the mental set of many women who perceive that we have made gains and cannot lose them, while others – including the institutions that predominate – act as if women's status has progressed too fast and too far since the 1960s. On the other hand, in the media and in academia there are those who argue that in some realms women may have lost more than they have gained since the 1960s, and there is evidence of a similar downward trend in women's status after women received the vote in the United States (Knudsen, 1969).

In 1969 sociologist Dean Knudsen of Purdue University published an article in the journal *Social Forces* on "The Declining Status of Women: Popular Myths and the Failure of Functionalist Thought." Knudsen shows that women's status declined in the United States during the 30-year period from 1940 to 1970 as evidenced by occupation, income, and education as indicators of status. Knudsen argues that women's status is relative to men's status, and that any apparent improvements must be compared to improvements for men in the same area. In most cases the author found that men gained significantly more than women over time, and that women had suffered a loss in status.

Beyond his central empirical finding, Knudsen makes two additional observations that are instructive. He poses the first in the form of a question: "In the face of an official equalitarian normative structure, and the later reinforcements of legal sanctions, what explanations can be offered to account for this evidence of apparent incremental inequality? Further, *how does one account for the persistent failure of social science to reveal this trend?"* (Knudsen, 1969: 191, emphasis mine). Knudsen's second observation describes the thought patterns that justify the sources and perpetuations of institutionalized inequality as to what are thought to be "appropriate sex roles." He concludes that "the conservative nature of modern social science also has contributed to this development, through the use of an individualistic perspective and the dominance of functionalist interpretations" (1969: 191). Knudsen continues:

> given the conviction that women should not pursue occupations in competition with men, women and employers together develop a self-fulfilling prophecy. . . . The effect is the perpetuation of a belief that sexual equality exists and that only effort is lacking, to which social scientists have offered their support (1969: 192).

In a personal communication, Knudsen reported that he had had a difficult time in finding a journal willing to publish his findings because they were not believable or because they were obvious. Social scientists are caught in the same mindset as others in their culture, and if they attempt to deconstruct, as Knudsen did, justification for not publishing such work will be plentiful, and in so doing the status quo control of women will remain intact.

The Use of Revolution in Gender Control

Status quo is not always the goal in relation to controlling processes. In many revolutionary governments the opposite is sought – to change the traditional control over women as part of the transfer of power over women from the kinship group to the state. The strategy of positional superiority is then enveloped by the strategy of modernization, a form of progress, sometimes by means of legal engineering.

Gregory Massell (1968), an American political scientist, published a classic article on "Law as an Instrument of Revolutionary Change in a Traditional Milieu." Massell describes the mid-1920s Soviet experiments to break up the Muslim family. The assault was a deliberate attempt to stimulate and manipulate

> sexual and generational tensions that would help to induce an upheaval in a traditional system of values, customs, relationships, and roles, beginning with the primary cell of that system: the extended, patriarchal Muslim family (1968: 196).

Although the Soviet experiment was considered a failure, some years later a similar experiment was conducted by another revolutionary regime, that of the Libyans under the leadership of Muammar Qaddafi, under an Islamic umbrella. Qaddafi's experiment seems to be more successful in the destruction of women's support groups as well as in the breaking of traditional systems of values.

In a preliminary study of the change in control over women in Libyan society, "Powerful Mothers, Powerless Daughters: Libyan Women and the Bitter Fruits of Change," Saddeka Arebi uses ideal types to look at the changing position of women in Libyan society comparing the experience of mothers and daughters at different points over two generations. The mothers were born from the 1920s and the daughters from the late 1940s and early 1950s. At the outset Arebi notes (1984, 1–2) that:

> the change in women's position is not considered as a process of transformation from tradition to modernity, but rather from tradition to alienation. The latter refers to a situation whereby the culture structure is no longer able to offer a means to integrate, create and make meaningful new experiences.

She observes that social change in Libyan society:

> has stripped women of their powerful independent position and has resulted in dependency and subordination . . . my conceptualization of mothers' and daughters' positions extends beyond the politics of interpersonal relations to account for the impact of the broader social, political and economic systems that structure and control their experiences.

The discovery of oil in late 1959 resulted in a high rate of internal migration which transformed Libyan society from 80% rural in 1956 to 80% urban by 1969 and brought a large number of foreigners to work for the oil companies. Arebi tells us that change for Libyan women was symbolized by the shift from veiled women living within their homes to young women dressed in the latest Western styles, driving their cars, working outside the home in offices, schools, factories, and hospitals, and attending the universities and entering the military.

Arebi sees three sets of variables as important in expanding, contracting, or redefining women's rights and obligations: the impact of institutionalized education, the effect of the emergence of the nuclear family (and, I would add, the concept of the couple), and finally the impact of women's work outside the home. By an examination of these variables Arebi demonstrates how women's subordination is institutionally structured to bind women to situations of deference, dependency, and powerlessness. Schools mean that the family no longer provides primary socialization and entail the loss of the family life experience that was previously exchanged among women of different age groups. School peer groups become important in constructing a life outside the family, which includes the reading of romance novels. These novels stress the search for individual identity and personal freedom unencumbered by the constraints of family and society. They glorify Western marriage and its emphasis on companionship and shared activities, and fit well with the move toward the nuclear family, itself an outcome of a high rate of internal migration.

The emergence of the conjugal unit, Arebi argues, did not always work to the advantage of Libyan women. Although the form was Western the content was Eastern – husbands and wives still tended to lack the shared interests and emotional bonds characteristic of Western *ideal* couples, and could not change the belief that the Libyan man is first and foremost attached to his mother. Living in a nuclear family meant giving up women's groups, which formed the source of mutual aid, exchange and companionship, all of which were important to the mothers' generation. In fact, she tells us, the isolation from personal networks of female solidarity changed the women's position from autonomy to dependency and the show of deference to the husband. The complete isolation of women from female networks enabled men to exert total control. Arebi (1984: 27) quotes the mothers who sense their daughter's dilemma: "We used to be free . . . go wherever we want and visit whomever we wish, we never were under men's mercy the way you are . . . women of today."

Men have come to make decisions in domestic matters that were once reserved for women, and women to depend on their husband for their status in society. Such changes lay the basis for a hierarchical relationship between husbands and wives in contrast to the traditional egalitarian relations resulting from an interdependent division of labor for men and women.

In her final assessment of the meaning of women's work outside the Libyan home, Arebi is even more emphatic about women's loss of power and control over their lives. Going out to work for Libyan women further enhanced the control of men over them as working wives. In the mothers' generation, women's control over their own property was institutionally based. In the daughters' generation women are "allowed" to work while still being completely responsible for the home and children. Men control their wives' material resources as well as their definition of themselves.[10]

In the Libyan case, education, the conjugal family, and work outside the home have all operated as controlling processes that restrict the range of options for women and confront them with dilemmas that they have to solve alone and without their women's support group. In addition, the perception of the mother in the mind of her child is changing:

> The change in the whole pattern of social networks has affected the socialization process of their children. Children isolated with their mothers, also lose touch with those intergenerational gatherings which functioned as an important socialization agent a generation ago . . . [and which] reinforced children's sense of their mother's high position. Activities such as sport clubs and scouting have become the new agents of socialization. The perception of the mother in the mind of the child is determined by and confined to the nature of her relationship to them and to the father (Arebi, 1984: 22).[11]

Multiple Systems of Female Subordination

Different systems of repression sometimes exist side by side. One can compare the lives of women living under pastoral conditions (Abu-Lughod, 1986), where they are under the protection of their fathers and brothers and where they may experience the solidarity that comes with being segregated by gender, to those of urban women, who live under strict Islamic conditions that include husbands (along with father and brothers) being in positions of protection and control and whose resistance to control may be supported by women's groups (Altorki, 1986: 99–121; Rugh, 1984.) Under the conditions of a modern nation-state the laws are written to include the state as a protector of women's rights, but there are also the unwritten laws of the modernizers, the developers whose systems destroy women's support groups (Joseph, 1982; Rassam, 1983). Some women get trapped by the most repressive part of each system. For those women who are caught up by the male-dominant extremes of the East and the West, there is resistance in the form of Islamic movements, either as a retreat or as a way to regain control over their own destinies. Others gather the modes of resistance and the support groups from each system and live a life of their choice, often without men (Jansen, 1987).

Nikki Keddie (1979: 225–240) underscored the need for an extension of historical and comparative understanding of the experience of Eastern and Western women:

> The transition to a modern and Western-influenced life structure has not been a simple progressive one for Middle Eastern women. Too many scholars use "modernization" as a simple equivalent to the more obviously ethnocentric "westernization," retaining the implication that modernization is essentially a straight-line progressive process, which either immediately or very soon improves everyone's way of life. . . . It should not be expected that there will necessarily be a single answer to the question of whether the Western impact, or modernization, made things better or worse even for a single class or group. Regarding women, even in Western Europe we find the rise of

capitalism in the seventeenth century removing women from many productive tasks and sources of income that had been theirs since the Middle Ages, but the same century saw the voicing and advancing of the first feminist ideas as another side of the rise of Capitalism. . . . The influence of Western and indigenous capitalism in the Middle East was similarly two-sided. . . . Female peasants, nomads, and city craft workers have increasingly lost their productive role as the goods they made came to be purchased from distant producers, although a very few women's products . . . found greatly increased markets.

Keddie also points out that Middle Eastern men who were tied to Western businessmen and wanted to qualify as modern were supportive of women's demands for liberation when it meant modern education, unveiling, and professional careers. A difference in lifestyles gradually emerged between upper- and middle-income urban women and the women of lower-income groups whose men saw no advantage in the change of customary ways.

While Keddie describes the separate evolution of different classes of women in the Middle East, in the West the presence of multiple immigrant groupings creates a situation in which a woman may be caught between two or more female subordination systems as in the example of a Mexican-American woman married to an Egyptian male and living in the United States in an isolated nuclear family, without association to a women's solidarity group. By virtue of the diffusion of female systems of subordination into urban centers and by virtue of the absence of comparable movements of women's support groups (which are usually rooted to locale and not easily moved) and the ubiquitous presence of the isolated nuclear family, conditions for women may be worsening in both the East and the West. Anthropologist Evans-Pritchard (in Etienne and Leacock, 1980) may have been correct in asserting that regardless of the differences, "*in all societies men are always in the ascendancy, and this is perhaps the more evident the higher the civilization*" (my emphasis). The manner in which Evans-Pritchard stated the case was imbued with the contradictions spoken about earlier. If progress is incremental then the place of women continuously improves, and evidence to the contrary is either minimized, or denied, or dealt with by turning the lens on the image of women in other cultures. Common sense tells us that change is incremental, that things should have improved. As I have argued elsewhere (Nader, 1987), explicit comparison between the First and Third Worlds may begin to loosen the hold of an ideology of progress so that we can see more clearly what is actually happening. By focusing on the similar plight of women in both the West and the East we may recognize sources of bias which are yet obscured. Two examples of this kind of comparison come to mind.

In "Subordination and Sexual Control: A Comparative View of the Control of Women," Gita Sen (1984) examines the impact of sexual control on women's place in family, community and labor market in India and the West. She distinguishes the Indian direct or non-commodity form of sexual control from that of the West, which is more impersonal and commodified. With diffusion both forms end up in India. In a second article on women's role in economic development, Lourdes Beneria and Gita Sen (1981: 289) indicate that "capital accumulation may weaken traditional forms of patriarchal control over women and introduce new forms." In Southeast Asia "patriarchy within the family has been replaced by a capitalist control that takes patriarchal forms; young women's lives and sexuality are circumscribed by the firm's labor control policies" (Beneria and Sen, 1981: 289; see also Ong, 1987). In addition, increasing male migrations may give women greater autonomy in the area of subsistence farming, but with land shortages a new situation emerges in which women become dependent on male wage earners.

Female subordination ideologies and organizations diffuse with Western production technologies, and feminist scholars, as I have indicated, have been alert to the impact of the global economy on women's lives. Scholars have also realized the importance of technologies that are soft. The idea systems that spread with the export of American goods and production technologies play an important part in the diffusion of ideologies of female subordination, like, for example, the isolated nuclear family, the concept of the couple, the idea of mother as maid, and the idea that dyadic relations between mothers and their daughters are somehow inherently antagonistic rather than cooperative (Nader, 1987). The ideal of mother–daughter separation was, according to some authors, well suited to the social mobility of Americans, whereas attachment was an impediment to mobility (Low, 1984: 1). Mother–daughter separation was also compatible with the ideal of the couple. Let me indicate how such ideas work in both the East and the West with further examples from ethnographic works.

Changing Veils: Women and Modernization in North Yemen (Makhlouf, 1979) is a study of women in a traditional, stratified, complex, yet isolated society. It deals with changes in ideologies, sexual segregation, veiling practices, and women's power since the 1962 revolution in North Yemen. Carla Makhlouf analyzes the changes that came with modernization, indicating that the key to women's changing position is the transfer of solidarity from women to husbands, or more specifically a shift from mother–daughter to husband–wife relationships in which the husband is the more powerful. As these changes penetrate Yemeni society, the Yemeni start celebrating Mother's Day (not Father's Day), an indication that the role of mother has declined. Mother's Day dramatized a role that is of lesser importance as women become increasingly dependent on their husbands rather than on their children for future welfare and present status.[12]

Yemeni women are westernizing their lives and, because of this change, they will be able to exercise greater power over their personal lives, in the area of choice of marriage partner, for example. However, as Makhlouf's study indicates, women are exchanging solidarity with their natal family and with others of their sex, for individuation and increased dependence upon their husbands. Women are now torn between a new ideal of attachment to husband and a traditional pattern of attachment to mother and other female kin. The ideal of mother–daughter separation and the introduction of the concept of the couple is not particularly well suited to the social mobility of Yemeni men, unlike the earlier argument for American parent–child separation patterns (Low, 1984). Yemeni men who migrate to work leaving their wives and children behind will increase the number of isolated nuclear families with an absent father.

It has been interesting to recognize how the pressure towards coupledom and mother–daughter separation works in the West. At the time of the birth of my first child I was teaching at the University of California at Berkeley where there was no maternity leave. The child was born three weeks before the beginning of the academic year, and my mother came to help. Her stay was accompanied by four successive greetings during the first four weeks: "Mrs. Nader, isn't it nice that you are here"; "Mrs. Nader, are you still here?"; "Mrs. Nader, who is taking care of Mr. Nader?"; and "When are you leaving, Mrs. Nader?" My parents' reactions were simple and indicative of Eastern structure – "Laura is Mr. Nader's daughter too; and I will stay as long as Laura needs me." And my father's response, "Are they foolish to think that I can't take care of myself when Laura has just had a baby and is teaching full-time?" For those who think in terms of the couple and mother–daughter separation, it was "natural" that husbands should attend their wife's birthing while the mother could not.

Actually, there is another time prior to the event of a birth when parent–children separation is insisted upon in the United States – when the child goes to college. At colleges across the country parents invited to campus are told that they must let go of their children if the children are to grow up and develop into mature adults (Coburn and Tree, 1988). Parents are told early on to let go. Furthermore the colleges do not continue guardianship, for example, in the form of housemothers in dormitories who check on "the girls," believing *in loco parentis* to be an outdated concept.

The anthropological literature is replete with examples of the difficulty and high cost for family relations that result from breaking with kin. When there is a separation of mother and daughter there is a break in the dissemination of women's culture from one generation to another. At the individual level the consequences are serious, as illustrated by the prize-winning work of Nancy Scheper-Hughes who, while working in northeast Brazil, discovered that daughters without their mothers do not know how to nurse their babies, one result of which is undernourishment (1985). At the level of modernization strategies and centralized government, breaking kin relations facilitates the introduction and acceptance of new forms and new ideologies.[13]

Thus, in addition to control by means of positional superiority there is the control that accompanies the development of global economy, the widespread migration of peoples, and the development of the nation-state. As dogmas of female subordination spread, the control over women multiplies. As previously noted, for women, coping with subordination or mobilizing against gender inequalities is often tied to women's support groups. Women's support groups are commonly localized and break up with the mobility of women. Beliefs related to gender travel more easily and are more likely to stay intact; female solidarity that is rooted in groups does not transfer so easily. The result, I believe, is increasing subordination of women. The cumulative effect of the multiple systems of female subordination patterns results in a crisis in gender relations which is not the creation of particular men or particular women, but a result of the evolution of a set of ideas about gender relations that do not include the adaptive responses (or the resistance) of women which are linked to enduring structures.

Colonialism, Development, Religion, and Gender Control

Although the main cultural arm of European gender control today is economic development, gender control was often key to political control under colonialism. Political scientist Peter Knauss describes the persistence of patriarchy in Algeria (Knauss, 1987). French colonialists were driven to "civilize" the Algerians by "cleansing" them of Arab patriarchy. As part of the civilizing mission, the French directed themselves to dismantle Islam, its economic infrastructure, and its cultural network. In the process, "Everything possible was done to make the Algerian male ashamed of the fate that he metes out to women" (Knauss, 1987: 27). Arab patriarchy – a hierarchy of authority that is controlled and dominated by males and in which women are subordinated to the role of permanent minors – persisted, however, as part of an Islamic longing, as part of the structure of the revolution, and, after the revolution, as part of the socialist effort to decolonize or to restore an Arab, Muslim Algeria.

Those most threatened by cultural assimilation and changing roles for Algerian women were the new middle peasantry and the new urban petite bourgeoisie. Knauss reports that, as conditions worsened for the Algerians, as the system of Islamic education was destroyed or allowed to collapse, as the peasants lost their lands and moved to employment and the money economy, a Muslim consensus slowly developed that reaffirmed Arab patriarchy. The revolution evolved, and ideas of liberating women were subsumed into the new revolutionary patriarchal family. Algerian women became dual victims of colonialism and this family setup. Post-revolutionary Algeria places women in a double bind. Over 200 000 Algerian women have employment outside of the home, yet they are expected to play the traditional role of custodians of Arab-Islamic values. Their dissatisfaction became manifest in mass demonstrations over the Family Code of 1981, only to be silent when it was reenacted in 1984 in the wake of the revival of Muslim fundamentalist activity.

Neocolonialism of a Western sort penetrates by manipulating the control of women, "Under the Banner of Development" (Rahnema, 1986). Under the banner of development there is a universal model of life that represents the ultimate any society can hope to attain, a replacement for no longer viable forms of social organization, as represented by segregated societies where women wear the veil. As I mentioned earlier, developers export technologies that carry gender ideas, such as farm machinery, which was to be run by men because of the assumption that farmers were always male, or "the pill," which carries the idea that women are to be responsible for population control (even though the pill might endanger their health), or with Western cosmetics that are often the first step in a process that is socializing women to a certain conception of beauty that implicitly carries a command for women to complete the rest of the fashion picture (which may include not aging as rapidly as their mothers), and to acquire the behavior that accompanies the form of dress.[14]

In the East the Islamic movements function as counterhegemonic resistance to Western patterns of gender control. Opposition to them is articulated by means of religion. With such opposition, economic policies that are "open door," like those of Sadat in Egypt, or "closed door," like those that preceded Sadat under Nasser, are recognized as conditioning the way in which gender relations are structured. Needless to say, open-door policies invited in gender constructions that competed with Arab constructions while closed-door policies discouraged multiple systems of female subordination. The reverberations of gender structure will inevitably, as in the examples previously presented (Saddeka Arebi for Libya and Makhlouf for Yemen), have a bearing on parent–child relations. A battle to colonize the mind is inevitable, and each form of domination inevitably brings a response – which may be different for the men and women of East and West, but in both places the discourse on gender is restricted. Looked at with some detachment, it becomes clear that part of the competition between East and West is over the control of Eastern women, who play a key role in maintaining a continuous Eastern tradition.[15]

History is helpful in understanding the dynamics of competition between males of different cultures. Knauss's technique (1987) is to examine Algerian patriarchy and its persistence through four time periods – traditional, modern and neo-traditional, revolutionary, and post-revolutionary socialist Algeria. The dilemmas, the resistance, the adaptations for women take on different forms and meanings in each period. History provides a window for us to see that part of the contemporary Middle East which is a product of a precolonial period. Historical research that extends back to the period prior to Western colonization provides a test of the theory that the mingling of Eastern and Western cultures has produced two patriarchies for women rather than an amelioration of their condition. Ethnographic work on the past or contemporary ethnography in areas isolated from colonialism allows us to test assumptions regarding the contemporary and colonized Arab world.

Historians are exploring life in the premodern Islamic world that is at some variance with the usual stereotypes, as my earlier reference to Keddie's work indicates. Another example comes from the work of Abraham Marcus (1985), who examined the court records for mid-eighteenth-century Aleppo, Syria, (home to 100 000 people), and the administrative capital of a large Ottoman province. The Islamic court was the official clearinghouse for disputes dealing with property, and both men and women of all classes and neighborhoods used the courts as plaintiffs. An unexpected finding of his analysis concerns the position of women in relation to home ownership and real estate dealings. For women, real estate was one of the more available avenues for investment and it appears that the spirit of material accumulation was not incompatible with the emphasis on female segregation. Marcus's work forces a rethinking of assumptions held by contemporary scholars about phenomena like modernization and industrialization as they affect roles and relationships between people. The relationship between men and women in Aleppo may appear extraordinary only because we harbor certain assumptions about the role of women in Islamic society (Nelson and Olesen, 1977). But in eighteenth-century Aleppo, both men and women seem to have been comfortable in matters of real estate, money, endowments, and the like. In this context, it is instructive to see how capital formation and the productivity of women are effected by dual economies in Third-World countries more generally (Boulding, 1976; Tucker, 1986).

Conclusion: The Need to Separate Identities

To understand dogmas of female subordination in dynamic patriarchies, we must examine gender ideologies in the larger framework of attempts by nations and societies, as in the US Afghanistan war, to maintain separate identities within the context of increasing interaction. In short, female subordination can be viewed as attempts to maintain moral authority in nations that are increasingly threatened by the dynamics of international power relationships. In this context, gender ideologies emerge not only as a product of internal debate over inequalities between males and females in a particular society, but also out of debates between the prevailing ideologies of different societies. Gender arrangements are complex wholes that can be related to macro-level distinctions between "us and them." Ruth

Benedict (1934) was one of the first anthropologists to suggest that distinctions between "our group" and "outsiders" reinforced in-group moral authority. Benedict's idea gains new significance today in Said's work, in which he suggests that the Muslim world is constructed by Westerners for their own purposes. Missing from Said's work is a consideration of the way images of gender relationships fit into Western views of the Muslim world or the ways in which the Arab Muslim world constructs visions of the West. These issues become crucial when we approach constructions of "the other" with a desire to understand changing structures of economic and political dependence and interdependence.

A major challenge to studies of the cultural construction of gender identity is the failure to take into account changes in gender ideologies. Cultural analysis of gender at times produces static images which are no less deterministic than biological explanations of male/female roles in society. Sanday suggests that "the logic of sex role plans is transmitted from one generation to the next almost intact" (1981: 15), unless there is a serious disturbance in the social and economic environment. With the expansion of US and Western European influence on the rest of the world, however, there are few places in which gender roles have not been altered dramatically by economic and political change, and certainly the Middle East has been a partner in change as a result of contact.

In this chapter I suggest that historical and comparative methods are useful in illuminating processes that may otherwise remain invisible, processes that inhibit knowledge as well as action. Strategies of resistance are often not feminist in origin, but are directly related to the shape of the male power structure. When women's conditions in both the Western and Arab patriarchiess are analyzed as part of a common discussion and when they are examined in juxtaposition to each other and to global economic movements, it becomes clearer the extent to which male forms of domination are associated with patterns of male competition (as between East and West) and the view that by virtue of their custodial positions, women are key to larger indigenous control systems.

In the West both governments and business corporations have created and consolidated a cultural hegemony and disseminated it to their own populations and to the Arab world by means of media, educational, and developmental organizations. In the East, nationalism and then religion have been powerful agents in the construction of gender hegemony as well as in counterhegemonic efforts. The dynamic of both processes catches women in a spiral. By not discussing both systems as part of an interactive process, the Arab world is discriminated against because of the way we construct their treatment of women. At the same time a self-satisfied incremental view of progress is perpetuated in the West which serves to divert attention from the varied mechanisms of gender control in Western Europe and the United States.

Images of women in other societies reinforce norms of subordination of women in one's own society. Also there may be an overall decline in the power of women with the rise of centralized states and the evolution of multiple systems of female subordination. There is strong support for both the appearance of multiple systems of female subordination in single locales which serve to exacerbate the condition of women and the appearance simultaneously of increasingly vocal critiques of conditions of female subordination as expressed by men and women of the other society. Resistance appears in the form of the co-occurrence of indigenous critique with a westernized form of feminism.

If mechanisms of subordination are to be found in development aid programs and short-term optimism in the West, and religious fundamentalism in the East, then the academic or anthropological means to an approach unencumbered by filters of the orientalist or occidentalist sort are to be found in a change in thinking about women, a conception in gender studies that is historical, comparative, and geared towards assumption testing.

Cultural theory, and in particular hegemonic theory, provides some help in understanding how particular idea systems operate as control and how they may appear as common sense to a set of group interests. While the principle of "internal contrastive comparison" has been productive in understanding gender arrangements (including the power of women) in societies, more attention should be given to how whole complexes of male/female relationships can be organized around contrastive comparison *between* societies of the First and Third worlds so as to illuminate the controls inherent in positional superiority strategies.[16]

Acknowledgments

Chapter 4 contains material quoted from *The Islamic Impulse* by Stowasser, Barbara Freyer; Georgetown University Center for Contemporary Arab Studies. Copyright 1987.

Notes

1 Throughout the text, I use dogma advisedly, to highlight the problem of meaning in such descriptions as "male dominance" or "female subordination." These are often used as articles of faith, assumed but not examined. For an attempt to explicate different types of "male dominance," see Peggy Sanday's *Female Power and Male Dominance* (1981). As Foucault (1978: 93) points out, power "is not an institution, and not a structure: neither is it a certain strength we are endowed with; it is the name that one attributes to a complex strategical relationship in a particular society."

2 The differences between orientalism and occidentalism were brought to my attention through a fruitful discussion with my graduate student Saddeka Arebi of texts that were written in Arabic on the West. In this context it is instructive to refer to Eric Wolf's *Europe and the People without History*. Wolf argues (1982: 6–7) that the categories of East and West encourage us to create false models of reality. However, the indigenous peoples of the East and the West use these two categories as folk categories that describe "the other."

3 While this is generally true, some think that Boserup's study advocates policy prescriptions no different from those of development agencies (see, for example, Beneria and Sen, 1981).

4 See also the discussion of this same point in Chapter 2, pp. 24–50.

5 The male bias in ethnographic reporting is being documented. See for example, Nelson (1974), Pastner (1978), and also Rattray (1955: 84 – quoted in Rogers, 1980: 145). When Rattray's informants commented that they did not stress the role of women to the anthropologists because "the white man never asked us this; you have dealings with and recognize only men, we supposed the Europeans considered women of no account and we know you do not recognize them as we have always done!"

6 See for example, Bullough (1973: especially pages 134–135). Stereotypes, by definition, may carry part truths or no truths. These areas of seeming contrast are based on the assumption that veiling, the cult of virginity, forced marriage, clitoridectomy and polygyny are characteristically "Islamic." These institutions predate Islam as Herodotus reported in the fifth century BC, and cross-cultural research reveals that they are known to different religions and cultures in Latin America, India, sub-Saharan Africa, Sri Lanka and Europe.

7 An exhibition in the College Library at Harvard University arranged by Alice C. Deyab in 1988 reported that women in the Arab world had published their own magazines for almost 100 years and these magazines then numbered over 300. In contrast to the owners of Western women's magazines, who were predominantly male, some 95% of those who owned, published, edited and wrote Arab women's magazines were female (Harvard University Library Notes, March 24, 1988).

8 The fact that women constitute the majority of the poor and impoverished is evident enough in American culture (see, e.g., Scott, 1984). In the Third World the same is true (see e.g., Sarri, 1985). Sarri discloses that, while women comprise more than half the world's population, they own less than 1% of its property and earn only 10% of its income.

9 See Diamond (1974) for a discussion of the notion of progress as inherent in Western civilization.

10 See also Hochschild (1989) for an analysis of the double shift problem for American women wage workers.

11 See also Ervin-Tripp *et al.*, 1984.

12 See Johnson (1988) for a discussion of the dynamics of these two roles in American culture.

13 See for example, Ashraf Ghani, *Order and Conflict: Consolidation of Power through Law: Afghanistan 1880–1901*. Unpublished manuscript.

14 Jane Collier (1986) provides an example of how fashion enters in to control even the anthropologist's observation of what is beautiful.

15 Fanon's *A Dying Colonialism* (1967) illustrates how the French colonialists planned and based their strategies and tactics in Algeria on this conception of women as a key to culture.

16 For an example of positional superiority, see the front page article in the San Francisco Chronicle, June 27, 1988, "Women Called Poor, Pregnant and Powerless." In worldwide studies of the status of women, Western categories of wage, numbers of children and levels of schooling, show Western societies are among the top dozen societies, while, not surprisingly, the women of Muslim societies are found at the bottom of a ladder that looks very much like a nineteenth century unilineal model of social evolution.

References

Abu-Lughod, Lila (1986) *Veiled Sentiments: Honor and Poetry in a Bedouin Society.* Berkeley, Los Angeles, London: University of California Press.

Altorki, Soraya (1986) *Women in Saudi Arabia: Ideology and Behavior among the Elite.* New York: Columbia University Press.

Arebi, Saddeka (1984) *Powerful Mothers, Powerless Daughters: Libyan Women and the Bitter Fruits of Change.* Unpublished paper, Department of Anthropology, UC Berkeley.

Benedict, Ruth (1934) *Patterns of Culture.* Boston and New York: Houghton Mifflin.

Beneria, Lourdes and Gita Sen (1981) Accumulation, Reproduction, and Women's Role in Economic Development: Boserup Revisited. *Signs: Journal of Women in Culture and Society,* 7, no. 2, pp. 279–298.

Berger, Peter. L., Brigitte Berger, and Hansfried Kellner (1973) *The Homeless Mind: Modernization and Consciousness.* New York: Vintage Books.

Boserup, Ester (1980) *Women's Role in Economic Development.* New York: St. Martin's Press.

Boulding, Elise (1976) *Dualism and Productivity: An Examination of the Economic Roles of Women in Societies in Transition. Paper presented at the Conference on Economic Development and Income Distribution,* Estes Park, Colorado, April 23–24.

Bullough, Vern (1973) *The Subordinate Sex.* Baltimore: Penguin Books.

Chaney, Elsa, M. and Marianne Schmink (1976) "Women and Modernization: Access to Tools." In *Sex and Class in Latin America,* J. Nash and I. Safa, eds. New York: Praeger Publishers, pp. 160–182.

Coburn, Karen and Madge L. Treeber (1988) *Letting Go: A Parents' Guide to Today's College Experience*. Bethesda: Adler and Adler Publ.

Collier, Jane (1986) From Mary to Modern Woman: The Material Basis of Marianismo and its Transformation in a Spanish Village. *American Ethnologist*, 13, no. 1, pp. 100–107.

Dangler, Sue (1976) *The Poor Rural Woman and Western Development Plans*. A Perspective Paper submitted to Asian Studies, University of the Philippines.

Diamond, Stanley (1974) *In Search of the Primitive*. New Brunswick, NJ: Transaction Books.

El-Guindi, Fadwa (1981) Veiling Infitah with Muslim Ethic: Egypt's Contemporary Islamic Movement. *Social Problems*, 29, no. 4, pp. 465–485.

Ervin-Tripp, S., M. O. O'Connor and J. Rosenberg (1984) Language and Power in the Family. In *Language and Power*, C. Kramarae, M. Schultz and W. M. O'Barr, eds. New York: Sage Publications, pp. 116–135.

Etienne, Mona and Eleanor Leacock, (eds) (1980) *Women and Colonization: Anthropological Perspectives*. New York: Praeger.

Fanon, Frantz (1963) *The Wretched of the Earth*, New York: Grove Press.

Fanon, Frantz (1967) *A Dying Colonialism*, New York: Grove Press.

Foucault, Michel (1972) *The Archaeology of Knowledge*, trans. A. M. Sheridan. New York: Pantheon Books.

Foucault, Michel (1978) *The History of Sexuality, Volume I: An Introduction*, translated by Robert Hurley. New York: Vintage Book Edition.

Ghani, Ashraf (n.d.) *Order and Conflict: Consolidation of Power through Law: Afghanistan 1880–1901*. Unpublished manuscript.

Goody, Jack (1983) *The Development of the Family and Marriage in Europe*. London and New York: Cambridge University Press.

Gramsci, Antonio (1971) *Selections from the Prison Notebook*, Quinton Hoare and Geoffrey Nowell-Smith (eds). New York: International Publishers.

Guichard, Pierre (1977) *Structures sociales "occidentales" et "orientales" dans l'Espagne musulmane*. ["Occidental" and "oriental" social structures in Muslim Spain] Paris-La Haye: Mouton.

Hochschild, Arlie (1989) *The Second Shift*, New York: Viking Publications.

Jansen, Willy (1987) *Women without Men: Gender and Marginality in an Algerian Town*. Leiden: E. J. Brill.

Johnson, Miriam M. (1988) *Strong Mothers, Weak Wives: The Search for Gender Equality*. Berkeley: University of California Press.

Joseph, Suad (1982) The Mobilization of Iraqi Women into the Wage Labor Force. *Studies in Third World Societies*, no. 16, pp. 69–96.

Keddie, Nikki R. (1979) Problems in the Study of Middle Eastern Women. *The International Journal of Middle Eastern Studies*, 10, no. 2, pp. 225–240.

Knauss, Peter R. (1987) *The Persistence of Patriarchy: Class, Gender and Ideology in Twentieth Century Algeria*. New York: Praeger.

Knudsen, Dean (1969) The Declining Status of Women: Popular Myths and the Failure of Functionalist Thought. *Social Forces*, 48, no. 2, pp. 183–193.

Low, Natalie (1984) Mother–Daughter Relationships: The Lasting Ties. *Radcliffe Quarterly*, December, pp. 1–4.

Mahdi, M. (1977) Foreword. In *Middle Eastern Muslim Women Speak*, Elizabeth W. Fernea and Basima Q. Bezirgan, eds. Austin: University of Texas Press, p. xi.

Makhlouf, Carla (1979) *Changing Veils: Women and Modernization in North Yemen*. Austin: University of Texas Press.

Marcus, Abraham (1985) Real Property and Society in the Premodern Middle East: A Case Study. In *Property, Social Structure and Law in the Modern Middle East*, Ann Elizabeth Mayer, ed. Albany: State University of New York Press, pp. 109–128.

Marcus, George and Michael M. J. Fischer (1986) *Anthropology as Cultural Critique: An Experimental Moment in Human Sciences*. Chicago: University of Chicago Press.

Massell, Gregory (1968) Law as an Instrument of Revolutionary Change in a Traditional Milieu: The Case of Soviet Central Asia. *Law and Society Review*, 2, no. 2, pp. 179–228.

Mead, Margaret (1926) *Sex and Temperament in Three Primitive Societies*. New York: W. Morrow and Company.

Naddaf, Sandra (1986) Mirrored Images: Rifa'ah al Tahtawi and the West: Introduction and Translation. *Alif, Journal of Comparative Poetics*, 6, Spring, pp. 73–83.

Nader, Laura (1987) The Subordination of Women in Comparative Perspective. *Urban Anthropology*, 15, no. 3–4, pp. 377–397.

Nader, Laura (1994) Comparative Consciousness. In *Assessing Cultural Anthropology*, Bob Borofsky, ed. New York: McGraw Hill, pp. 84–96.

Nash, June and María Patricia Fernández-Kelly (1983) *Women, Men and the International Division of Labor*. Albany: State University of New York Press.

Nelson, Cynthia (1974) Public and Private Politics: Women in the Middle Eastern World. *American Ethnologist*, 1, no. 3, 551–563.

Nelson, Cynthia and Virginia Olesen (1977) Veil of Illusion: A Critique of the Concept of Equality in Western Thought. *Catalyst*, 10–11, pp. 8–36.

Ong, Aihwa (1987), *Spirits of Resistance and Capitalist Discipline: Factory Women in Malaysia.* Albany: State University of New York Press.

Pastner, C. (1978) Englishmen in Arabia: Encounters with Middle Eastern Women. *Signs: Journal of Women in Culture and Society*, 4, no. 2, 309–323.

Rahnema, Majid (1986) Under the Banner of Development. *Development*, 1, no. 2, 37–46.

Rassam, Amal (1983) *Political Ideology and Social Legislation: Women and Modernization in Iraq.* Graduate Center in Queens College, CUNY, New York.

Rassam, Amal (n.d.) Toward a Theoretical Framework for the Study of Women in the Arab World. Unpublished manuscript.

Rattray, R. S. (1955) *Ashanti.* London: Oxford University Press.

Reiter, Rayna. R. (1975) Introduction. In *Toward an Anthropology of Women,* Rayna Reiter, ed. New York and London: Monthly Review Press.

Rihani, May (1978) *Development as if Women Mattered: An Annotated Bibliography with a Third World Focus.* Overseas Development Council, Occasional Paper No. 10. Washington, DC: New TransCentury Foundation.

Rogers, Barbara (1980) *The Domestication of Women: Discrimination in Developing Societies.* London and New York: Tavistock Publications.

Rugh, Andrea B. (1984) *The Family in Contemporary Egypt.* Syracuse, NY: Syracuse University Press.

Said, Edward (1978) *Orientalism.* New York: Vintage Books.

Salama, Ghassan (1981) Aseb Al-Istishrag [The Essence of Orientalism]. *Almustagbal El-Arabi*, no. 23, January, pp. 4–22.

Sanday, Peggy (1981) *Female Power and Male Dominance: On the Origins of Sexual Inequality.* Cambridge: Cambridge University Press.

Sarri, Rosemary (1985) *World Feminization of Poverty.* Report prepared for the University of Michigan's School of Social Work.

Scheper-Hughes, N. (1985) Culture, Scarcity and Maternal Thinking: Maternal Detachment and Infant Survival in a Brazilian Shantytown. *Ethos*, 13 no. 4, pp. 291–317.

Scott, E., S. Ervin-Tripp, and E. Colson (1970) *Report of the Subcommittee on the Status of Academic Women on the Berkeley Campus.* University of California, Berkeley. Available at http://www.eric.ed.gov/ERICWebPortal/search/detailmini.jsp?_nfpb=true&_&ERICExtSearch_SearchValue_0=ED042413&ERICExtSearch_SearchType_0=no&accno=ED042413 (accessed April 12, 2012).

Scott, Hilda (1984) *Working Your Way to the Bottom: The Feminization of Poverty*. London and Boston: Pandora Press.

Sen, Gita (1984) Subordination and Sexual Control: A Comparative View of the Control of Women. *Review of Radical Political Economics*, 16, no. 1, 133–142.

Smart, Barry (1986) The Politics of Truth and the Problem of Hegemony. In *Foucault: A Critical Reader*. David Couzenshoy, ed. New York: Basil Blackwell, pp. 157–174.

Stowasser, Barbara F. (1987a) *The Islamic Impulse*. London: Croom Helm.

Stowasser, Barbara F. (1987b) Religious Ideology, Women, and the Family: The Islamic Paradigm. In *The Islamic Impulse*, Barabara Stowasser, ed. London: Croom Helm, pp. 262–296.

Tinker, Irene (1976) The Adverse Impact of Development on Women. In *Women and World Development*, Irene Tinker and M. Bo Bramsen, eds. Overseas Development Council, Washington, DC, pp. 22–34.

Tucker, Judith (1986) *Women in Nineteenth Century Egypt*. Cairo: American University of Cairo Press.

Wolf, Eric (1982) *Europe and the People without History*. Berkeley, Los Angeles and London: University of California Press.

Further Reading

de Beauvoir, Simone (1953) *The Second Sex*. New York: Alfred Knopf Publisher.

Ortner, Sherry (1974) Is Female to Male as Nature is to Culture? In *Woman, Culture and Society*, Michelle Z. Rosaldo and Louise Lamphere, eds. Stanford, CA: Stanford University Press, pp. 68–87.

5

Corporate Fundamentalism
Constructing Childhood in the United States and Elsewhere

When parents feel powerless, it is not because they really need reform, therapy, or education, but because they are relatively powerless in today's society.

(Keniston and the Carnegie Council on Children, 1977)

Introduction

Corporate fundamentalism as a movement has its roots in nineteenth-century America with the rise of industrialization of a particular sort and the rise of wage labor. That corporate fundamentalism has played an important role in the construction of childhood in the United States is known at some level, but it has not been given the attention it deserves, sometimes as a result of equating the politics of childhood solely with national government reform. What has been hardly recognized is the ripple effect of the interaction

Culture and Dignity: Dialogues between the Middle East and the West,
First Edition. Laura Nader.
© 2013 John Wiley & Sons, Inc. Published 2013 by John Wiley & Sons, Inc.

between American corporate fundamentalism and American religious fundamentalism, and how that interaction stimulates fundamentalisms couched in religious terms in the Arab world, for example. In the Arab world, where family and kinship are the predominant units above all others, people fear that traditional family cultures are under attack. Indeed, it may be that linkages between American corporate policies and wars against "terrorism" create the social breakdown of families everywhere and are the components that unite parents here and elsewhere and invite religious innovation. My intuitive thinking about these connections was stimulated by the publication of several histories covering one part or another of the construction of childhood in the United States. American foreign policy, the serious problems facing the American family, the reconstruction of American industry by design, evangelicalism, marketing to children, pharmaceutical drugs, educational testing, and activism both direct and indirect here and in the Islamic world, all have a domino effect. But I need to step backward and document, insofar as possible, how the processes evolved in the United States and Europe such that families were transformed.

Fundamentalisms of a religious bent are a worldwide phenomenon and not just Islamic. We in the United States take for granted that childhood is constructed and experienced within the politics of government, of families, of schools, and of media entertainment. It would hardly be controversial to observe that the world has been radically changed by new electronic technologies. Under any canopy of power we find children. We in the United States have also had warnings about the conflation of democracy with commercial markets eroding civil society and reinforcing the politics of the right. What has been missing, with few exceptions, is an integrated analysis that explains the ways in which all of these variables (of grossly unequal power) interact and affect families and children. In 2005 I argued that in both American and Arab society, the rise of religious fundamentalism may be related to the parental loss of control in child rearing, when family values are experienced as under attack by powers mostly invisible to the untutored, but felt nevertheless. All of this needs to be refined and understood in historical context.

Manufacturing Culture Bit by Bit

In *An Irresistible Empire* (2005), historian Victoria de Grazia tells the fascinating story of how United States industrialists conquered twentieth-century Europe in the American struggle for the "peaceful conquest of the world." She begins her tale with President Woodrow Wilson positing two strategies of conquest through "democracy of business." One was "to force the tastes of the manufacturing country on the country in which the markets were being sought." The other was "to study the tastes . . . of the countries where the markets were being sought" (de Grazia, 2005: 1) and through manufacturing satisfy those tastes and needs – this latter strategy he considered to be the American way. Desire and taste were at the core of this sales philosophy. For Wilson, salesmanship and statesmanship were inter-related. According to de Grazia, Wilson's message, delivered in 1916 to the World's Salesmanship Congress in Denver, is clear:

> The great barrier of this world is not the barrier of principles, but the barriers of taste. . . . Let your thoughts and your imagination run abroad throughout the whole world, and with the inspiration of the thought that you are Americans and are meant to carry liberty and justice and the principles of humanity wherever you go, go out and sell goods that will make the world more comfortable and more happy, and convert them to the principles of America (2005: 1–2).

Wilson's policy was seductive. The world was to be won over by calculated mass marketing and an American notion of democracy based on sharing habits of mass consumption by watching the TV ads, wearing the same clothes, and learning the same "facts" in schools.

What is particularly fascinating about de Grazia's book is that Wilson and the large US manufacturers targeted Europe, the place whence most of them were descended. She describes how they did it: they measured Europeans by American tastes, introducing Hollywood films, mass marketing, and American consumer goods, in the last case through the department store. Europeans traded their cultural values of thrift for goods. However, such moves have been resisted. For example, today the Italian slow foods movement serves as a critique of the fast food life, and other critiques of Extreme West consumption values have been carried out by a number of other countries, from the Netherlands to Scandinavia, respectful of organic agriculture and opposed to genetically modified foods.

Before de Grazia, historians in the United States described how these same manufacturing interests target US citizens, using most of the same techniques to persuade them to become captive consumers of standardized goods and services. David Noble documents how this was done in his now classic *America by Design* (1977). Interlocking interests of the industrialists, educational institutions, and the military were all involved, their roles redesigned to match corporate interests, first in the manufacture of goods and then in the manufacture of a lifestyle. The rise of mass marketing techniques was also the subject of Stuart Ewen's *Captains of Consciousness* (2001 [1977]), and, later, the counterpunch of contemporary business culture was dealt with in Frank and Weiland's *Commodify Your Dissent* (1997). Such books give an idea of how modern American corporate culture came about, how its agents worked on shopping and manufactured American wants and desires and psychic goods. Advertisements, installment plans, easy credit, and the mass standardization of taste were processes that created a new ethos. Some see this as a continuation of *The Great Transformation* (Polanyi, 1944) – a fundamentalist movement that may be related to, and may even have ignited, certain fundamentalist religious movements in the United States and elsewhere. What happens when such a movement spreads throughout the world, going beyond the conquest of domestic and European markets? Such questions require multifaceted and interwoven analyses of how American family loyalties – and increasingly family loyalties across the world – are transferred to brand loyalties. It may be hard, nonetheless, to imagine such transformations happening in the Middle East where family and tribal loyalties are traditionally primary.

We might start to understand outcomes by delineating the consequences for childhood in the United States where this kind of corporate fundamentalism began. But first a sketch of the major characteristics of corporate fundamentalism as a movement, one that had its roots in nineteenth-century America with the rise of industrialization and the accompanying rise of wage labor. Corporate fundamentalism's important role in the construction of childhood in the United States was analyzed early on through the provocative work of Christopher Lasch (1977; 1978) on the transformation of the family under American industrialism. Nevertheless, for the most part social scientists have not paid enough attention to understanding the corporate construction of the American family through marketing to children, the atomization of American culture linked, as I believe it is, to the rise of evangelical Protestant religious fundamentalism in the United States in response to the erosion of parental authority. Lasch described specifically how corporate capitalism expropriates parental authority by enlisting the helping professions and by the use of narcissistic techniques that create insecurities among the young that marketers can then exploit. Toward the end of this essay I shall indicate the irony of the combination of American corporate fundamentalism and American religious fundamentalism serving to stimulate fundamentalisms of a religious nature in other parts of the world such as the Middle East.

John Gray in *False Dawn: The Delusions of Global Capitalism* (1998) spelled out the instability produced by the system of global capitalism that Sir Edmond Leach was referring to some 70 years earlier. Gray is one of Britain's leading political economists who was at one time a close adviser to Margaret Thatcher and the New Right in Britain. A *New York Times* book reviewer had this to say: "Gray's new book argues – actually, thunders – that the global economic system is immoral, inequitable, unworkable, and unstable. . . . He recognizes that the movement toward free markets, goods and ideas is not a naturally occurring process but rather a political project that rests on American power" (Zakaria, 1999).

Early on in his argument, Gray expresses outrage at what he sees as core consequences of the increased shift away from the more socially rooted markets that had existed for centuries in England before the mid-nineteenth century to neoliberalism as practiced today. Mid-nineteenth-century England was a time of experimentation in social engineering. In the free market it constructed a new institution creating a new type of economy in which prices of all goods, including labor, changed without regard to the effects on society. The goal of the experiment, according to Gray, was "to demolish social markets, and replace them by deregulated markets that operated independently of social needs" (1998: 1), the experiment that Polanyi called the Great Transformation, "the political and economic origins of our time." Gray points out that there is a similar transformation operating today in the guise of the World Trade Organization, the World Bank, and the International Monetary Fund together with what has been referred to as the Washington Consensus – institutions with a philosophy that seeks to impose the so-called free market worldwide. Connecting personal with political, Gray opines (1998: 2) "In the United States free markets have contributed to social breakdown on a scale unknown in any other developed country. Families are weaker in America than in any other country." Later in his book Gray (1998: 112) reiterates this same point: "The increases in economic risk that go with the mutation of capitalism in twentieth-century America have occurred in a society in which families are more fragile and more comprehensively fractured than those of any European country, including Russia, where the extended family has survived over seventy years of communism." And finally he notes, "Through effects on the family the American free market weakens one of the social institutions through which a liberal capitalist civilization renews itself" (1998: 114).

Thus, although the young Edmund Leach (mentioned earlier) felt that something was unbalanced about "the terrible tyranny that is typified by American business . . . the logical succession to the more sober commerce of the last century" (Tambiah, 2002: 28), Gray is looking at the consequences of the false dawn of the global free market in terms of social instabilities: a weakened family, exacerbated inequalities, elevated incarceration levels, and more. What Gray does not do is indicate exactly how those effects come about, the process by which, in this case, American families become fractured.

It involves understanding something about corporate fundamentalism as well as American evangelism as they combine to impact the American family, and understanding the missionary-like zeal with which childhood is corporatized.

Fundamentalisms: Corporate and Religious

When I first composed the title "Corporate Fundamentalism: Constructing Childhood in the United States and Elsewhere," I had not thought about the origins of the term corporate fundamentalism; it just seemed logical that there should be such a concept from reading about marketing to children in the United States. However, the term had been coined, probably independently, by a number of thinkers and scholars. We found two definitions on the Internet, neither of them complimentary. The first was "Corporate fundamentalism: a brutal indifference to anything that threatens profits" (Yankowski, 2001). The second "Corporate fundamentalism: entreats most of the world's people to accept an unjust economic order in which they have no power, promising rewards in some rosy future" (Guma, 1997).

Such definitions resonate with what Gordon Sherman, a former CEO of Midas Muffler, said in a lecture to my anthropology class on controlling processes in the mid-eighties. Sherman's big picture concern dealt with the corporate process as it affects the environment, and at the outset he asked: "What permits or encourages us as a society to tolerate that, to allow it to happen? What influences of control . . . tempt us to succumb and not only tolerate but to be a part of this horrible calculation, extermination, and destruction of the globe?" (Sherman, 1987) Gordon Sherman was no ordinary American CEO, but one of those few corporate managers who had been speaking truth to power over the past decades.

Sherman was director and creator of the Midas franchise system, which he described as a modern adaptation of feudalism. He well understood how the corporate process worked when he compared corporate ethics with Judeo-Christian ethics. The corporate ethic in counterdistinction to Judeo-Christian ethics is opportunistic:

"It simply says . . . we will do whatever we can carry off" (Sherman, 1987). Sherman called this opportunism "the raw ethic." He spoke about how corporations keep 'us in willing compliance with what they are up to, even if it means polluting what we need to survive, and how corporations entice people within their own ranks to be obedient and subservient, so that subordinates willingly do as they are told and suspend judgment and values in pursuing corporate goals. He also spoke about the free enterprise system and how American practitioners of free enterprise close ranks to protect the system. Corporations have no sense of consequence, no sense of legacy – "They live . . . in a sea of expediency." But in the end Sherman concluded that the controlling corporate process can be summed up in two words: "universal complicity." We Americans are all implicated in the whole corporate cycle as consumers, employees, stockholders: "Technology and its amenities sweep up everyone." For Sherman, those who oppose the system are the true heroes of our time but they are in short supply. His empathy with corporate executives as hostage to their own success led him to repeat that the corporation will continue to march on until opposed (Sherman, 1987). The inherent irresponsibility, exploitation, and expediency need to be checked, as outlined by Charles Reich in *Opposing the System* (1995) and by others since (Ho, 2009; Tett, 2009)! But many decades have passed since the initial drift in mid-Victorian England away from socially rooted markets to the market mentality free from social and political control. Thus social markets were replaced by "deregulated markets that operated independently of social needs" (Gray, 1998: 1, also 12–14). As Sherman pointed out in the 1980s, the corporate juggernaut is part and parcel of our life; we're all aboard.

Others in the corporate world have invoked the word corporate fundamentalism to conceptualize what Sherman described in detail, although it may be more commonly used by those involved in the grass roots movements. John Galvin, a psychologist and psychotherapist, put it starkly in a 2002 editorial: "Corporate fundamentalism is a threat to America and we need to mobilize all of our resources to combat it. The fight will be far more difficult than the fight against Al-Qaeda. Our great military and economic power will be useless against this foe. To win the war against corporate fundamentalism, we must rely upon moral fitness and courageous self-knowledge" (2002: 4). We must, Galvin continues, "overcome our natural tendency to depend . . . on the powerful. We must dig deeper into ourselves to the core of our American values to reclaim a balance that has been lost. This will be a war where the battlefields are in the homes, schools and workplaces of America, not the hills of Afghanistan. This will be a citizen's war." A version of this is currently being articulated in the Arab Spring and the Occupy movements.

We hear often from political camps in the United States about American values, but rarely with respect to corporate fundamentalism. Gordon Sherman is partly driven by his concern for environmental degradation and by the Enron debacle that some later likened to the tragedy of September 11. Along the same lines, others are outraged at the role of corporate marketing in fracturing the American family: "Enron, just like the World Trade Center attack, reveals the presence of a network of people whose values and behaviors threaten the security of our families, the integrity of our institutions, and the future of our children" (Galvin, 2002: 4).

Simon Western (2004), a young business scholar writing about "The Social Dynamics of Fundamentalism," posits a connection between the rise of Christian fundamentalism in the United States and the emergence of transformational corporate managers. He asks the question, "How can leadership be potent without leading 'the flock' into the totalizing corporate cultures that are reminiscent of fundamentalist movements?" The convergence that he notices is between two different fundamentalisms – one religious, the "New Christian Right," and one secular, "Corporatism and the Neo-liberal Free Marketers." The two form an unlikely alliance that needs unraveling. To that end, Western turns to the underlying dynamics from which religious fundamentalism assumes its power, and brings these two entities together under one umbrella: shared culture. Corporate secular fundamentalism and religious fundamentalism share certain values and assumptions – conviction of righteousness, a certainty of the truth, intolerance of difference, evangelizing zeal, and paranoid mindsets (Western, 2008: 141–161). He summarizes all this in a chart highlighting similarities (2008: 145).

Similarities between Christian Fundamentalism and Corporate Culture

Transformational leadership

Based on mythos, signifying powers, and normative control to create conformist, homogenous, and yet dynamic cultures. Predominantly gendered as male.

Conviction of righteousness, certainty of truth

Free market corporate culture believes "there is no other way" but the free market, and fundamentalist Christianity, believes that "there is no other way" but their form of Christianity.

Intolerance of difference, refuting pluralism

Again, both believe "there is no other way." The only pluralism accepted by corporate culture is the pluralism within the bounds of westernized market democracy. Other forms of governance and economic functioning are blasphemous. Conflict is encouraged to defeat opposing ideologies; anything which challenges the hegemony of either belief systems.

Growth

Both fundamentalists and corporate culture aim for gaining "greater market share" in their own terms.

"Religious" evangelizing zeal

Both have this in abundance and both aim to convert/conquer new markets and new believers.

Structural organization

Charismatic leadership with flattened hierarchies, organized around family-sized teams/groups, dispersed leadership, set within a larger homogenous community, held together by visions, values, and normative control.

Corporate Fundamentalism

The term corporate fundamentalism may also be used to describe a global agenda of the sort that was attributed to President Wilson at the beginning of this essay, an agenda now functioning through advertising, TV, Internet, billboards, and signs that pollute public spaces. Ursula Franklin, emeritus professor at the University of Toronto (see Klein, 2000: 311), puts it starkly: "We are occupied the way the French and Norwegians were occupied by the Nazis during World War II, but this time by an army of marketers. We have to reclaim our country from those who occupy it on behalf of their global masters." Naomi Klein (2000) describes the colonizing of everyday life by means of a powerful socio-political as well as an economic force, what she calls "McGovernment." Other commentators speak of a Westernized fundamentalism, a hegemony with totalitarian tendencies, creating mono-cultures, denying difference, colonizing public and private spaces, tolerating other cultures only to the extent that they assume consumerist values (see Friedman, 2000; Hertz and Nader, 2005, on Friedman). In addition, a bevy of critical voices are being heard that describe the impact of corporate fundamentalisms – Monbiot (2001) on the corporate takeover of Britain, Habermas (1987) on the colonization of the life world, and Hertz (2001) on the silent takeover. But Simon Western challenges the way in which religious and corporate fundamentalism are discussed separately as if there were no link, only similarity one to the other. What he has to say about corporate management reiterates Gordon Sherman's observations – control is not located specifically but is aimed generically. To be different is not an option; the lack of privacy precludes dissent; the management aims at forming a one-dimensional company person, a culture of surveillance by peers. How all this affects the construction of childhood and the lives of American youth follows. This longish prelude about the context in which childhood is constructed is critical for combating those who normalize "modernity" and who buy into a singular definition of progress as consumerist development such as the gentleman from Morocco (mentioned in Chapter 1) who said, "We have to modernize, Laura."

Marketing and Children: The United States

The marketing onslaught targeting young people in the United States operates twenty-four hours a day, all year, and is driven by tens of billions of dollars in sales and profits. For the most part, American parents do not have the resources and organizations to protect their children from the onslaught should they want to. About all they can do individually is limit their children's exposure to marketing, for example, by not allowing television viewing. But they would also have to limit their children's use of computers, and their viewing of billboards and much else, a near impossibility even for those who home-school their children. Virtual reality, the Internet, and interactive technologies enable the kind of "one-to-one marketing" difficult to control. It is not an easy task to monitor exposure. Not surprisingly, many American parents feel that marketing is separating them from their children, while drawing the children into a world of commercialism that knows little restraint.

For the most part, parents were not prepared for the corporate construction of childhood. This is because it had moved in little by little over dozens of years. Government and the mass media were supportive of families in the 1930s through the 1950s, but by the late twentieth century, starting at a very early age, children's time had been taken over by images including materialism, money, sex, violence, junk food, and products from Disney to Pepsi. Slowly the impact of corporations was to atomize, to break up families into individual consumers. And the anxieties of American parents are now being felt by parents in other countries. Their children, too, are bombarded by globally modulated fashions coming to them through TV, video games, billboards, and even word of mouth. The main difference is that in other countries such flagrant commercialism is thought to be equivalent to American culture, not to an American corporate culture that has been imposed on Americans as well. The presumption that American parents want the corporate ethic is assumed, while parents everywhere need to be aware of common concerns regardless of nationality.

In the United States, parents are seen as a primary obstacle by marketeers: "Parents are in the way but they provide the dollars" (Nader, Ralph with Coco, 1996: vii). Marketing firms deal with this problem by sending messages of liberation directly to children. Prime examples are McDonald's ads that portray adults as lame, stupid, a pain, and overall out of touch. Video companies from the time of Nintendo do the same in their advertisements – they degrade and devalue parents. So do television programs like *The Simpsons*. The advertiser's message is "We understand you better than your parents do." Today, there are a plethora of academic and popular books that instruct salespeople on how to sell to children. Some strategies target a vacuum existing in many households and neighborhoods, given the increasing number of single-family and two-earner households in the United States. They take advantage of struggling families, playing their roles as hucksters to the hilt. Their strategy even plays upon the parental anxieties that advertising itself has helped to create. Strategies such as "cradle-to-grave" brand loyalty miss the full costs of ills created.

Although it has been remarked that anthropologists have paid relatively little attention to American children or childhood over a century of research (Hirschfeld, 2002), there seems to be today some growing interest in children in anthropology. In 1996, Linda Coco investigated the marketing-to-children industry. She attended advertising conferences, interviewed marketers, studied their publications, and interviewed children – the "target population." At the beginning of the essay *Children First* (Nader, Ralph with Coco, 1996: 1), Coco quoted a renowned marketing-to-children expert, James McNeal, who affirmed "children times dollars equals markets." The more children control money, the more money they have at their disposal, the greater the need for marketing to find hooks that reach into their lives and minds. The first challenge for the marketer then is to find ways leading directly to children, limiting parents' roles while not completely alienating the holders of the purse strings. Market researchers have pointed to three techniques that can be used toward achieving this goal: children can be effective agents inasmuch as they can nag their parents to buy products for them;

parents can be induced to buy products for their children as a compensation for overworking and not spending time with them; and, finally, by undermining parental authority, both parents and children can be led to look to corporations themselves for answers and guidance.

Coco (Nader, Ralph with Coco, 1996) collected and presented examples of all three strategies. Marketers studied the developmental process by which children learn to ask parents for products and get requests filled. Fueled by a marketing system, techniques of persuasion are used to foment nagging of parents, what some marketers call "pester power." In particular, the guilt factor is used in advertising to latchkey children and their parents. Many parents see little of their children, either because the family has only a single parent or because both parents work outside the home or for other reasons. In 1996 more than 7 million children were left at home after school to take care of themselves, at times with only a television to keep them company. The figures are more like 10 million today. Latchkey products can be bought and left on the counter for the child coming home from school to an empty house. Microwaveable entrées make it possible for a child to make "My Own Meals." The most insidious ads are those that portray parents as stupid and out of touch with the world of children, and mock parental concern for safety and health, parents who are nurturers, teachers, and guardians to their children.

Market researchers have used a variety of methods to find out what makes children tick, and what can be made to appeal to them. Some market researchers call themselves ethnographers because they use participant observation, in addition to focus groups and surveys, in an effort to better target children's values as well as shape them to fit commercial interests. Some of the hooks marketers use are related to a child's desire for acceptance by its peers, for love, power, independence, and "aging up," or wanting to look and be older than they really are. In this context, the focus groups are planned and premeditated control mechanisms that some anthropologists call "guerilla research"; others question the ethics of such marketing practices. The film *The Corporation* includes some shockingly candid interviews with marketers who dismiss ethical concerns.

One company applies child development research to marketing. Development schemes for marketing target 0–2 as the dependency/ exploratory stage, ages 3–7 as emerging autonomy stages, 8–12 as rule/role stages, and so on, associating specific characteristics for marketing hooks appropriate to each stage of development. For example, ages 13–15, described as early adolescent stage, focuses on biological development of the right and left brain hemispheres and self/social categories of identity, independence from parents, and peer approval. The teen market, in the United States over 30 million strong, is big business and big money, not the least because by their teens youth have jobs, and in the United States teens are very brand- and fashion-conscious. They want to be "cool" and that is an obvious entry for the marketers of health and beauty ads. In other words, as is common in advertising more generally, marketers target the inse- curities and ambitions of developing youth. As Coco points out, this focus on exploiting fears and concerns of teens ends up exacerbating the problems that teens face, and marketers in effect intensify inse- curities for the sake of the sale (Nader, Ralph with Coco, 1996: 20). *Frontline*, a prime time television show, produced a documentary, *The Merchants of Cool* (Goodman, 2001), on how such marketing affects teen ideas about sex, clothes, beauty aids, self-worth, and dignity.

Other observations have focused on technologies such as video games, with most commenting on the violence in and outside gam- ing. One early example, Mortal Kombat, is a game played between two persons that involves ripping hearts out, ripping off heads and spines, people cut in half, electrocution, people blown up, and so forth. Home video games are not much better, causing havoc in terms of adolescent rebellion, moving our teens into a virtual reality that has its own rules, beliefs, fantasies. Best-selling role-playing games in some formats (XBOX, Playstation) include many games such as Call of Duty and Medal of Honor where one can play a sol- dier in Afghanistan and other sites around the world. *Stop Teaching Our Kids to Kill* (Grossman and DeGaetano, 1999), a book coauthored by a US West Point professor and a psychologist, calls attention to the consequences of the desensitization of children to violence by the media. American parents and others who have pressed for some kind of government regulation of the video game industry have had little success, partly because the government is itself in on the act, as consumption, war, and entertainment connect in Army video games an important recruiting tool for the Pentagon (Gonzalez, 2010).

A final choice among many possible examples is the marketing of music. As one anthropologist put it: "There is probably no other human cultural activity which is so pervasive and which reaches into, shapes, and often controls so much human behavior" (Merriam, 1964). Since the 1950s, according to Coco, commercial music has been exercising enormous influence over young people, spurred by a music industry that is age-segmented and -subsegmented to separate the younger generation from the adult world, and even pre-teen from late teens, or "boy bands," and so on. It produces music for a world of peers, a youth culture with its own set of ideas, styles, and behavior, and a desperate need to belong. The giant recording companies glorify rape, murder, promiscuity, drug use, abuse of women and children for a youth music industry that is twice as large as the adult market.

Given increasing youth violence, youth music has been blamed for encouraging hedonism, violence, and disregard for civility. Coco excerpts some of the explicit lyrics, but I shall only mention that they are excellent examples of how far a commercialized industry will go without any sense of introspection or responsible business ethics. By some estimates, the pornography industry in the United States, which abuses youth, is larger than either major league sports or Hollywood (Rich, 2001). In his letter to his parents, Edmund Leach referred to American commercialism as a huge monster that has lost control of itself, leaving it to the parents or the child consumers themselves to buy or not to buy. Even in schools, as well as on television and the Internet, commercials push food brand names and various other addictions aimed at enticing young Americans (see, for example, Schor, 2004, *Born to Buy: The Commercialized Child and the New Consumer Culture*). There are those who defend advertising as educational, but from an analytical point of view the process is manipulation pure and simple, a form of manipulation that causes the young to feel alone, to lose connections to their roots, and to feel abandoned in a world of peer pressure, competition, and insecurity. Coco concludes her work with a warning: "The despair of many children should be understood not as a new manifestation of the age-old generation gap, but as the consequence of a huge shift in our culture and values" (Nader, Ralph with Coco, 1996: 105). Nor is it only a shift in "our" culture. There are huge shifts in cultures around the world – what starts in US corporate headquarters travels far and wide, and appears not just in buying patterns. After all, *Brave New World* (Huxley, 1932) was centered on soma – the happiness drug.

In a chapter on the disintegration of love in contemporary Western society, Erich Fromm (2006 [1956]) had the following to say about economics and religion:

> Capitalistic society is based on the principle of political freedom on the one hand, and of the market as the regulator of all economic, hence social relations on the other. . . . Human relations are essentially those of alienated automatons, each basing his security on staying close to the herd, and not being different in thought, feeling or action. While everybody tries to be as close as possible to the rest, everybody remains utterly alone. . . . Our civilization offers many palliatives which help people to be consciously unaware of this aloneness . . . man overcomes his unconscious despair by the routine of amusement, the passive consumption of sounds and sights offered by the amusement industry . . . by the satisfaction of buying ever new things, and soon exchanging them for others (2006: 79–80).

> Just as automatons cannot love each other they cannot love God. . . . This fact is in blatant contradiction to the idea that we are witnessing a religious renaissance in this epoch (2006: 96).

Juliet Schor's research on the commercialized child (2004) does not link consumerism with happiness in children. Rather, she notes that those who consume more are likely to become more depressed, and the more they consume the more their relationship with their parents deteriorates when the two value systems come into conflict. More recent research merely details the extension of such observations.

Drugs, Commercialism, and the Biomedical Paradigm: An American Example

In my undergraduate course on Controlling Processes, students are assigned a term paper in which they are asked to locate a controlling process in their everyday life and describe how that control works. Women students often write about how advertising affects their "self-esteem," their sense of self-worth as they measure what they see in the mirror against a standardized conception of beauty and body shape. They often end by noting that, although they know they are "being controlled," they feel helpless to do anything about it, they feel "caught" in a net of self-victimization, and are often depressed. Both male and female students write about drugs – not the kind you get off the streets, but those that are purchased with a medical prescription. The following counterintuitive excerpt is not unusual:

> The summer before my freshman year of college, my parents divorced, my dad moved in with his secret girlfriend of 3 years, my mother moved to Northern California, we sold the house holding my lifetime of memories, my cat died, and both my grandmother and my twenty-eight-year-old cousin were diagnosed with terminal cancer. Then I went to college. . . . I was distraught due to these events and some unresolved insecurities . . . I was advised to speak to a counselor. The psychologist . . . listened . . . and she told me that I should start taking Prozac. . . . I responded that I didn't want anti-depressants. . . . She then informed me that I had a chemical imbalance, that Prozac would cure me . . . and that if I continued to refuse treatment, the college could ask me to leave. I maintained that I was simply going through a difficult time and just needed to speak with someone. . . . Disheartened, I shared my story with several other students, only to find that the health center had a reputation for imposing anti-depressants on the students.

The same student went on to write a prize-winning essay on how normalized the use of psychotropic drugs has come to be in the United States (Laleuf, 2004). What is marketed, in this case, is a constant "happy" state, an emotional condition that is marketed as the most desirable.

Pharmaceutical drugs allow people to meet the criteria of being "normal," and such definitions of "normal" have spread world-wide. Laleuf understands that there is mental illness and that pharmaceuticals do help individuals who are sick, but she argues that pharmaceutical companies capitalize on the ambiguities of mental illness diagnoses by appealing through marketing techniques for a kind of normalcy that they have themselves defined. By using their drugs, an individual can be normal, balanced, happy, and released from the stresses of life. In this way the pharmaceuticals are shaping what constitutes "normal" behavior. The effect of this shift in a moral system on the younger generations is dramatic.

As Laleuf notes, "Between 1988 and 1994, there was a three to fivefold increase in the use of antidepressants among 900 000 youths in the United States between the ages of 2–19 (Mahoney, 2002: 53). Another study done in 2002 showed that between 1985 and 1999 central nervous system drugs had an increase of 327%, with Ritalin standing as the most prescribed drug." Laleuf cites a number of studies indicating that the prescribing of antidepressant drugs to treat very young American children – preschoolers 0–5 – is growing fast. Parents are often pressured to conform to the use of antidepressants in order to help their children, sometimes with disastrous results for the children, as in cases brought to light by recent studies linking antidepressants with suicides. In most public schools children are being required to undergo testing for attention deficit (ADHD) problems, and if they have this "disease" (now designated as mental illness under the new Diagnostic and Statistical Manual) they are required to take the appropriate drugs in order to be allowed in the classroom. Whether in most cases it is for depression, boredom, or simply excess energy, millions of American children are being given antidepressant drugs. Since young children's brains are still developing, experts, parents and the children themselves worry that long-term use of these drugs could injure the development of the child's brain, it being very "elastic" (Kluger, 1998: 94). Some studies also indicate that Ritalin has addictive and cardiac side-effects similar to those of cocaine (Williams, 2003).

This collaboration between pharmaceutical companies, the schools, and the political realms teaching children to depend on drugs to fit into what is acceptable behavior in society, is a very dark aspect of social standardization and control found in corporate fundamentalism. In Aldous Huxley's *Brave New World* chemical stabilization and mind control are used to control society. In the contemporary United States pharmaceutical companies are redefining the way psychiatric medicine is taught and practiced, and we now have enormous numbers of television advertisements for prescription drugs, reaching $5 billion worth in 2010.

As in other domains, corporate fundamentalism knows no boundaries beyond the bottom line – a shift away from the more socially rooted markets written about by Polanyi (1944) and later John Gray in *False Dawn* (1998). Self-knowledge, which John Galvin spoke about, is what college students are searching for in themselves and others by examining medical drug use in the United States. They find that corporate secular fundamentalism shares with religious fundamentalism the conviction of righteousness, and exhibits evangelizing zeal. They ignore recommendations made by the prestigious Carnegie Council on Children in *All Our Children: The American Family under Pressure*. The report pointed out that "we must have corporations with a high sense of social responsibility, even when the exercise of that responsibility produces no new profits or increases in the rate of corporate growth" (Keniston and the Carnegie Council on Children, 1977: 70). If the 2010 British Petroleum environmental disaster in the Gulf is any indicator, there is no sign of any reawakening of corporate ethics, whether dealing with children or the environment, although victims of such disasters may be awakened to the implications of the lack of governmental regulation of big businesses.

When Corporate Profits and Education Meet: The Educational Testing Industry

The original intent of those who started the educational testing industry in the United States may have been to make entrance into college fairer and less dependent on class, privilege, or social networks, but the results have been almost the opposite. An early ground-breaking report documenting this fact was written in 1980 by Allan Nairn (now a journalist of East Timor fame, then a sophomore at Princeton). He described the standard assessment test (SAT) as a poor measure of creativity, academic potential, and performance in the United States let alone for applicants in the Middle East. Since then a number of increasingly sophisticated critiques of test-making and test-preparation for American students have been developed, some of them by anthropologists. With the implementation of President Bush's No Child Left Behind law, the critiques are increasingly coming from parents and the children themselves. As Penny Owen, an educational anthropologist, put it to me recently:

> Testing children as young as third grade produces inaccurate results. I have seen students break down in tears, incapable of functioning when presented with another test. More significant than a child's anxiety level, however, is their own awareness that their brains develop at different times than other children, an awareness that adults do not seem to have no matter how much brain research has been done. Teachers call it the 'Ah Hah' moment, the moment the light comes on and abstractions finally make sense to students. Expecting all children to be at the same place at the same time defeats the children, their schools, and in the long run the country (personal communication, 2009).

The public education business in the United States has a budget of more than $300 billion. The testing initiative is a corporate inroad toward eventual control of public education. Psychologists who have been working on the concept of multiple intelligences suggest that the tests only gauge linguistic and mathematical intelligences, if that, and ignore other kinds of intelligence, and as more schools feel pressure to *teach to the test*, these other forms of intelligence are put to one side even if they are necessary for critical thinking. Formulaic learning becomes the rule, and standardized thinking the result. The pool of creative teachers also suffers, since teacher-proof curriculums and authoritarian management intended to raise test scores often drive away the best teachers. At the same time, students hire personal tutors and corporate programs like Sylvan Learning Centers, which benefit a select few to the detriment of broader public schooling.

When school is boring and merely a drill, students often fidget and do not pay attention. It should come as no surprise, therefore, that one of the concerns of American educators is student inability to concentrate, which may be a result of new media. Concentration seems to be defined as stillness and an ability to sit focused on a teacher who may herself lack focus. Concentration is especially difficult when the school day is divided into disciplinary areas, when students are expected to be still and listen rather than partici-pate actively. If they get diagnosed as ADHD, youngsters who can't sit still find themselves on drugs. If they do sit "still," our young are increasingly obedient, docile young adults. The choice is to be eccen-tric or to be a clone. It's a horror story (Roberts, 2006). *And American aid institutions are aggressively exporting our school system to the Middle East!* There is a fundamental shift in thought processes that accompanies development of new media – computers, cell phones, iPods – that is startling even without inclusion of culture difference. Exporting American school ideologies without consideration of cultural settings is planned failure.

Fundamentalisms: Economic, Religious, Political

The last chapter of the report by the Carnegie Council on Children, (Keniston and the Carnegie Council on Children, 1977) contains a remarkable statement – remarkable because so many theories of the American family have been cast in psychological terms that blame only parents for difficulties. This conclusion is cast in relation to culture and society:

We may yearn for the storybook picture of untroubled families in charge of their own destinies, but we now live with a reality very different from this. It is time for parents, citizens, private business, and public officials to face up to the many new shapes that are emerging for the old family and to bring our ideas and policies into line with reality. When parents feel powerless, it is not because they really need reform, therapy, or education, but because they *are* relatively powerless in today's society. Changing that fact requires not just individual change, family therapy, or childhood education, but social, economic, and political change. Most children's problems are also social problems. Change must be not just personal but also political (1977: 213–214).

What followed was an outline of "A Policy for Children and Families" that could be achieved in a decade, a "Vision of the Possible," and the book jacket noted, "*All Our Children* is a book that must be read by everyone who wants to restore the traditional primacy of the family in American life." This in the United States, not in the Middle East – not yet.

In the years following the Carnegie Report, there was a flurry of activity in both the public and religious spheres on the American-family-under-pressure, most of which was *not* coordinated. Public interest groups like Commercial Alert were organized to warn Americans of the consequences of rampant commercialism. A campaign was launched recommending a worldwide ban on the marketing of junk food to children of 12 years of age and under. *Commercial Alert* also pushed measures called a "Parents' Bill of Rights" to help combat the destructive commercial influences on children. This Parents' Bill of Rights included nine proposed pieces of legislation, a few of which have already been introduced in Congress: the Leave Children Alone Act, Child Privacy Act, Advertising to Children Accountability Act, Commercial-Free Schools Act, the Fairness Doctrine for Parents Act, Child Harm Disclosure Act, and so forth. But for the most part not much has resulted. Many citizen groups have formed around these and other issues such as the corporatization of school lunch, now largely taken over by the fast food industry, and as a reaction more school gardens flourish. Issues have been raised about school safety, tobacco, alcohol, and drugs from the streets, and also, of course, television and electronic gaming. Now also addressed are privacy issues – commercial brokers are selling lists of the names and personal information of children as young as two years of age. Two United States senators, Ron Wyden from Oregon and Ted Stevens from Alaska, introduced legislation to stop the practice. Their proposed bill would prohibit corporations from selling without parental consent the personal information of children below 16 years of age for commercial marketing purposes. A similar law passed in 2010 on information-sharing with military recruiters. Such legislation has a precedent. *Hammurabi in his code in 1750 BC made selling to minors punishable by death.*

Of course, the commercialization of childhood is a subset of a larger phenomenon, as indicated earlier: the corporatization of the United States as a whole. As my colleague Paul Bohannan put it to me in a personal communication, "Historically, treasured cultural values are either viewed as marketing impediments, or are commandeered, co-opted, or outright commodified in the service of corporate profits." Nothing in the past is remotely comparable to the unrestrained corporate intrusion into formerly noncommercial space. For the most part we have routinely come to accept what would once have been considered unthinkable: public schools allowing commercial television into the classroom replete with product advertising, on the grounds that schools could not otherwise afford the donated television equipment. Christopher Lasch pointed out early on that social scientists and historians have failed dismally to theorize how broader public policies have impinged on the family. Taboo subjects are often those closest to the sources of power, and as I said in "Who Is Raising American Children?" (Nader, Laura, 1980), cutting-edge research on children might tell an interesting story of the evolution of responsibility among all the people involved in feeding, clothing, sheltering, and influencing the way our children think and act. It may take a village to rear a child (Clinton, 1996), but a corporation is not a village. In fact villages are hard to find, although still plentiful in the Middle East.

Back to Corporate Fundamentalism: Future Directions

As I mentioned earlier, some business academics have posited a convergence between two different US fundamentalisms – one religious (the New Christian Right), and the other secular (the neoliberal marketers). Apart from the observation that both fundamentalisms share certain traits (righteousness, certainty of the truth, intolerance of difference, evangelizing zeal, paranoid mindsets), there seems to be a complementary domino effect operating here. Rampant political and economic commercialisms destroy family stability and aspects of culture that transmit dignity. This leads some powerless parents to turn to religious rhetoric to buy power, and to recruit other adherents. This can be seen in the United States with evangelical conservatives rallying around "family values," a phrase that is often vaguely referenced. But this reaction from powerlessness occurs overseas as well. The globalization of commercial interests, coupled with military operations, feeds a turn to fundamentalisms the world over, the Middle East being only one example (see Munoz, 2000).

Just as multinational corporate marketers disrupt traditional society in the United States, so too do they disrupt traditional culture elsewhere. In Middle Eastern societies youth are increasingly subject to disruptions, ruptures, and traumas due mainly to economic change and the scarcity of work, state politics as associated with Israeli occupation, or the harsh policies of authoritarian US-backed Arab governments, or the American war as in Iraq. Stefania Pandolfo documents (2007) what she calls "the burning" in relation to clandestine migration to Europe and the Islamic ethical-political configuration of their economic predicaments in the context of changing family roles. Even ideas about basic *age* categories are being challenged. Soraya Altorki (2002) asks whether "youth" is a local category or an imported one as she and other local scientists study the gaps opening up between the young and their parents over things like language, violence, dress, and consumption patterns more generally – problems precipitated by globalization and youth accommodation to Western influences. Egypt is a clear case.

144

Egyptian President Gamal Abdel Nasser's bloodless revolution led to Arab pride and socialist economies. With the death of President Nasser in 1970, the Egyptian economy moved from income redistribution schemes that benefited lower economic classes to an open door policy (*infitah*) (open to foreign investment) under President Anwar Sadat (1978–1981) and this continued incrementally under President Hosni Mubarek (1981–2011). Egyptian policies also moved from Nasser's confrontation with the West to an accommodation with the West, which included most immediately corporate advertising (El Guindi, 1981) as well as a change in relations (political and economic) with Israel. Some have dubbed this shift economic fundamentalism or part of the new corporate colonialism (one that now includes Japanese, Korean, and Chinese corporations, not just Western ones), in either case retaining all the rigidities of global religious fundamentalism (Smith, 1999). The difference, however, is that, unlike in the United States, in Middle Eastern societies there is no popular sympathy between religious fundamentalism and that of the corporations; rather there is opposition. Thus in Egypt we have the appearance of new forms of Islamic dress characterized by covering the body, as opposed to its opposite found in advertisements featured in Western media that increasingly bare the female skin.

The question of whether fundamentalisms are inherently conservative and wedded to the past or whether their ideas are essentially modern and innovative (Armstrong, 2000) is being hotly debated by secular theorists (Hirschkind, 2006; Mahmood, 2005). Hardt and Negri (2001: 148) note the "return to the traditional family is not backward-looking at all, but rather a new invention that is part of a political project against the contemporary social order" (or what is better labeled as corporate fundamentalism) a challenge to atomization, a form of resistance against a perceived threat sometimes referred to as secularism or modernity but here called corporate. What Simon Western has pointed out, and what needs further exploration, is how American Christian fundamentalists, initially a site of resistance to family breakdown, have broken the trend of most fundamentalist religious resistance by adapting to and aligning

145

their values with the business world (Western, 2004: 29). In this light, consumerism becomes the key weapon in exporting religious ideas about American values that are not traditionally American at all (like waste or disposability, for example), but rather corporate owing to the dysfunction of the corporation and the marketplace. Western further posits that the alignment of values between Christian fundamentalists and free-market fundamentalists provides an arena that offers easy access to more converts who find a new enemy in social agendas. Evangelicals see traditional family values as under attack from liberals (Frank, 2004), when really the destruction of such values in the United States may emanate from those with whom the Christian believers align.

Anthropological insight provides the building blocks afforded by ethnographic specifics. The business corporation is the most powerful institution of our time, and the paucity of ethnography on this dominant institution needs to meet up with the rich documentation that anthropologists have labored over in examining the consequences of corporate dominance over time (Doukas, 2003; Mattei and Nader, 2008). We suffer from historical shallowness. In order to explain unexpected alliances that do not seem apparent upon initial observation, we need to connect fundamentalizing processes, much as Weber did when he drew parallels between Protestantism and a certain kind of capitalism.

In the instance described in this essay the connections are between American corporate fundamentalism (now no longer solely American) and the siege mentality it invokes elsewhere among Islamic fundamentalists in the Arab East, although the threat of contemporary corporate fundamentalism has, by the twenty-first century, penetrated the entire geopolitical world scene. Thus, it is worthwhile connecting youth, wars, and violence and instances of the Arab Spring more generally, and the nexus merits attention beyond the study of national or small localized practices. Corporate fundamentalism has triggered the rise of non-Western religious fundamentalism against these now disparate forms of imperialism often embroiled in military incursions. But economic determinism, fundamentalist or not, is not the issue. It is the accompanying cultural manifestation, the construction of childhood so that family members become individual consumers separate from larger family units – individuated. In this sense fundamentalism is as intimately connected to a type of economic system as it is to religious belief.

Education researcher Mayssun Succarie tells the story of a class in entrepreneurship taught by Save the Children to youth in Jordan. The message was that, to be successful businesspeople, young people had to put a goal before themselves and not be swayed from this goal no matter what. At the end of the semester, a youth is asked by the teacher to imagine what he would do if he had saved 500 dinars for a new start-up business, his neighbor's house burned down and the homeless neighbor asked him for a 400 dinar loan. What would he do? The youth answered that he would give him the loan. "Wrong answer," said the teacher! He should plow ahead with his business plan. The youth then responded, "You want me to refuse my neighbor? He's my uncle!" Success in this case requires shifting priorities from the family to neoliberal principles.

References

Altorki, Soraya (2002) *Age, Gender, and Class: Youth in the Changing Society*. Unpublished paper presented at American Anthropological Association.

Armstrong, Karen (2000) *Islam: A Short History*. New York: Modern Library.

Clinton, Hillary Rodham (1996) *It Takes a Village: And Other Lessons Children Teach Us*. New York: Simon & Schuster.

de Grazia, Victoria (2005) *An Irresistible Empire: America's Advance through Twentieth-Century Europe*. Cambridge, MA: Belknap Press.

Doukas, Dimitra (2003) *Worked Over: The Corporate Sabotage of an American Community*. Ithaca, NY: Cornell University Press.

El Guindi, Fadwa (1981) Veiling Infitah with Muslim Ethic: Egypt's Contemporary Islamic Movement. *Social Problems*, 28, no. 4, 465–485.

Ewen, Stuart (2001 [1977]) *Captains of Consciousness: Advertising and the Social Roots of the Consumer Culture*. New York: Basic Books.

Frank, Thomas (2004) *What's the Matter with Kansas?* New York: Henry Holt.

Frank, Thomas, and Matt Weiland (1997) *Commodify Your Dissent: Salvos from the Baffler*. New York: Norton.

Friedman, Thomas L. (2000) *The Lexus and the Olive Tree*. New York: Anchor Books.

Fromm, Erich (2006 [1956]) *The Art of Loving*. New York: Harper Collins.

Galvin, John (2002) Terrorism Within. *Ripsaw*, 4, no. 33, 4.

Gonzalez, Roberto (2010) *Militarizing Culture – Essays on the Warfare State*. Walnut Creek, CA: Left Coast Press.

Goodman, Barak (2001) *Merchants of Cool*. *Frontline*. PBS, February 27.

Gray, John (1998) *False Dawn: The Delusions of Global Capitalism*. London: Granta Books.

Grossman, Dave, and Gloria DeGaetano (1999) *Stop Teaching Our Kids to Kill: A Call to Action Against TV, Movie and Video Game Violence*. New York: Crown.

Guma, Greg (1997) Winning a Global Vote. *Toward Freedom Magazine*. Available at http://www.thirdworldtraveler.com/Democracy/Global_Vote.html (accessed April 12, 2012).

Habermas, Jurgen (1987) *The Theory of Communicative Action: A Critique of Functionalist Reason*, trans. T. McCarthy. London: Polity Press.

Hardt, Michael, and Antonio Negri (2001) *Empire*. Cambridge, MA: Harvard University Press.

Hertz, Ellen, and Laura Nader (2005) On *The Lexus and the Olive Tree*, by Thomas L. Friedman. In *Why America's Top Pundits are Wrong: Anthropologists Talk Back*. Catherine Besteman and Hugh Gusterson, eds. Berkeley: University of California Press, pp. 121–137.

Hertz, Noreena (2001) *The Silent Takeover: Global Capitalism and the Death of Democracy*. New York: Free Press.

Hirschfeld, Lawrence (2002) Why Don't Anthropologists Like Children? *American Anthropologist*, 104, no. 2, 611–627.

Hirschkind, Charles (2006) *The Ethical Soundscape: Cassette Sermons and Islamic Counterpublics*. New York: Columbia University Press.

Ho, Angela (2009) *Liquidated: An Ethnography of Wall Street*. Durham, NC: Duke University Press.

Huxley, Aldous (1932) *Brave New World*. London: Chatto & Windus.

Keniston, Kenneth, and the Carnegie Council on Children (1977) *All Our Children: The American Family under Pressure*. New York: Harcourt Brace Jovanovich.

Klein, Naomi (2000) *No Logo: Taking Aim at the Brand Bullies*. Toronto: Vintage Canada.

Kluger, Jeffrey (1998) Next Up: Prozac. *Time, November* 30, 94.

Laleuf, Marianne (2004) *Psychotropic Drugs: The Candy of the Twenty-First Century.* Undergraduate honors thesis, Department of Anthropology, University of California, Berkeley.

Lasch, Christopher (1977) *Haven in a Heartless World: The Family Besieged.* New York: Basic Books.

Lasch, Christopher (1978) *The Culture of Narcissism: American Life in an Age of Diminishing Expectations.* New York: Norton.

Mahoney, Diana (2002) Use of Antidepressants in Pediatric Populations Skyrockets. *Family Practice News,* 32, no. 21, 711–723.

Mahmood, Saba (2005) *The Politics of Piety: The Islamic Revival and the Feminist Subject.* Princeton, NJ: Princeton University Press.

Mattei, Ugo, and Laura Nader (2008) *Plunder: When the Rule of Law is Illegal.* Malden, MA: Blackwell.

Merriam, Alan P. (1964) *The Anthropology of Music.* Evanston, IL: Northwestern University Press.

Monbiot, George (2001) *Captive State: The Corporate Takeover of Britain.* London: Pan.

Munoz, Gema (2000) Arab Youth Today: The Generation Gap, Identity Crisis, and Democratic Deficit. In *Alienation and Integration of Arab Youth: Between Family, State and Street.* Roel Meijer, ed. Richmond, UK: Curzon Press, pp. 17–26.

Nader, Laura (1980) Who is Raising American Children? Talk given at the Carnegie Council on Children, Washington, DC.

Nader, Ralph with Linda Coco (1996) *Children First: A Parent's Guide to Fighting Corporate Predators.* Washington, DC: Corporate Accountability Research Group.

Nairn, Allan (1980) *The Reign of ETS: The Corporation That Makes Up Minds.* Washington, DC: Ralph Nader.

Noble, David F. (1977) *America by Design: Science, Technology, and the Rise of Corporate Capitalism.* New York: Oxford University Press.

Pandolfo, Stefania (2007) The burning: Finitude and the politico-theological imagination of illegal migration. *Anthropological Theory,* 7, no. 3, 329–363.

Polanyi, Karl (1944) *The Great Transformation.* Boston: Beacon Press.

Reich, Charles A. (1995) *Opposing the System.* New York: Crown.

Rich,, Frank (2001) Naked Capitalists – There's No Business Like Porn Business. *New York Times,* May 20. Available at http://www.nytimes.com/ 2001/05/20/magazine/20PORN.html?pagewanted=all (accessed June 8, 2012).

Roberts, Elizabeth J. (2006) *Should You Medicate Your Child's Mind? A Child Psychiatrist Makes Sense of Whether to Give Kids Psychiatric Medication.* New York: Marlowe and Co.

Schor, Juliet (2004) *Born to Buy: The Commercialized Child and the New Consumer Culture.* New York: Scribner.

Sherman, Gordon (1987) The Corporate Ethic. Unpublished lecture delivered as part of the course "Controlling Processes" in the Anthropology Department of the University of California, Berkeley. From a transcript of a videotape of the lecture.

Smith, David G. (1999) Economic Fundamentalism, Globalization, and the Public Remains of Education. *Interchange*, 30, no. 1, 93–117.

Tambiah, Stanley J. (2002) *Edmund Leach: An Anthropological Life.* Cambridge: Cambridge University Press.

Tett, Gillian (2009) *Fool's Gold: How the Bold Dream of a Small Tribe at J.P. Morgan Was Corrupted by Wall Street Greed and Unleashed a Catastrophe.* New York: Free Press.

Western, Simon (2004) The Social Dynamics of Fundamentalism. Available at http://www.ispso.org/Symposia/Boston/Western.htm (accessed June 15, 2010).

Western, Simon (2008) *Leadership: A Critical Text.* London: Sage Publications.

Williams, Armstrong (2002) The Mental Health Industry. *The Alliance for Human Research Protection.* Available at http://www.ahrp.org/informail/0702/25.html.

Yankowski, D. M. (2001) War Diary: Let Cipro Be Our Guide. *Friction Magazine.* Available at http://www.frictionmagazine.com/politik/columns/wardiary_112501.asp (accessed April 10, 2012).

Zakaria, Fareed (1999) Passing the Bucks. *New York Times*, April 25. Available at http://www.nytimes.com/1999/04/25/books/passing-the-bucks.html?scp=1&sq=zakaria+passing+the+bucks&st=cse&pagewanted=all (accessed April 20, 2012).

Further Reading

Hertz, Ellen (1998) *The Trading Crowd: An Ethnography of the Shanghai Stock Market.* Cambridge: Cambridge University Press.

Leach, Edmund R. (1967) *A Runaway World?* New York: Oxford University Press.

Orwell, George (1961 [1948]) *Nineteen Eighty Four.* New York: Signet Classic.

6

Culture and the Seeds of Nonviolence in the Middle East

The Arab world that is; not the one that isn't; the real lives of real people, not the conjured lives of stereotypes

James Zogby (2010: 6)

Introduction

The Middle East, and the Arab world in particular, are places of great diversity. The many traditions that have met in this region over the millennia make it difficult to isolate what is indigenous to it in the realm of nonviolent regulation, if there ever was such a thing. Nevertheless, in my 1985 American University in Cairo (AUC) lecture I thought it useful to call attention to cultural and social dimensions that might be at least ubiquitous in the area. It might then be possible to generate some ideas about dealing with individuals' behavior in

Culture and Dignity: Dialogues between the Middle East and the West,
First Edition. Laura Nader.
© 2013 John Wiley & Sons, Inc. Published 2013 by John Wiley & Sons, Inc.

cases of social and cultural control that fit more with the values of the region than do the models of forced harmony or human management used by contemporary Western nation-states and imported to the Arab world.

Let us look first at Middle Eastern law behavior. Islam, we are told, is a way of life. The most striking aspect about Islam is the primary place of law. Law as expressed through religion is society's chief regulatory force. In the Middle East people are apt to discuss life in a religious idiom, or at least this is how it strikes the observer from the West, and Arabs in particular often confront their social problems with legal language, whether or not they are in a legal forum. Middle Easterners, as compared with Americans for example, emerge as a law-conscious, law-active population (Mayer, 1985). Thus, those who make and apply law (whether customary, sharia, or state law) in the Middle East play to a law-conscious audience. It has also been observed that, in the struggle for limited resources (wealth, prestige, or honor and dignity), law imposes order. Although lawyers exist in the Middle East, the tradition in courts of law is to have litigants speak for themselves. The relative absence of lawyers and lawyering shifts the courtroom focus to the judge, or *qadi*. *Qadi* justice pulls the lay person into the legal process in a way that lawyers' justice cannot.

In a comparative study of *Courts* Martin Shapiro (1986: 195) makes several additional observations that are useful: "Islamic law treats not only of what is legally right or wrong, but also of what is morally good, better, and best." Embedded in Islamic legal thought, he notes, is the concept that what is true in law and religion is determined by the consensus of the faithful rather than the command of any living being. In Islam there is acceptance of a very great diversity of opinion within this overall consensus. "Not only are there many differing schools of law but, as we have seen, differing opinions within a single school are tolerated. Even the Islamic notion of consensus is generally one of spontaneous evolving agreement rather than one of imposition of uniformity" (1986: 203).

Law in Middle Eastern nations consists of a multitude of principles, scattered in innumerable quarters, which are combined, selected from, and sometimes ignored in the course of judicial decision-making. Islamic law, customary law, and the inheritance of colonial law are melded into parts of the national legal systems. Some argue that the colonial period expanded options used by present-day governments. Others also argue that when the new nations borrowed from the administrative, commercial, and criminal law of the West they increased options from precolonial times. It may be, however, that nation-state law has introduced a rigidity into the system that forces governments to turn from less to more customary or sharia law. In the context of the nation-state, Islamic courts and customary law are both a social and a civil means of control, and nowhere is this more true than in decentralized states like Afghanistan.

What about control outside institutions like courts? In much of the scholarship on the Middle East (orientalist or otherwise) great emphasis was laid on the fact that primary groups were strong, and that this emphasis on the primary group (whether nuclear family, lineage, or clan) functioned to the detriment of secondary group development not based on familial relationships. The primacy of kinship groups was used to explain the absence of hierarchy, in courts, for example, or in government more generally. The observation that family holds great significance in the area is certainly true, but the second part of the generalization, which underscores the absence of secondary/civic groups, does not seem to recognize Islam as an organizing and regulatory force that is characterized by a large number of "automatic" controls.

During a summer field stay in Morocco in 1980 I was able to observe some of these automatic controls. The Moroccans were celebrating Ramadan. On the day before Ramadan the beaches of Rabat were as usual crowded. On the first day of Ramadan not a single soul was on the beach. There were no police or other officials to monitor visits to the beach, nor were there police watching to see who went into restaurants during the day to eat. The constraints were internal and rested on individual discipline. Cigarette and food addicts had to regulate their own intakes in observance of the fasting. In observations of court room encounters during Ramadan, I noted

that only a few alcoholics were brought to the court by the authorities for shaming. The overall discipline was remarkable, at all levels
of society, and particularly in the public sphere; and it was achieved
by means of cultural control, not social control by the police to monitor people's behavior, which on such occasions would require more
resources than Morocco or any other nation might be able to muster.
In the West the decrease in self-regulating mechanisms has meant an
increase in police and police technology. In the poorer countries of
the world self-regulating mechanisms are cheaper than policing.
Without self-regulating mechanisms religious occasions such as
Ramadan or the yearly pilgrimage to Mecca, the Hajj, would be very
difficult activities to carry off. It is self-discipline, self-regulation,
then, that is an important feature of fasting or pilgrimage, at least
traditionally, and the mechanism that is central here is the shared
regional one, rather than an imported culture.

Disharmonic Westernization and Pilgrimage

What part of culture operates through self-regulation and what
mechanisms undergird it? In some societies the mechanism may be
fear, in others it may be guilt; in the Middle East the mechanisms are
likely to be related to ideas of shame and honor. The focus on honor
and shame led Bourdieu (1958: 95–96) to observe that internal
dissensions, failures, and shortcomings must not be displayed
before a stranger to the group. Such ideas are often described by
scholars in relation to the place of women in the code of honor, but
honor and shame have a much wider impact. For example, the code
of politeness provides linguistic formulas, rules of politeness,
sayings for each circumstance reflective of dignity and reserve. The
group is powerful and affects "the most trivial actions of daily life"
(Bourdieu, 1958: 95).

We should also examine the communal connotations of honor
and shame, for both honor and shame spread beyond the limits of
the particular group. People attach themselves to a group that has
gained honor, and drop the less significant, less honorable segments

of their kin groups. Good deeds and proper action enhance the prestige of a family; shameful blunders tarnish the reputation of the group. A number of rights are associated with honor, such as the right of refuge: immunity should be given to an enemy who surrenders to his foes in wars and raids; even a killer can go to the house of his victim and claim immunity. As will be noted elsewhere, tolerating the enemy who becomes a guest involves a high degree of self-control. The reward is sublime honor for behaving in an honorable way; failure to comply with these rules brings shame and disgrace. The highest grade of honor is achieved when the ideal is realized at the expense of the performer. As one researcher notes, "The best example of this is the obligation to grant sanctuary to an enemy when he asks for it. In such cases a man gives practical proof that in his consideration honor is larger than life" (Zeid, 1966: 258). In a segmentary society that has only recently submitted to the authority of a government, as with the Bedouins of Egypt, honor plays an important role in the field of social control. And since honor and shame are found more widely in Arab society, one can speculate that they play an important role in regulating social behavior for better or worse. In democratic contexts, for example, shame (public) holds more possibilities for the common good than guilt (private).

In this part of the world, there are many means of nongovernmental control. Controls are decentralized and internalized, and escalation of conflict is often diffused by respected middlemen, people who have power through respect, who find remedies for their constituencies by means of *wastas* (*not* to be confused with bribes) that make good use of restitution and compensation to inhibit escalation (see Nader, 1965). The theoretical model inherent in the *Majjlis* is essentially that of an open meeting between ruler and ruled, to address and resolve problems. I do not wish to indicate that force is not used to achieve ends in this region; the Middle Eastern dictatorships have displayed their share of violence toward their citizens. The modern nation-state often comes equipped with unbridled police and military; still, nonviolent means of control are potentially strong cultural seeds in the area that could be further developed.

What does not travel with imported ideas of control and government are the nonviolent means found in the West. Thus, the new nations often lean too heavily on force for control, in part because of disharmonious importations such as centralized nation-states and in part because modernization works in competition with regional means of control, especially when Western powers support dictatorships, and also because of the inheritance from colonial regimes.

Contradictions appear in the means of control in relation to pilgrimage, for example. The history of this region indicates how little governments have historically interfered with the private lives of citizens whose mutual relationships have been channeled through other kinds of structures such as the customary and religious, some of which I have already referred to. As noted, new nation-states are, unfortunately, accompanied by an apparatus of force that serves to undermine traditional means of control. In addition, like every government in the world, a Middle Eastern government is built to face two kinds of crises – those from within and those from without. In the Arab world, however, crises classified as "from within" at some level traditionally include those originating in other Muslim countries, Arab or not (as with Iran and Saudi Arabia or Iraq and Saudi Arabia – Shia/Sunni); states composed of nonbelievers would clearly fall into the outsider category. Dissention may be internal to the Islamic world, yet, as members of nation-states, people are required to have a passport to move from one country to another, thereby marking differences during pilgrimage. This kind of contradiction is part of what scholars speak about when they refer to a disharmonic Westernization.

The problem of disharmonic Westernization does not usually appear in the analysis of political scientists when they speak of the role of external parties in the context of civil strife, since the presence of a nation-state is taken for granted. But, for anthropologists, it follows that conflict behavior generated by external parties since the end of colonialism is now intimately connected with situations of internal strife, and that external allies have been already to some extent involved in domestic affairs in a great number of interstate conflicts since the end of World War II with the Iran/Iraq war a prime example.

Although mostly in the shadow of our discussions, the comprehensive perspective presented is critical for any question of the means available for control of individuals. Indirect controls in the forms of honor and shame, intermediary regulation as with the use of *wasta,* more public forums such as the *Majjlis* and the Islamic courts are front and center to nonviolence in cases of pilgrimage, as when literally thousands of people from all over the world converge on Mecca and Medina. If these means are ignored in favor of the police force apparatus that is part of a European-style nation-state, the consequences that might follow include escalation of the problem, or the internationalization of problems that start as domestic issues, or challenges of brutality no matter who the instigators were or what they provoked. Few Middle Eastern peoples would argue that brute force is the solution to anything but particular incidents. The majority favor the use of nonconfrontative tactics or Islamic solutions involving law or those means of control such as shame that have been part of Middle Eastern culture for hundreds of years, which in the case of pilgrimage includes the role of the crowd itself in controlling individuals who violate cultural norms.

Between the Stereotype and Reality

After 1960 I devoted a good part of my research to the study of disputing processes and dispute-resolution processes. My students have studied disputing or peace-making from West Irian in New Guinea, to Bavaria, from Ghana to Lebanon, from Turkey to Ecuador. The ethnographic results of that research were published in *The Disputing Process: Law in Ten Societies* (Nader and Todd, 1978). As that book makes clear, some societies were at the time of study more violent or more contentious than others (see, for example, Koch on West Irian New Guinea and Nader on the Oaxacan Mexican Zapotec), and the prevalence of litigiousness or violence or its absence could be associated with historical trajectories or different aspects of social structure. Indeed, we found that social structure could not always be said to be the origin of violence. Sometimes violence, its conception, and its perpetuation, originated outside of particular cultures, as in the relation between Sardinians and their Italian governors (Ruffini, 1978) or between the indigenous people of Mexico and the Spanish conquerors (Nader, 1990).

The work on disputing is useful in thinking about the distribution of violence in relation to culture in general and Middle Eastern culture in particular. Though such an approach may not offer easy solutions to problems in the Middle East, it could outline new ways of thinking about and dealing with violence. In particular, it could point toward a policy whereby Arab publics could take control of their own destiny vis-à-vis when, how, and for how long violence should be used as an instrument of control, with clear recognition of how violence is induced by cultures, societies, and special interests beyond the Middle East. It is obvious to many by now that the type of violence overtaking the Middle East is a type not traditional to the area – a hi-tech violence that does not distinguish between men, women, and children, or between civilians and soldiers, one that will leave ecological traces of war for long periods, sometimes centuries after, in addition to personal memories.

A broader frame of reference for understanding violence might ask who has more of it, and in particular how the Middle East fits into the broader frame. In the United States, stereotypes of members of violent cultures include Latin Americans and Middle Easterners, particularly Arabs. Both are placed high on the list of violent peoples even though hi-tech war machinery was first produced in Euro–American countries (unless you consider guns and cannons as "low-tech"). There is a growing literature on how Arabs in particular are stereotyped as violent in US textbooks, movies, TV, newspapers, and other media – and looking at this literature is instructive of the way in which stereotypes preclude objective realities (Shaheen, 2001; 2008).

The stereotyping of Arabs in American cinema often has Israelis played by popular American actors, while the Arabs are portrayed as cruel terrorists, unseen or seen only from a distance. This stereotyping has a fairly long history. In the film *Exodus* (1960), an Arab brutally kills a 15-year-old refugee girl. In *The Wind and the Lion* (1975) an Arab terrorist kidnaps an American woman. In *Network* (1977) during a bitter anti-Arab Semitic report a crusading TV news commentator warns that the Arabs are taking control of America; he calls the Arabs medieval fanatics. The film won four Academy Awards. In *Beach Sunday* (1977) the story concerns an Arab terrorist plot to kill the spectators at the Superbowl, including the President of the United States, with a horrible device to be detonated in a TV blimp over the stadium. In *Rollover* (1981) "the Arabs" destroy the world financial system. In publicity interviews, Jane Fonda made the movie's message explicit: "If we aren't afraid of Arabs, we'd better examine our heads. They have strategic power over us. They are unstable. They are fundamentalist, anti-woman, anti-free-press" (quoted in Parenti, 1992: 30). In *Wrong is Right* (1982) the story involves "an Arab King" who seems ready to turn over two mini atom bombs to a Khaddafi-like revolutionary leader, with devices to be detonated in Israel and later New York. Paramount Pictures was reportedly considering a $15 million dollar version of a novel that concerns Palestinians with Libyan support planting a bomb in New York. Yes there are counterexamples – for example, films by Syrian-American Moustafa Akkad; still, stereotypes of the Arabs as a violent people may serve to actually encourage a certain kind of violence in and on the Middle East, and may even serve to rationalize violent aggression as acts of defense. In the novel by Leon Uris, *The Haj*, which was third on the bestseller list and covered the 1944–1956 time period, Arabs are described as "lazy, cowardly, boastful, deceitful, untrustworthy, lustful, murderous, thieves or rapists," and Jews are quoted as saying, "We Jews are once again stuck with the job of dealing with the cruelty and evil of the Moslem world," and the Arab hero of the novel himself says, "We are a people living in hate, despair and darkness. Islam is unable to live in peace with anyone . . . we have contributed nothing to human betterment in centuries unless you consider the assassinations and terrorists as human gifts." Both prejudice and ignorance feed hate and violence.

The world has, of course, seen much violence: wars of conquest, wars of liberation and incorporation; the civil war in El Salvador; in Nicaragua the Contras attempting to overthrow the Sandinistas; the Soviet and later American-led invasions of Afghanistan, as well as the Israeli invasion of Lebanon; the genociding of the Mayan Indians in Guatemala and the Amazonian Indians in Brazil; also the struggle against the Khmer Rouge and the invading Vietnamese in Cambodia; the tribal wars of Zimbabwe and the violence in South Africa; the Hindu–Muslim violence and the massacre of Sikhs after the assassination of India's Gandhi; and, of course, IRA violence in Northern Ireland and England. All of these examples, with the exception of IRA violence, were located in the Third World. But in the background there was also the arms race of the USA and the USSR, and the involvement of the super powers in many of these examples of Third World violence. Yet if you read an American newspaper daily you see how the stereotypes of the Arab world and the "darker peoples" are fed – *they* are violent, not the ubiquitous arms dealers.

At the same time, there are also nonviolent groups and movements worldwide. Less attention is paid to them, but the ones that we know about are primarily, though not entirely, motivated by questions of civil rights, nuclear arms, and environmental/survival questions. The US Civil Rights movement under Dr Martin Luther King, Jr in the 1960s; the Chipwa group in North India in the Himalayas (environmental, mostly women, "hug the trees"); Bishop Tutu and his followers in South Africa against apartheid; the Sanctuary Movement in the United States to protect refugees from Central America whose lives are in danger – violating civil law in protecting these people; and, of course, the nonviolent antinuclear movement: in Great Britain the Women of Greenham Common; in the United States the Livermore Action Group and War Resisters League; the Greens in West Germany, the peace groups in Eastern Europe, about which we knew less, and the Free Palestine movement.

Understanding violence and the potential of nonviolence in the Middle East specifically requires us to stand back and take a look from afar, to understand the *dynamics of violence* and nonviolence over time. Countries, cultures, and societies are not "born violent"; they may evolve toward violence or toward peaceful behavior during different periods. The Swedish Empire under Gustavus Adolphus in the seventeenth century ravaged Europe and killed thousands; now we see the Swedes as peacemakers and peace-oriented. The Japanese and the Germans were violently militaristic up until World War II, but because of the conditions of losing a war they turned away from the arms business to ecological and energy development; they are the best modern argument against those who say that our US economy would falter without an arms business, without a defense industry, although the Japanese may be selling arms in the near future after the Fukushima disaster. Then, too, there are peoples who make the transition from peaceful to violent. The Jews as a people belonged to a humanist tradition and were not violent until Hitler unleashed his murderous policies, which led to the further development of Jewish nationalism associated with Zionism and the Israeli state. And Egyptians were a peace-loving people who only in the twentieth century were moved to build up their military might.

If we focus our attention on the technology of violence, the Euro–American nations are among the first and foremost in creating the most devastating war technology the human species has ever known – the USA, USSR, Britain, France, Germany, Japan, and Israel – technologies that caused wholesale violence, such as the calculated dropping of two nuclear bombs by the United States on civilians in Japan in World War II. War technologies now form the basis of much international trade; the arms exports to places like Central America or the Middle East are made in the USA, Russia, France, the United Kingdom, Germany, China, or Israel.

Little Worlds in the International Grip

With the larger context as background, let me move back to the little world that the anthropologist usually studies in the Middle East. In the Levant area, nationals are causing violence to one another, and

161

we find international violence operating on a wide scale. The context of this violence is multi-faceted and has both external and internal aspects. When I first began anthropological fieldwork in the Middle East, I went to south Lebanon, to a Shia Muslim village, which later came under Israeli control in 1982. There I studied the effect of dual organizations and the prevalent factionalism that sometimes leads to violence. This tobacco-growing village was divided into two factions: A and B, as defined by kinship. The village was homogenous Shia: the A's married within their half and the B's married within their half; there was no third party in the village. So when an A had a conflict with a B, the conflict could escalate into all-out village warfare. The solution – in order to prevent dangerous factionalism in the village, at times when violence surfaced the two opposing parties would leave the village in search of a *wasta*, a mediator, and even if they were Shias, they might go to a respected man of another religion, most likely a Christian Orthodox, to mediate.

Ten years after initiating research with the Shias in 1971, I sat on a Ph.D. economics dissertation at the University of California Berkeley that dealt with development in Lebanon. One of the conclusions of the candidate was that development was leading to increasing disparities between the rich and the poor, and that this was likely to cause or exacerbate political instability later. The Shia were among the poorest. In both the early 1960s (after the 1958 shakeup in Lebanon) and in the mid-1970s (with the Lebanese civil war), most American news broadcasters cast the conflict as a purely religious one, Christian/Muslim, with little or no mention made of economic or other determining factors. As a matter of fact, in the Levantine village areas, we find many mixed Christian–Muslim villages. The one combination we rarely find in the same village is Shia–Sunni. But again, outside interpretations fit the stereotype of the Arab as broadly divided Christian/Muslim.

In 1982, with the invasion and occupation of Lebanon by Israel, again the reason for violence – in this case Israeli violence – was garbled in the international reporting, at least in the United States. Although American opinion began to turn, a majority of Americans still thought that the Israelis were defending themselves from terrorists operating in south Lebanon. It was next to impossible for US educators who wished to enlighten the public to change the grid through which the Arab world is seen, even in such a blatant situation as the 1982 invasion of Lebanon by Israel. In *Orientalism* (1978) (or better yet *Covering Islam*, 1981), Edward Said pointed out this grid through which the Arab world is being and has been analyzed, and which has been rooted in the exteriorized Western view of the East for centuries. In the discussions following the 1982 invasion attempts to explain Israeli violence and aggression in terms of greed and expansionism – the control, political or economic, of cheap labor and abundant cheap water from the Litani River – fell on deaf ears and was selected out by the grid, by the stereotyped image of the Arab as violent aggressor. Arabs were terrorists, the Israelis were protecting their borders. The attempt to explore the psychological components of Israeli aggression in displaced aggression theories (whereby the Palestinians become for Israelis the Nazis of the Middle East) or with the battered baby syndrome (Jews who have been battered become the batterers) also fell outside the grid.

To summarize, the external events operating in the Middle East interrelate with many of the internal observations. Foreign interference from Europe has been endemic for centuries now, whether those doing the interfering are Eastern Europeans – like, for example, the Soviets in Syria or Egypt or Yemen – or Western Europeans or their dependents – as with Israel in Lebanon and later US invasions of Iraq and Afghanistan. Ever since the Crusades and for centuries after Napoleon invaded Egypt in 1798, the region has been a pawn of the West and a pawn of the East: all the Cold War European peoples came to the Middle East to take out natural resources such as oil and then sell the Middle East their products such as arms. Today the major products are arms: the arms business and hi-tech killers lead the way in products exported to the region.

The American Educational Trust has repeatedly noted in its publications that the Middle East has become one of the most heavily militarized areas in the world. The Arabs, Iranians, and Israelis together have more tanks and combat aircraft than all of

NATO in Europe. In addition to five wars involving the state of Israel since 1948, there have been large-scale hostilities around the periphery of the Arab world involving Somalia with Ethiopia, Iraq with Iran, Moroccan and Mauritanian forces with Algerian-supported guerillas in the western Sahara, and Libyan forces in Chad. East of the Arab world the 1980s Soviet invasion of Afghanistan, and the upheavals in Iran raised fears among both Arabs and Westerners of possible disruption of supplies of oil and gas and other resources, even invasions.

During the Cold War, Great Power involvement in Arab problems was expressed in sales of sophisticated weapons, the stationing of foreign military advisers in some Arab states, the prepositioning of both US and Soviet military equipment in certain Arab countries, and unequivocal US support for Israel, the Saudi Arabian monarchy, and other authoritarian governments. All such activity provides a powerful incentive to mute any intraregional disputes, which could disturb stability and provide the catalyst for outside intervention, or any pro-democratic uprisings (as were seen from the spring of 2011 onwards in Tunisia, Egypt, Yemen, Bahrain, Syria, and elsewhere).

The East–West struggle was being carried on in the Middle East – why? Think a minute about who lives there: Muslims, Jews, and Christians. These peoples are described in terms of problems: the Jewish problem – persecuted; the Muslim problem – expendable; the Christian problem – outnumbered. The technique once again, as in colonial times, is to divide and conquer. The British were past masters at this strategy; so were the French; and the American version was symbolized early in the person of then Secretary of State Henry Kissinger whose policies of shuttle diplomacy were usually followed by thousands if not hundreds of thousands dead. The contemporary versions of colonial policies of divide and conquer are only exacerbated by war technologies aimed at annihilation. But the core issue has been oil.

Among many sources, Noam Chomsky early in *The Fateful Triangle* (1983) and Robert Fisk later in his comprehensive *The Great War for Civilization – Conquest of the Middle East* (2005) describe US hypocrisy in criticizing Israeli violence against Lebanese citizens since we (the United States) supply Israelis with the "hi-tech killers." These include cluster bombs dropped in heavily populated areas to "get maximum kill per hit." Films of the 1982 siege of Beirut show supersonic Israeli Mirage fighter-bombers attacking the city while Palestinians vainly try to shoot them down with anti-aircraft guns. In the Iran–Iraq war US arms manufacturers did well, having sold arms to both sides at one point. But these are now seen as mere previews of the first Gulf War in 1991, the invasion of Afghanistan in 2001, the Iraq war in 2003, later Israeli forays into Lebanon, and, most recently, American and NATO involvements in the Libyan rebellions.

Culture and Nonviolence: Who Stands to Gain From Peace?

There are two models of Middle Eastern society pertinent to this discussion: *the ties that bind,* and *the structures that divide.* Propaganda in the West often focuses on the aspects that divide not only for purposes of conquest but because of external fears of Arab unity. But there are ties that bind and it behooves the people of the Arab world to emphasize them. It used to be a joke in the 1970s that if Arabs disagreed about everything at least they agreed about the beautiful voices of Um Khaltoum and Fairouz. The first attempt for nonviolence or violence prevention is to find the common bonds, particularly in music and poetry, and to emphasize them here and abroad to change the grid through which the Middle East is viewed by outsiders, one sometimes shared by Middle Easterners themselves. There is more cultural exchange between Israel and the United States than between the United States and the entire Arab world. Furthermore, there are *social structural principles*. The shepherds' conflicts in north Lebanon were mediated by the highly respected elder statesman Emile Bustani in the 1940s and written up in the *New York Times*. *Third-party intermediation* is a principle as old as tribalism in the Middle East, and, by the way, it is being borrowed

165

by the United States in the shape of Alternative Dispute Resolution movements, not to mention by General Petraeus as he seeks a "tribal strategy" in Iraq and Afghanistan. Negotiation or face-to-face techniques have not been useful in this part of the world, which values third-party interventions first and foremost.

The principle of segregation in neighborhood quarters (sometimes described as cell-like) is a way of making and keeping peace that should be highlighted. It contrasts with Western principles of desegregation, but segregated neighborhoods have worked for centuries of close urban living lasting from ancient Mesopotamia to the present ward system in urban areas throughout the Middle East. In more modern contexts, ethnic or religious or craft segregation may be giving way to segregation on the basis of class, both rich and poor, which, as we know in the urban United States, has its own divisive problems.

The Middle East has traditions. The educated have a role in addressing social inequities, of being concerned with social progress; this may mean not imitating the West but finding an Eastern pattern of social betterment. All of these things go together as part of any evaluation of modernity, whatever that means, as progress. Speaking at Berkeley in the early 1980s, the brother of King Hussein of Jordan asked: Who stands to gain from peace? He then launched into social development as his response, depicting an era of trade and intellectual exchange across all borders including Israel, again a tradition with a long history. The audience ignored his talk, which was meant to be uplifting. Rather, the first questions Berkeley professors asked were: Are the Israelis going to invade Lebanon? The West has pushed on the East a conception of war, an imported idea that neither they nor the human race can afford. This is why infusing philosophies of nonviolence is indeed visionary. A first step is more exchange with those who would unfairly stereotype Arabs as violent and therefore dispensable. The Israelis who invaded Lebanon pillaged educated Palestinian homes in Beirut and were surprised to find they contained books. The other side of the stereotype is when the Arab starts to act as he is expected to by the anti-Arab Semites.

If the seeds of nonviolence are cultural, social structural, and political, how are nonviolent practices used to attain political ends? In the struggle of the Palestinians, nonviolence is not a new method. Palestinians have used nonviolent methods since the 1930s side by side with armed tactics. Two of the most prominent examples of the use of nonviolence in the Palestinian cause are the strike of 1936 and later the Arab boycott of Israel (Swedenburg, 1995).

There are 3.5 million Palestinians living in the West Bank and Gaza. The Judaization policy changes every one of the possibilities. Methods of resistance cannot include brute force. Thus, especially when people are not permitted to possess weapons, nonviolence has been the most effective method for waging the struggle – indeed the only possibility open. If the world knew this, it would do much to remove the irrational fear of "Arab violence" and would, on the other hand, do a great deal to reveal the racist and expansionist aspects of Israeli militaristic forces. In 1985, I mentioned demonstrations, obstructions, such as the refusal to work in building Israeli settlements, the refusal to sign or fill out forms that are printed or written in Hebrew, and the building of an infrastructure – universities, factories, institutions, libraries, hospitals, schools, etc. – independent of Israel.

In the occupied territories the school and commercial strikes, the petitions, protest telegrams, and attempts to boycott Israeli goods are manifestations of nonviolent strategies. The Syrian citizens in the occupied Golan Heights were also conducting a powerful and concentrated campaign of nonviolent resistance to Israeli attempts to impose Israeli law on the Syrian Golan Heights. This campaign was reported to be well organized and intelligent in its use of nonviolent methods.

The tactics of nonviolence were different in Lebanon to deal with violence between nationals. Public opinion was developed (among women) as a form of social control that operated to isolate and shun groups or individuals who jeopardized the stability of the country. Light was shed on those Lebanese who were benefitting from the arms running that resulted in internal violence. Such tactics start small but can snowball into a movement that articulates nonviolence independent of government, for governments, and government officials, are often powerless to take positions that can only come from nongovernmental organizations or charismatic individuals.

My general argument in the 1985 AUC lecture was that solutions to the Middle East problem of violence, or any other Third World violence situation, have to be adapted to several fronts simultaneously. Simultaneously changing the stereotyping means that Arabs become humans and therefore perhaps less dispensable from a Euro-American point of view, and the first place to start is to re-educate Arabs in their own traditions of self-respect followed by mutual respect. Among the longest-lasting civilizations was that of Egypt – a civilization not dependent on the outside, on external forces. I reiterated that in Middle Eastern society there are many existing principles of social organization that work as violence prevention. Studying these principles and elaborating upon them would be part of the blueprint. If external forces have chosen to confront each other on your land, do not give them a reason to do so. It may be that the Arabs, even more than other nations, can provide models for unraveling the vicious circle of rapid change followed by increased violence that we find elsewhere in the developing world. The type of violence overtaking the East was in part filling the role that has been determined for the East since the Crusades. The Middle East *can* become a place where the East and West try out hi-tech new medicines, forms of renewable energy that have long roots in the area, an area also known for its poetry, art, and architecture, a participant in strengthening planetary cultures.

Dignity Becomes Reality

By 2012, a quarter of a century after my Cairo lecture, the possibilities for nonviolence have become reality. As if to welcome what is referred to today as the Arab Spring, a bevy of books have been published documenting the pro-democracy, secular path to what appears to some as sudden eruption of nonviolent actions. In 1990 *Arab Nonviolent Political Struggle in the Middle East* (R. Crow,

P. Grant, and S. Ibrahim, eds) was published, to be followed by *Live from Palestine: International and Palestinian Direct Action against the Israeli Occupation* (N. Stohlman and L. Aladin, eds) in 2003. In 2007 *A Quiet Revolution: The First Palestinian Intifada and Nonviolent Resistance* (M. King) appeared, followed in 2009 by *Civilian Jihad: Nonviolent Struggle, Democratization,* and *Governance in the Middle East* (M. Stephan, ed.). *Refusing to be Enemies: Palestinian and Israeli Nonviolent Resistance to the Israeli Occupation* (M. Kaufman-Lacusta, ed.) came out in 2010, and in 2011 M. Qumsiyeh's *Popular Resistance in Palestine: A History of Hope and Empowerment.* These works cover in detail material that was not available for my 1985 lecture – from the Golan Heights to the Western Sahara, from the Lebanese intifada to North Africa, from Israel to Hezbollah to Iran, boycotts, strikes, street theater, protests, humor, rooftop chanting, sit-downs, parliamentary walkouts, nonviolent defiance – all of this in the Middle East, not typically thought to be a place where civil rights could take root and succeed. Fear was gone; people's patience was at an end; a youthful population less risk-averse than their parents took to the streets. In addition, the usual proponents of violent strategies, Egypt's Muslim Brotherhood, Turkey's Justice and Development Parties, Jordan's Islamic Action Front, have taken violence off the table.

Why did the Western world not celebrate such happenings before spring 2011? One of the least reported was the example mentioned earlier of the efforts of the mainly Druze population of Syria's Israeli-occupied Golan Heights to resist forced assimilation by Israel after the Israeli capture of Golan during the June 1967 war. In 1981 Israel passed legislation to effectively annex the territory forcing the Druze to accept Israeli identification. The Druze first petitioned for a reversal of the Knesset action; when that failed, they announced a campaign of noncooperation by workers, defying curfews, confronting Israeli soldiers in nonviolent defiance until the Israelis lifted their siege (R. Scott Kennedy, 2009: 119–130).

Reading these scholarly works about nonviolence in Middle Eastern lands puts a different frame on journalistic explanations of the Arab Spring attributing new democratic uprisings to Facebook and similar technologies or to *al Jazeera.* The *New York Times* (Stolberg,

2011) attributed Arab nonviolent revolution to the writings of American Gene Sharp, whom Arab youth have never heard of, while As'ak Abu Khalil, a Lebanese political scientist, complained that Western journalists were using colonialist tactics to deny credit to Arabs. But if one takes a historical frame the immediate attributions become moot. Throughout the recorded history of the Middle East the seeds of nonviolence have been nourished by the realization that violence is not producing desired results – thus the oscillation from violence to nonviolence.

Although there is a good deal of ethnographic reporting on Arab and Middle Eastern traditions governing social and cultural control, Khalid Kishtainy's overview, "Violent and Nonviolent Struggle in Arab History" (1990), pretty much covers the range of regional, religious, and cultural variations and movements, as well the area's high vulnerability to intervention by outside powers since the seventeenth century (I would say since the first Crusades). Of the Arabs of the seventh century, Kishtainy (1990: 10) says that the ruling classes "were inherently merchants and looked upon such things as military grandeur with the cynical and opportunistic eye of the mercantile class." And later he notes that Arab history has "no Carthage, Troy, Gallipoli, Stalingrad, or Berlin" and quotes General John Glubb as saying, "even the pre-Islamic 'long wars' were in fact, no more than skirmishes and raids that caused little loss of life" (1990: 10). Of course, he speaks of elites when he notes, "Leaving war and soldiering to other Muslims (Persians, Turks, and Tartars), Arabs turned their attention to the attractive aspects of civilization . . . the translation of Greek and Indian classics; the development of science, mathematics, and philosophy; and the enjoyment of art, poetry, literature, music, love, sophisticated cuisine, and travel" (1990: 12). Kishtainy also caveats that it "would be naïve to think the Arabs a nonviolent people as no people on earth can be so described," but "there are very few wanton murders in the Arab World" (1990: 12). His overview is worth reading if only to shake up the usual stereotypes of Islam and Arab culture as inherently violent.

In the same vein, ethnographic writings on tribal justice provide continuing insight. "The Settlement of Violence in Bedouin Society" by Sulayman Khalaf (1990), a scholar of Bedouin tribal background from the northeast of Syria, describes the pendulum of war and peace and Bedouin efforts to repress violence and settle conflicts, a complex system of protection in cases of homicide. The Bedouin consider it their duty to take revenge, but, because each Bedouin home is a sanctuary, culprits have sought sometimes refuge in the home of their foes and were granted protection. They also provide a protector and guardian against possible dangers from the victim's group while mediation gets worked out. (Again worth reading in light of the discovery of Osama bin Laden "hidden in plain sight" in Pakistan). Bedouin conflicts are short, limited in scale, and healed rather quickly.

Although over long periods the Middle East has developed mechanisms to prevent the escalation of violence, during the contemporary period adapting to rapid change has thrown much of this askew. Thus we have the colonial wars, independence, the balkanization of the Arab World into different "states" with boundaries set arbitrarily, a settler colony, Israel, five Arab/Israeli wars since 1948 (1956, 1967, 1973, 1982); add the civil wars in Lebanon, the Sudan, Iraq – all of these relatively recent events make the Arab Spring appear as a surprise. As has been reiterated many times, the Middle East has less than 10% of the world population, yet in the past five decades 20% of the world's armed conflicts. Its strategic location and its reserves of oil and gas have made it susceptible to intervention by outside powers since the nineteenth century and its own build-up of military capability provided by Euro-American powers since the development of nation-states (Khalidi, 2006).

In Khalid Kishtainy's thought one has to focus on the right mechanisms in planning nonviolence and he suggests one: "the well-established concept of *sabr* (patience) which is a primary ingredient in all nonviolent action" (1990: 17–19). In the Quran there are over a hundred verses dealing with *sabr*. He also adds the historic use of civil disobedience and withdrawal of cooperation, and reminds us of the guidelines of Islam: "those who pledge their allegiance to an unjust ruler have no religion." Imam al-Ghazalil (1058–1111) was also clear, arguing that the overthrow of an unjust ruler must be carried out without violence, although some Islamic sects allow overthrow of rulers by force. But for anyone who wants to find the seeds of non-violence in the Arab world, Arab history is complete with practical possibilities. Antecedents going back centuries are well established.

Although new attention is finally being given to nonviolent potential, it is clear that one reason for the shift to interest in non-violence is that military power disparities have led to death, destruc-tion, and the loss of individual and collective dignity. The young are seen as models for a new kind of mobilization. As has been said, they have lost fear. The term dignity now appears repeatedly – the dignity of each person and the dignity of their state, whether it be Egypt, Iraq, Tunisia, Lebanon, or Palestine. Stability is purchased by Western powers when they support dictatorships, but at the cost of individual and collective dignity. Humiliation by dictators and also humiliation by imperialist powers sabotages dignity as demonstra-tors throughout the Arab world are indicating by putting their bodies on the line from one end of the Arab world to the other. Dignity means freedom, social justice, and respect.

References

Bourdieu, Pierre (1958) *The Algerians.* Boston: Beacon Press.

Chomsky, Noam (1983) *The Fateful Triangle.* Boston: South End Press.

Crow, Ralph, Philip Grant, and Saad Eddin Ibrahim (eds) (1990) *Arab Nonviolent Political Struggle in the Middle East.* Boulder, CO: L. Rienner Publishers.

Fisk, Robert (2005) *The Great War for Civilization – Conquest of the Middle East.* New York: Alfred A. Knopf.

Kaufman-Lacusta, Maxine (2010) *Refusing to be Enemies: Palestinian and Israeli Nonviolent Resistance to the Israeli Occupation.* Reading, NY: Ithaca Press.

Kennedy, R Scott (2009) Noncooperation in the Golan Heights: A Case of Nonviolent Resistance. In *Civilian Jihad*, M. Stephan, ed. New York: Palgrave Macmillan, pp. 119–130.

Khalaf, Sulayman (1990) The Settlement of Violence in Bedouin Society. *Ethnology*, 29, no. 3, pp. 225–242.

Khalidi, Rashid (2006) *The Iron Cage: The Story of the Palestinian Struggle for Statehood.* Boston, MA: Beacon Press.

King, Mary Elizabeth (2007) *A Quiet Revolution: The First Palestinian Intifada and Nonviolent Resistance*. New York: Nation Books.

Kisthainy, Khalid (1990) Violent and Nonviolent Struggle in Arab History. In *Arab Nonviolent Political Struggle in the Middle East*. R. Crow, P. Grant, and G. E. Ibrahim, eds. Boulder, CO: L. Rienner Publishers, pp. 9–24.

Mayer, Ann Elizabeth (ed.) (1985) *Property, Social Structure and Law in the Modern Middle East*. Albany, NY: State University of New York Press.

Nader, Laura (1965) Choices in Legal Procedure: Shia Moslem and Mexican Zapotec. *American Anthropologist*, 67, no. 2, pp. 394–399.

Nader, Laura and Harry Todd, Jr (eds) (1978) *The Disputing Process: Law in Ten Societies*. New York: Columbia University Press.

Nader, Laura (1990) *Harmony Ideology: Law and Justice in a Mountain Zapotec Village*. Stanford, CA: Stanford University Press.

Parenti, Michael (1992) *Make-Believe Media: The Politics of Entertainment*. New York: St Martin's Press.

Qumsiyeh, Mazin (2011) *Popular Resistance in Palestine: A History of Hope and Empowerment*. London – New York: Pluto Press.

Ruffini, Julio L. (1978) Disputing over Livestock in Sardinia. In *The Disputing Process: Law in Ten Societies*. Laura Nader and Harry Todd, Jr, eds. New York: Columbia University Press, pp. 209–246.

Said, Edward (1978) *Orientalism*. New York: Vintage Books.

Said, Edward (1981) *Covering Islam: How the Media and the Experts Determine How We See the Rest of the World*. New York: Pantheon Books.

Shaheen, Jack G. (2001) *Real Bad Arabs: How Hollywood Vilifies a People*. New York: Olive Branch Press.

Shaheen, Jack G. (2008) *Guilty: Hollywood's Verdict on Arabs after 9/11*. New York: Olive Branch Press.

Shapiro, Martin (1986) *Courts: A Comparative and Political Analysis*. Chicago: University of Chicago Press.

Stephan, Maria (ed.) (2009) *Civilian Jihad: Nonviolent Struggle, Democratization, and Governance in the Middle East*. New York: Palgrave Macmillan.

Stohlman, Nancy, and Laurieann Aladin (eds) (2003) *Live from Palestine: International and Palestinian Direct Action against the Israeli Occupation*. Cambridge, MA: South End Press.

Stolberg, Sheryl Gay (2011) Shy U.S. Intellectual Created Playbook Used in a Revolution. *New York Times*, February 17, p. A1.

Swedenburg, Ted (1995) *Memories of Revolt: The 1936–1939 Rebellion and the Palestinian National Past*. Minneapolis: University of Minnesota Press.

Zeid, Abou A. M. (1966) Honor and Shame among the Bedouins of Egypt. In *Honor and Shame – The Values of Mediterranean Society*. J. G. Peristiany ed. Chicago: University of Chicago Press.

Zogby, James (2010) *Arab Voices: What They Are Saying to Us, and Why It Matters*. New York: Palgrave Macmillan.

Further Reading

Geertz, Clifford (1999 [1971]) *Islam Observed: Religious Development in Morocco and Indonesia*. Chicago: University of Chicago Press.

7

Normative Blindness and Unresolved Human Rights Issues
The Hypocrisy of Our Age[1]

Introduction

Human rights is a phrase in common use since the 1948 Declaration of Human Rights, but common use does not imply common meaning. This chapter addresses the growth and spread of human rights with particular regard to women's human rights. Although the declaration itself was a marker in the history of the human community, the present is more a time for reflection than celebration. As we know from the media, personal contact, and our own analysis of what is happening worldwide, we need more human rights activists today than ever – activists who are part of a world citizenry, people who are alert to the speed of technological impact, the centralization of power and its impersonal aspects as reflected in warring at a distance as with the American drone wars in Pakistan and Yemen. There is work to be done.

Culture and Dignity: Dialogues between the Middle East and the West,
First Edition. Laura Nader.
© 2013 John Wiley & Sons, Inc. Published 2013 by John Wiley & Sons, Inc.

This chapter covers several topics. First, I review the constraints governing the original declaration in order to recognize the major conceptual progress made since the 1940s. Second, I comment on the unresolved issues of the declaration, issues that, when spearheaded, led to more inclusive frameworks for human rights work, including views from the margins – the Third and Fourth World, the world of women. Finally, I call attention to a recognition of the human rights abuses resulting from wildly out of control commercialism. Throughout I use a comparative outlook, one that requires us to look in the mirror from the start, to be self-conscious of the role of Euro–American human rights activists. It has been remarked that a leap forward is needed by human rights activists in this century. However, such a leap forward in dealing with specific human rights violations needs to be grounded in a broad-gauged philosophy about human suffering, one that cuts across positions that are at cross purposes.

Early Constraints

The importance of the UN Declaration lay in the attempt itself. Imagine the post–World War II scene. Delegates from Western, Communist, and Third-World nations were discussing in philosophical terms the content of the future declaration of human rights, each from their particular points of view – the Chinese representatives insisting that Confucian philosophy be incorporated into the declaration, the Catholics the teachings of St Thomas Aquinas, the liberals advocating the views of John Locke and Thomas Jefferson, and the Communists those of Karl Marx. To find agreement among such diverse parties as to what constituted human rights was a daunting task. But they took a first step, at least.

Eleanor Roosevelt chaired the UN Human Rights Commission and was ever persistent in reminding her collaborators that they were charged with writing a declaration acceptable to all religions, ideologies, and cultures. Yet, even with all her efforts, there were enormous disagreements as well as gaps. There were no representatives from the indigenous peoples of the so-called Third World, from the peoples of Islam, and little input from women in spite of Mrs. Roosevelt's presence. Roosevelt was a practical woman and as such she dealt with what was in front of her – Eastern countries who wanted to confine the charter to social and economic rights on the one hand versus Western declarations of the liberties listed in the American Bill of Rights and the French Declaration of Human Rights on the other. In the end the group found compromise by including socialist-inspired articles that guaranteed full employment, adequate housing, decent health care, and cradle-to-grave social security.

Mrs Roosevelt should also be credited with not compromising fundamental rights merely for the sake of reaching unanimity. In her own words: "We hope its proclamation by the General Assembly will be an event comparable to the proclamation of the Declaration of the Rights of Man by the French people in 1789, the adoption of the Bill of Rights by the people of the United States, and the adoption of comparable declarations at different times in other countries" (Bergen, 1981: 73). The early years at the United Nations were heady. Years later, in nominating Mrs. Roosevelt for the Nobel Prize, which she was not awarded, Jean Monnet, father of the Common Market, eulogized her (Lash, 1972: 337): "Fundamentally, I think her great contribution was her persistence in carrying into practice her deep belief in liberty and equality . . . to her, the world was truly one world, all its inhabitants." In Mrs. Roosevelt's words:

> Where after all, do universal human rights begin? In small places, close to home – so close and so small that they cannot be seen on any map of the world. Yet, they are the world of the individual person; the neighborhood he lives in; the school or college he attends; the factory, farms or factories where he works. Such are the places where every man, woman or child seeks equal justice, equal opportunities, equal dignity, without discrimination. Unless these rights have meaning there, they have little meaning anywhere (quoted in Romany, 1994: 90).

Eleanor Roosevelt and the New Deal women belonged to their era. They were and remained reformers first, social welfare workers first and foremost: *they knew what was best for others* (Hoff-Wilson and Lightman, 1984; Berger, 1981). As others have noted, in their advocacy for women their accomplishments proved transitory: the meager gains of political women stemmed from their structural class position, one rooted in cultural ideology and social institutions, and any analysis of these factors and an agenda for their change was beyond the reach of those who focused narrowly on political participation and individual aspirations and rights, rather than on root causes.

Unresolved Issues

The complex unresolved issues of Mrs. Roosevelt's period are still our issues today, when debates are formulated as binary. Should we focus on individual rights to the exclusion of collective rights? Should we be concerned with public issues to the exclusion of private issues? The balance between national sovereignty and international human rights presents further problems. Finally, the issue of human rights as part of a Western and mainly American hegemonic movement is an issue increasingly taking front stage (Renteln, 1990). After all, the Commission on Human Rights and the UN as a whole *were* predominantly Western. Indeed, the movement to create a new international apparatus for the promotion of human rights was led largely by Americans. The US Department of State orchestrated the early drafts; the crucial meetings took place in the USA, and even the goal itself – drafting an International Bill of Rights – had an undeniable American flavor. Everyone has a right to life, liberty, security of person, freedom of thought, conscience, and religion, freedom of movement . . . no one shall be held in slavery, subjected to torture, subjected to arbitrary arrest, detention, or exile. And all but two drafts were written in English. It is imperative that we understand something about the history of the drafting in order to understand the challenges that still face us. Let me take these issues one at a time.

The focus on individual rights versus collective rights was critical for indigenous peoples. It meant that indigenous people would be poorly served by the UN Declaration. Many Native Americans believe that the *group* rights of Indian peoples are the most important and most endangered of all Native American Indian rights. The right to self-government, the right to maintain communal owner-ship of land and resources, the right to preserve their cultures and languages, and their religion, all argue for a protected group human right. Indian groups need their own lands and water for group survival, and the taking or denying of such lands or water is a policy of ethnocide in its effect (Nader and Ou, 1998).

Richard Falk (1992), a scholar who has distinguished himself for his lucidity on human rights issues, writes of "normative blindness" – a blindness that accompanies a modernization outlook that regards premodern culture as a form of backwardness to be overcome for the sake of indigenous peoples, not from deference to their cultural autonomy but rather from a perspective of orderly and equitable assimilation into the more benevolent space of the modernizing ethos. In the name of development, indigenous people have been and are being destroyed and displaced in many parts of the third world (Falk, 1992: 47–48). Their wealth in plant diversity and intel-lectual property is being stolen. Exclusion from the rights-forming process is itself a denial of human rights, according to Falk, and one can easily see why. Indigenous issues were not part of the 1948 effort. And, ironically, neither were the Palestinians who were ousted from their homes in 1948.

Similarly, a concern with the state to the exclusion of the private domain of intimate interaction excluded many human rights that particularly concerned women: torture, wife battering, a right to reproductive selves, sexual harassment, life itself. Since 1948 the real-ization of the public/private dichotomy has stimulated volumes of legal research on the nonstate aspects of human rights as they affect millions of women's lives in their homes and in the workplace.

The emphasis on *international* human rights versus *universal* human rights has encroached on the touchy issues of national sovereignty and relativism. It is in this realm that we see the shrillest performances of human rights advocates, activists, often with reform in mind, absent introspection, and armed with huge dollops

179

of self-righteousness, who expound at international women's conferences on human rights often in the company of nationalists who
are similarly reform-minded. More on that later.

And finally there are the issues of western positional superiority
that Edward Said (1978) wrote about – the human rights discourse
as part of a western discourse or even a western hegemonic
discourse. Anyone sensitive to cross-cultural issues, or any alert
member of a so-called Third-World country, knows that these issues
engender cynicism about the whole notion of human rights. Often
such discourse appears in our newspapers and goes unnoticed as
anything but a universal or should be universal idea of human
rights. For example, in the New York Times (Eckholm, 1998) there
appeared a headline – A LOOK AT RELIGION IN CHINA BY US
CLERICS – with a subheadline "A Key Human Rights Issue:
Freedom of Worship in China." The article begins: "A high profile
delegation of American religious figures began arriving in Beijing
today for a three-week tour of China to examine the state of religious freedom here, one of the most volatile human rights issues in
American diplomacy." And later, "In its quest for dialogue, the
group will confront a sharp difference in perspectives about the
meaning of religious freedom" (Eckholm, 1998).

Contemplate the asymmetry for a moment. Imagine a Chinese
delegation to the United States to examine the right of Native
Americans to practice religious freedom whether it be the Ghost
dance, the peyote cult, or vision quests. In spite of the 1978 American
Indian Freedom Act, in the 1980s and 1990s the federal courts ruled
in over ten consecutive cases denying Native Americans religious
freedom. (See, for example, *Lyng vs. Northwest Indian Cemetery
Protective Association*, in Nader and Ou, 1998.)

Or, imagine a Chinese delegation that came to examine political
persecution of American minorities. Our country has one of the
highest rates (if not the highest) of prison intake in the world – into
prisons mainly peopled by American minorities.

From the start, human rights have been something that Americans
take to others. Boalt Hall Law School at the University of California
at Berkeley has a human rights clinic, a facility that provides free

legal services and investigations of human rights abuses for both international and national clients. Two of the clinic's first clients were from African nations, individual refugees seeking political asylum from the US Immigration and Naturalization Service – in itself not a bad service to provide, but, when viewed as part of the whole immigration picture, contributing to a lopsided view.

In preparing for this chapter I spent weeks reading the human rights literature, of which there is a prodigious amount. Much of it is technical and abstract. A very useful development found in the literature, however, is the presence of human rights advocates from other than Euro–American countries, people who have a good deal to teach us about ourselves. For example, an interesting article on Structural Adjustment Programs (Kuenyehia, 1994: 430) points to the negative consequences of Structural Adjustment on the human condition. The author points out that in Ghana there has been retrogression rather than development in the areas of nutrition, education, employment, and social welfare. Third-World advocates argue that rights to food, education, work, and social assistance have been rendered meaningless, due to conditions generally set by the International Monetary Fund, conditions which must be fulfilled by a recipient country prior to receiving financing from the World Bank or being considered as internationally creditworthy. As a result of Structural Adjustment Programs in Ghana and elsewhere the total burden of women's work has increased to an inhuman degree. A healthy deparochializing of human rights was recently published as *Human Rights: Southern Voices* (Twinning, 2009) in which four jurists presented "southern perspectives" from Sudan, Kenya, and India regarding claims to universality in human rights discourses. Others (Morsy, 1995) have documented experiments with American-originated reproductive technologies such as Norplant as gross violations of human rights in Egypt. Institutions are cancelling each other out. The specific point here is that American human rights advocates are being cancelled by their own government.

Such problems were not center stage in 1948, principally because the participants were limited. The targets at that time were nation-states, and globalization processes were limited by comparison.

Today, transportation technologies, travel and tourism, media attention, cross-cultural education, and a logarithmic increase in human interaction of all varieties has opened both opportunities and obstacles for human rights. On the plus side, tourists, for example, played an important regulatory role in the Chiapas uprising in southern Mexico, and tourists from many countries also played an important part in the defense of villagers from state violence in Morelos, Mexico. In addition to tourists, Americans picketed US investors in Morelos, and American, Canadian, and European as well as Mexican newspeople reported on human rights violations recorded by video technology.

The prospects for improving human rights depend upon an open process of communication, free from dogmatic interference. We need a more open human rights philosophy. Since the conception of human rights transcends the citizenship of the individual, the support for human rights can come from anyone, whether or not she is a citizen of the same country as the individual whose rights are threatened – all the more reason to employ practical reason. Humility is an important component of any action plan, as is passion, and, as we can see, the existence of a first, second, and third generation of human rights indicates that we are making some headway conceptually.

A Canadian law professor, Berta Hernandez-Truyol (1996: 343) puts the prospect for cultural reconstruction this way: "It is imperative that for any analysis of cultural practices to be valid, it must be conducted from the perspectives of both 'insiders' and 'outsiders.'" For example, industrial-state feminists need to think seriously about how certain practices can be explained to others. Consider, for example, the glass ceiling phenomenon, the feminization of poverty, the denial to mothers of welfare benefits if they have more children than a state thinks they should, while fathers are not part of the "welfare reform equation." She also underlines the recognition that "in no society today do women enjoy the same opportunities as men" and notes that "the observation that sex inequality is a global reality . . . prevents those in the US from considering gender problems and concerns as existing only in 'other places,'" such as Third-World states, or states with non-Western-based traditions (1996: 329). We speak of Saddam Hussein's use of biological warfare. A 1998 *Nation* magazine references work documenting the use of biological and chemical weaponry by the US on Cuba (*Nation*, March 9, 1998: 9). The point is *we all live in glass houses*.

A Nonstate Human Rights Effort

I now move the focus on unresolved issues to the Middle East where human rights violations by both insiders and outsiders have been rampant. Anyone with a fine-tuned sense of injustice would have been affected by Israel's forays into Lebanon, or by the 1991 Gulf War and the bombing of Baghdad, the Iraq War, which included random civilian bombing, as also by the more recent uprisings and state violence in Yemen, Bahrain, Syria, and Libya. I recall watching the Gulf War on television, a surrealistic experience that left a mark on many of us. Immediately after Clinton's election another targeted bombing took the life of a famous Iraqi artist. At the time I thought that if there were more symmetry, more mutual respect, such a bombing might not have happened. It sparked a human rights effort using the work of Arab women artists as an illustration. A friend and I came together with a third and a fourth to organize the International Council for Women in the Arts (ICWA). ICWA's first challenge was to find Arab women artists, plan an exhibit, and locate the opening in Washington, DC where it would be visible to American policy-makers. No small task. Our motive was to humanize the demonized and dehumanized Middle East situation, to open channels for communication.

ICWA was an organization that arose from the ashes of the Gulf War. The opening exhibit attracted more people than any previous show at the National Museum of Women in the Arts in Washington. Since we have written about this effort elsewhere (Nashishibi *et al.*, 1994), here I wish only to mention some of these Arab women artists who, in their own words and in their artwork, expressed their relation to human rights and dignity writ large in the context of armed conflict, occupation, and a destroyed environment. Their stories were punctuated by their reactions to war, pollution, emigration, the family life cycle, and other events. Their work revealed a political art actively resisting domination and creating new culture. The Arab East was a battleground in the nineteenth and twentieth centuries. Over the past 200 years Arabs have been subjugated by foreign rule, a state of affairs not lost on these artists. Violence and tragedy, destruction and death were, consequently, common catalysts. Here are a few examples.

Saloua Raouda Choucair – one of the first abstract artists in Lebanon and one of the best sculptors in the Arab world – recalled that her early commitment to art began as a challenge to her philosophy professor at the American University of Beirut, Charles Malik (one of the Eurocentric crafters of the Universal Declaration of Human Rights) who stated that "Arabic art is a decorative art of a lower degree, far from being pure art, because the Arabs were not inspired by the nude." A student of mathematics and physics, Choucair began to explore the geometry, form, and color of Islamic art.

Injii Efflatoun, an Egyptian artist, was part of the turmoil that engulfed the region following World War II, a turmoil that made women artists more overtly political. Her agenda was a Marxist one – to restructure the relationship between landowners and peasants. She spent four years imprisoned under President Nasser because of her political beliefs, an experience that provided the foundation for a number of her paintings.

The conflict over Palestine, which has led to five wars between Israel and Arab countries since 1948, added another dimension to human rights struggles. Mona Hatoum, a Palestinian artist from a refugee camp in Lebanon, was drawn into performance art. Her art involves the political use of binary opposites, contrasting order and chaos, oppression and resistance, always revealing the two sides of the same reality: victor/victim, strength/weakness, uniformed/naked.

The dialogue of colonial occupation was represented by Houria Niati of Algeria. Niati remembers being taken to prison by the

French authorities for writing anticolonial slogans on walls at the age of 12. Years later Niati started her series "No to torture," saying that "Women in Algeria were fighting and dying. They were tortured." Western notions of the Oriental imagined a fantasy world of women. Delacroix's Arab women were half-naked. Niati's women of Algeria do not replicate the splendor of Delacroix, rather they unmask the power dynamics inherent in Delacroix's picture. Niati says no to torture *everywhere*.

The dialogue of colonialism and occupation in Palestine inspired Lila Al-Shawa of Gaza to record the harsh realities of Israeli occupation. She photographed graffiti on the walls of Gaza before it was covered up by the Israeli occupation army. She photographed the map of Palestine that had been drawn on the sides of the cement-filled barricades that surround the streets of Gaza to prevent stone-throwing children from escaping. In speaking about her work and commenting on the silences of the "civilized," Al-Shawa said, "I recorded a method of communication and punishments which has been sanctified by the 'civilized world.'"

Perhaps the most poignant quote came from Leila Kawash, an Iraqi artist speaking about how her art was affected by the Gulf War:

> During the war with Iraq . . . when Americans hit on this shelter [with] a lot of children, and they all ran out and one of them called out "Allah el Akbar" [God is Great]. And I was painting this painting and when I went back to it, these words, it was like he gathered all the strength . . . it was like he was combating the whole war with two words . . . I spray-painted these words and it obliterated all the gold that I was putting on before.

It was Kawash who lost her sister, also an artist, as a result of pinpoint bombing early in the first Clinton administration.

Feelings of betrayal were articulated by the women artists and summarized by the artist from Gaza who spoke of the terrible feelings Arabs have about the West, "a power that is trying to destroy you without ever trying to understand what you are about . . . that you're a very old culture – that you're a people from a great civilization, that your roots go back thousands of years." As one commentator said about the work of Arab artists, "Their work appears less a search for identity than the expression of pain." They are about the kind of pain that human rights activists might understand. Yet the concerns, the human rights concerns, of Arab women artists are not the concerns of vocal human rights activists who have, for the most part, eschewed discussions of violations of human rights from *external* sources to focus on such subjects as female circumcision – *to the exclusion* of human rights concerns with the thousands of women and children who died in the bombings of Baghdad or with the children with stones whose human rights are regulated in Palestine/Israel. As the artists pointed out, there have been deafening silences from the "civilized" world.

Many of us *are* a part of the hegemonic silence on politically incorrect human rights issues. Remember that the objection to the notion of human rights in many countries is due to its Western origin. And with good reason. Privileging Western concerns with human rights is ethnocentric, and such concerns should not be attended to exclusive of broader-definition human rights concerns. The reason they are has to do with positional superiority. They have female circumcision, which is barbaric. We don't have such barbaric customs, maybe.

Health and Human Rights

The connection between health and human rights appears in a report on Public Health and the Persian Gulf War (Hoskins, 1997), a report on the consequences of random civilian bombing. For more than five years after the end of the Persian Gulf War, Iraqi civilians subsisted in a state of extreme hardship, in which health care, nutrition, education, water, sanitation, and other services were minimal. As many as 500 000 children are believed to have died after the war, largely due to malnutrition and a resurgence of diarrheal and vaccine-preventable diseases. Health services were barely functioning due to shortages of supplies and equipment. In 2007 such devastation was further documented by Barbara Nimri Aziz.

Iraq before the Gulf War was a high middle-income country with a modern social infrastructure. The breakdown of health, water, and sanitation, and other essential social services which followed the Gulf War led to a dramatic increase in infectious diseases like cholera and typhoid and diseases related to malnutrition. The impact on maternal and perinatal mortality was considerable. Iraqi women were loaded with considerable burdens. More than 10% of married Iraqi women became widows. International study teams documented widespread depression, anxiety, headache and insomnia, weight loss, menstrual irregularity, difficulty in breastfeeding, and other illnesses. Human populations were put at risk when their source of water was directly affected, and environmental problems that resulted in toxic contamination of various sorts wreaked further havoc.

Actually, the people who led the way out of this morass are active in the current health and human rights movement (Heggenhougen, 2000). Health professionals find that the human rights framework is a more useful approach to modern public health challenges than any framework in the biomedical tradition. Public health professionals increasingly realize that they must deal directly with the underlying socio-economic concepts that determine who lives and who dies, when and of what. Because of the realized importance of societal issues at the Harvard School of Public Health, the graduates, along with their diploma, receive a copy of the Universal Declaration of Human Rights, with special attention to article 25 on human rights and health. Public health workers do not have to decide which is worse – the Taliban takeover in Afghanistan (Faiz, 1997), or the Gulf War initiative, or Indonesian policies in East Timor. All of these happenings are bad for people's health. Furthermore, we can all agree with Jonathan Mann and others: "A male-dominated society is a threat to public health" (quoted in Rodriguez-Trias, 1992: 663; see also Mann, 1996). Assaults by husbands, ex-husbands, and lovers cause more injuries to women than motor vehicle accidents, rape, and muggings combined. The overall model for thinking holistically about the health and human rights movement may be illustrated by returning to the issue of circumcision and/or cliterodectemy.

Over the years I have formed an antipathy towards public lectures and discussions on cliterodectemy or female circumcision in Africa. Often, too often, the accusatory, holier-than-thou confrontations result in rigid resolve on both sides. They always remind me of *sati* in India: when condemned and outlawed by the British, self-immolation by widows only increased. I always thought that there was something wrong with the dialogue over sexual mutilation; that it was too ethnocentric, too lacking in introspection.

Not too long ago, my librarian handed me an interesting book titled *Sexual Mutilations – A Human Tragedy* (Denniston and Milos, 1997). *Sexual Mutilation* does what should have been done years ago. The work was the result of the Fourth International Symposium on Sexual Mutilations in Lausanne, Switzerland (the first having been held in 1989 in California). Permit me to quote from the preface so that you can sense the tenor of the approach: "Sexual mutilation is a global problem that affects 15.3 million children and young adults annually. In terms of gender, 13.3 million boys and 2 million girls are involuntarily subjected to sexual mutilation every year . . . The violation occurs with the first cut into another person's body" (Denniston and Milos, 1997: v) While such terms as "circumcision" and "genital cutting" are less threatening to our sensitivities, they ultimately do a disservice by masking the fact of what is actually being done to babies and children. According to the belief systems of those cultures that practice the sexual mutilation of children, the sexual organs do not belong to the person to whom they are attached: instead, they are regarded as community property, under the immediate control of physicians, witchdoctors, religious figures, tribal elders, relatives, or the state. The number of children who die as a direct result of traditional sexual mutilations is high. The number of children who almost die is higher; it is estimated that 229 babies die each year as a result of the complications of the sexual mutilation of routine foreskin amputation. Additionally, 1 in 500 suffers serious complications requiring emergency medical attention. Traditional sexual mutilations occur primarily in Saharasia (Africa and Saudi Arabia) and Melanesia in the Pacific. The preface continues: "the almost spontaneous genesis of sexual mutilation in historic times in the United States at the hands of physicians, [provides] insightful clues about the earlier origins of sexual mutilation in prehistory" (1997: vi).

I also began to notice that some newspaper reports on sexual mutilation are more even-handed. Perhaps something is changing. The *New York Times* (December 19, 1997: A3) reported on Egypt's highest court ruling that practices such as circumcision were not Islamic religious practices, and this was followed a few days later by an article on Canadian research advocating pain relief for *male* circumcision (*New York Times*, December 30, 1997: CT), and also followed by a number of letters to the editor relieved that the medical community is finally admitting that newborns feel pain, asking "So why do many hospitals perpetuate the practice when there is no compelling medical reason to do so?" Another noted: "You wisely reject genital mutilation in Africa, but how could you not mention the nearly 1.6 million infants who become victims of routine circumcision every year in the United States?" (*New York Times*, January 3, 1998: A28).

The *Sexual Mutilations* book covered the globe and included the United States in its survey. It was not solely about the human rights of others, it was also about the human rights of Americans. I learned a great deal I did not know or notice prior to reading the book. For example, interviews with people in both Africa and the United States who accept sexual mutilations claim that their respective sexual mutilation practices are minimal, painless, beautifying, medically indicated, hygienic, prophylactic, sexually improving, universal, medicalized, and harmless. Both excised African women and American men are usually reluctant to believe they have lost anything — regardless of the amount of tissue lost.

For human rights activists circumcision represents a violation of the fundamental human rights to autonomy, security of the person, physical integrity, physical and mental health, and self-determination. Female sexual mutilation is practiced in 22 countries. Many of these countries are Arab or Muslim; male sexual mutilation is practiced by approximately one billion Muslims, 300 million Christians, and 16 million Jews (Denniston and Milos, 1997).

But the chapter on the institutionalization of involuntary sexual mutilation in the United States was the most enlightening. As early as 1845 insanity was cured in the United States by excision of the external organs of women, with similar practices for men. It became a preferred treatment for masturbation, epilepsy, prevention of syphilis, hernia, bad digestion, inflammation of the bladder, hip joint disease, curvature of the spine and more (see, for example, Feibleman, 1997 and Sheehan, 1997). Sexual mutilation was used to cure paralysis in girls. It became moral hygiene. From 1914 on there was a crusade for mass involuntary circumcision that became a business. Justifications continued to elaborate – a cure for frigidity, for urinary tract infection, prevention of AIDS, cervical cancer of the female, penile cancer – and discarded foreskins are sold to bio-research labs and transnational corporations. The point of the historical treatise was to indicate that masturbation was the hysteria, then epilepsy, then sexually transmitted disease, then cancer, then HIV – and, in the name of science, sexual surgery continued to be the response in every case. What the contemporary situation is we cannot grasp. In casual conversation with an administrator at UC Berkeley she informed me that she had had sexual surgery at 17 because her doctor recommended it would make her more sexually attractive to her husband. The same doctor had her bind her breasts rather than nurse her babies for the same reason (see also Scheper-Hughes, 1991).

As of the late twentieth century, it was the doctors and the nurses who were opposing circumcision as an iatrogenic epidemic, an epidemic caused by doctors, sustained by the invention and proliferation of alleged medical reasons, and as each medical reason is scientifically disproven new reasons for circumcision are quickly invented.

Gender cannot be considered in isolation, and it cannot be essentialized. The approach needs to be multidimensional so that it can be humane. The Ashley Montagu Resolution to End the Genital Mutilation of Children Worldwide was A Petition to the World Court, The Hague. What is indicated by the above-mentioned sexual surgery example is a model for bridging the gap between them and us, between the ideal and the real, a way to reduce positional superiorities, a way by which human rights activists neither need to use culture as a shield to protect practices that violate women's human rights, nor need to use human rights as a weapon of moral imperialism to oppress other communities and ways of life. During the Persian Gulf War, I actually heard people say "Bomb 'em, those people do not know how to treat their women," or "Look what they did to the Kurds – bomb 'em!"

Human Rights and Commercialism

There is one last issue that I would like to mention in regard to women and human rights. Human rights have been conceptualized within the national and international arenas, in both formal and informal contexts. The state has been highlighted from the beginning, so too in the second generation has the private domestic and work context. Nowhere, however, have I heard a sustained examination of the role of an expanding and penetrating mercantile system which itself promotes mutilation justified by "it's her choice." Choice, as I have written elsewhere, is a complicated concept that needs to be unpacked, and many feminists have worked on exactly that in the area of standardized beauty concepts (Nader, 1997).

Well over a million women in the United States had had silicone-gel breast implants by 1994 – 80% of them for purposes of breast enlargement (Coco, 1994) – and the figures continue to grow and expand to Brazil, Iran, Lebanon, China, and elsewhere. How would we explain to a group of African human rights activists who saw such activity as mutilation why this surgery happens? How would we make people from other cultures understand the connection between a woman's breast size and her self-confidence, personal well-being, and social worth, when it might appear to the Africans as a form of insidious indoctrination, a patriarchal colonization of the female mind and body, an unnatural phenomenon?

As we all know, the beauty industry is well organized; there is a good deal of money at stake. The prominent messages in commercial beauty images are of youth, thinness, large breasts, European facial features, and passivity. Also sold is the promise of self-improvement by mass dissemination of the image of official beauty. What one writer called a saturation bombing of women's psyches leaves little room for the realities of physical existence. In sum, the commercial images of the model female represent the best beauty propaganda that money can buy, encouraging women to meet the requirements through surgery: face-lifts, eye-lid surgery, collagen injections, nose jobs, liposuction, and various forms of breast surgery. The beauty industry's insecure consumer becomes a patient, a deformed beauty invalid. Her social illness, ugliness, can only be cured with a scalpel. The key role of the plastic surgeon is to diagnose small breasts as diseased (a constructed disease called hypertropy), and to prescribe treatment or cure – the recreation and construction of the "official breast." It is not uncommon to find plastic surgeons advertising "body sculpting," but the focus has been on the women's breast.

Understanding silicone-gel breast implants in the United States requires exploring patriarchy, business marketing, and organized plastic surgery. The healthy female breast conceptualized through the rubric of lack, results in the creation of the "official breast." Does this example constitute a violation of women's human rights? Ask the women who suffered serious medical complications, or ask African women. In both the practice of circumcision and that of breast augmentation, mutilation is done for her and not to her, for the re-creation of the female appearance. The operation on the female breast in America holds much of the same social meaning as sexual mutilation in Africa. In both places the choice to have reconstructive surgery was determined outside the individual: in our country as a result of the commercialization process, whereby woman is mechanized, medicalized, and merchandized; in Africa by the family.

If, for some people, the issue of breast implants is in the grey area in terms of human rights abuses, perhaps the commercialization of life itself might be considered to fall clearly within the realm of human rights (Burrows, 1996). Ask John Moore, the origin of the "Mo" cell line, subject of United States Patent #4,438,032: "How does it feel to be patented? To learn all of a sudden, I was just a piece of material . . . It's so beyond anything you can really conceive of. There were so many issues involved . . . There was a sense of betrayal, I mean, they owned a part of me that could never be recovered" (quoted in Burrows, 2001: 246).

John Moore brought suit in 1984 against his doctor, the Regents of the University of California at Los Angeles, and the pharmaceutical companies that licensed the "Mo" cell line. In 1990 the California Supreme Court ruled that John Moore's doctor had breached his fiduciary duty to John by not revealing a research and financial interest in John's cells. However, the court also denied John Moore's claim to ownership of the cells removed from his body arguing that research on human cells plays a critical role in medical research. And so also goes the story about the US attempt to patent the cell line of a Guaymi Indian woman. Are these human rights issues? Whatever your answer, such cases argue for the inclusion of corporate human rights abuses in the larger equation, in the larger frame of reference. How can we speak about genocide in Africa without speaking about the arms industry? Indeed how can we speak about Iraq without considering the role of the military–industrial complex? The commercialization of life helps to trivialize life. So does the need to test weaponry. We need to take suffering seriously. In Texas under Governor George Bush a contract for the Sierra Blanca nuclear waste dump was especially targeted at a low-income predominantly Mexican-American community. Is this a human rights issue? It lies 16 miles from the Rio Grande and above an aquifer (*Nation*, March 9, 1998, p. 19). One of my colleagues at Berkeley says no because the primary purpose is not to destroy Mexican-American lives, that is only a by-product.

Concluding Remarks

As I hope to have indicated, a more inclusive notion of human rights serves to reduce hypocrisy by including us as well as them and by bringing us closer to root causes. Americans may not count President Carter as among our most illustrious presidents, but people of other nations do because *at the least* he gave symbolic importance to human rights in foreign policy. That was only a beginning because such symbolic capital only works if we are even-handed. In short, the credibility of a human rights spirit requires that we look at ourselves as well as those we seek to help. Credibility also requires a greater awareness of root causes and that will require us, among other things, to look particularly at industrial sales at home and abroad. Globalization need not have predominantly negative connotations; we know that from historical examinations of earlier pre-European globalization efforts (Abu-Lughod, 1989). But a great leap forward in human rights achievement will require person to person, group to person, or group to group work across the globe to be grounded in a philosophy of mutual respect, a knowledge of power distribution and of actions resulting from power inequities both at home and abroad that today produce anything but human rights based on culture and dignity.

Note

1   The paper on which this chapter is based was first presented in Houston, Texas at the Rothko Chapel on March 7, 1998. The author acknowledges with gratitude critical help from many colleagues including especially Dr. Alison Renteln, whose impressive knowledge of the human rights literatures launched this work, Dr. Rania Milleron for her input on health and human rights issues, and Suzanne Calpestri for her insightful attention to human rights material relevant to anthropological interests.

References

Abu-Lughod, Janet (1989) *Before European Hegemony: The World System AD 1250–1350*. New York: Oxford University Press.

Aziz, Barbara Nimri (2007) *Swimming Up the Tigris: Real Life Encounters with Iraq*. Gainesville: University of Florida Press.

Berger, Jason (1981) *A New Deal for the World: Eleanor Roosevelt and American Foreign Policy*. New York: Social Science Monographs, Columbia University Press.

Burrows, Beth (1996) Second Thoughts about U.S. Patent #4, 438, 032. *Genewatch*, 10, no. 2–3, October, pp. 4–7.

Burrows, Beth (2001) Patents, Ethics and Spin. In *Redesigning Life? The Worldwide Challenge to Genetic Engineering*, Brian Toker, ed. New York: Palgrave, pp. 238–251.

Coco, Linda (1994) Silicone Breast Implants in America: A Choice of the "Official Breast?" In *Essays on Controlling Processes*. Laura Nader, ed. Kroeber Anthropological Papers, no. 77, 103–132.

Denniston, George C. and Marilyn Fayne Milos (eds) (1997) *Sexual Mutilations – A Human Tragedy*. New York: Plenum Press.

Eckholm, Erik (1998) A Look at Religion in China by U.S. Clerics. *New York Times*, February 9. Available at http://www.nytimes.com/1998/02/09/world/a-look-at-religion-in-china-by-3-us-clerics.html?pagewanted=all&src=pm (accessed 25 April, 2012).

Faiz, Abbas (1997) Health Care under the Taliban. *The Lancet*, 349. April 26, pp. 1247–1248.

Falk, Richard (1992) Cultural Foundations for the International Protection of Human Rights. In *Human Rights in Cross-Cultural Perspectives – A Quest for Consensus*. Abdullahi Ahmed An-Na'im, ed. Philadelphia: University of Pennsylvania Press, pp. 44–64.

Feibleman, Peter (1997) Natural Causes. *Double Take Magazine*, Winter Issue. Available at http://www.fictionwriter.com/double.htm (accessed April 15, 2012).

Heggenhougen, H. K. (2000) More Than Just "Interesting!" – Anthropology, Health and Human Rights. *Social Science and Medicine*, 50, no. 9, pp. 1171–1175.

Hernandez-Truyol, Berta E. (1996) Women's Rights as Human Rights – Rules, Realities and the Role of Culture: A Formula for Reform. *Brook Journal of International Law, xxi, no.* 3, pp. 605–677.

Hoff-Wilson, Joan and Marjorie Lightman (eds) (1987) *Without Precedent – The Life and Career of Eleanor Roosevelt*. Bloomington: Indiana University Press.

Hoskins, Eric (1997) Public Health and the Persian Gulf War. In *War and Public Health*. Barry S. Levy and Victor W. Sidel, eds. New York: Oxford University Press, pp. 254–277.

Kuenyehia, Akua (1994) The Impact of Structural Adjustment Programs on Women's International Human Rights: The Example of Ghana. In *Human Rights of Women—National and International Perspectives*. Rebecca, J. Cook, ed. Philadelphia: University of Pennsylvania Press, pp. 422–436.

Lash, Joseph P. (1972) *Eleanor: The Years Alone*. New York: W. W. Norton & Co.

Mann, Jonathan M. (1996) Health and Human Rights. *British Medical Journal*, 312, pp. 924–925.

Morsy, Soheir A. (1995) Biotechnology and International Politics of Population Control: Long-term Contraception in Egypt. *SIGNS Journal of Women, Culture, and Society*, 20, no. 4, pp. 1054–1057.

Nader, Laura (1997) Controlling Processes – Tracing the Dynamic Components of Power. *Current Anthropology*, 38, no. 5, pp. 711–737.

Nader, Laura and C. Jay Ou (1993) Idealization and Power; Legality and Tradition in Native American Law. *Oklahoma City University Law Review*, 23, no. 1, pp. 13–42.

Nashashibi, Salwa, Laura Nader, and Etel Adnan (1994) Arab Women Artists. In *Forces of Change - Artists of The Arab World*. Washington, DC: The National Museum of Women in the Arts, pp. 1–36.

Renteln, Alison (1990) *International Human Rights: Universalism versus Relativism*. Newbury Park, CA: Sage Publications.

Rodriguez-Trias, Helen (1992) Women's Health, Women's Lives, Women's Rights. *American Journal of Public Health*, 82, no. 5, pp. 663–664.

Romany, Celino (1994) State Responsibility Goes Private: A Feminist Critique of the Public/Private Distinction in International Human Rights Law. In *Human Rights of Women – National and International Perspectives*. R. J. Cook, ed. Philadelphia: University of Pennsylvania, pp. 85–115.

Said, Edward W. 1978. *Orientalism*. New York: Vintage Books.

Scheper-Hughes, Nancy (1991) Virgin Territory: The Male Discovery of the Clitoris. *Medical Anthropology Quarterly*, 5, no. 1, pp. 25–28.

Sheehan, Elizabeth A. (1997) Victorian Clitoridectomy. Isaac Baker Brown and His Harmless Operative Proceedure. In *The Gender/Sexuality Reader: Culture, History, Political Economy*. Roger Lancaster and Micaela di Leonardo, eds. New York: Routledge, pp. 325–334.

8

Breaking the Silence
Politics and Professional Autonomy[1]

Introduction

The response of anthropologists to the Gulf War raised questions about violence and professional autonomy, about whether anthropology was unencumbered enough to contribute to the reduction of violence by breaking the silence about the Arab World, much as we did for Vietnam. My question then had to do with professional responsibility. Does anthropology only reflect dominant hegemonies, or is it possible to have an anthropology free of central dogmas originating outside the discipline?

The Islamic World in general, and the Arab world in particular, are a part of the world still among the least known ethnographically. They are a part of the world about which disinformation and misinformation are rampant, yet, in spite of the good work of numbers of anthropologists, since 1951 there has not been a *general* book about the area that has enjoyed the circulation of Carleton Coon's *Caravan*.

Culture and Dignity: Dialogues between the Middle East and the West,
First Edition. Laura Nader.
© 2013 John Wiley & Sons, Inc. Published 2013 by John Wiley & Sons, Inc.

Indeed since World War II our discipline seems predisposed to feed silence and starve informed opinion about the area. While this became crystal clear during the Gulf War, it is even clearer after September 11, 2001.

For example, when hiring ethnographers of the Arab world, major departments select people who work at a distance from "troubled areas" such as the Levant, Iraq, Sudan, or the West Bank. Harvard hires specialists in Turkey or Yemen, Columbia a specialist in Morocco, Michigan an anthropologist who works in Yemen (although more recently a hire who works in Jordan), Stanford one who works in Turkey, the University of California, Berkeley and Princeton University have hired Moroccan specialists, and later two anthropologists working in Egypt were taken on at Berkeley. Such hiring choices reflect nervousness in major anthropology departments that, whether conscious or not, diminish the possibility of breaking the silence about zones of serious violence.

Some anthropologists try to explain the silence, the absence of serious political debate. What little there is suggests that Anglo–American anthropologists are not learning fast, in spite of the fact that over the past several decades we have been pounding the table with relentless critiques of British structural functionalist anthropologists working in colonial Africa who ignored colonizers, settlers, power, and imperialism. The same was true for the Gulf War and since September 11, but with a new twist; few British or American anthropologists are speaking or writing or being invited to inform citizens in our country who may not only be uninformed but grossly misinformed about other peoples. Foreign-born anthropologists may be stepping into the breach.

Silence and Dominant Hegemonies

Again looking back to the Gulf War might be useful. Commenting on the massive disinformation campaign launched by the 1990s Bush White House, Susan Pollock and Catherine Lutz (1994) wrote about "Archaeology Deployed for the Gulf War." They discovered shameless uses being made of Iraq's archaeological past: the focus was on commoditized items (archaeological relics), not the lives of those now living with this past. The media made points about Iraq's ancestral ties to "our" civilization, suggesting that Iraq's heritage belongs to all of us (which it does if one is working in a world history frame). The archaeological sites were given great respect and Iraq's past humanized. It's ironic that the first Bush administration, while killing innocent Iraqi civilians, was making use of Iraq's ancestral ties by paying lip service to Arab allies while simultaneously bombing that heritage. In the same vein, when the Taliban were destroying archaeological monuments, these were rightly labeled barbaric acts by the same actors working in Iraq.

In a paper about internally generated state violence, William Young (1999) suggested that the sympathies of anthropologists are more easily mobilized if human rights issues involve tribal peoples in conflict against a state. But, he says, when it comes to the Middle East, where victims are commonly identified in the media and in scholarly writings as ethnicities or nations, few anthropologists feel ready to champion such causes. He goes on to confess that those anthropologists without tenured positions may be reluctant to offend their colleagues, who work in Israel, Turkey, Iran, Egypt, or any other state that does not accept scholarly criticism of national policies. Ted Swedenburg (1995) notes that researchers can be tainted by their informants. In the case of research on Palestinians he quotes *The Chronicle of Higher Education* as noting that studying Palestinians "was not always a wise career move for aspiring academics" (Coughlin, 1992: A8). He should know. In his search for a job at major anthropology departments he came in number two each time, in spite of an excellent book, *Memories of Revolt*, and superlative work on subjects ranging from Algeria to Egypt to the use of musical texts as political expression in the Levant.

Julie Peteet (n.d.) speaks of "permission from the academy and the public to narrate the violence experienced by the Palestinians." She notes that such permission is more forthcoming now than in the past, while also quoting a Palestinian who commented that the possibilities for such narration are greater now because it no longer matters. Containment or defeat may dilute the need for the imposition of silence and censorship.

Peteet is also exasperated that scholarship on Palestine must always be "balanced" by an Israeli speaker or presence to gain legitimacy in the academy, thus acquiescing in an ethnography of the silences and censorship of the scholarship itself. She adds that Palestinians are the largest group of refugees and the longest refugee presence, yet in a widely praised volume on refugees by Zolberg, Suhrke, and Aguayo (1989), there is hardly more than a paragraph or two on Palestine. The violence evaporates.

And speaking about silencing forces, I once assigned Peteet's book *Gender in Crisis* (1991), an ethnography of a Palestinian refugee camp in south Lebanon, in an introductory anthropology course. A lobby of parents came asking why Palestinians were being humanized when they were terrorists, while insinuating that, as a result, the class had an anti-Semitic outlook – one example of a campaign of accusations, echoing similar experiences in many past years. Fed up with the silence, Congressman Paul Findley (Republican, Illinois) documented the making of silence in his book, *They Dare to Speak Out: People and Institutions Confront Israel's Lobby* (1985), and later (2001) published *Silent No More – Confronting America's False Images of Islam*, while, more recently, political scientist Norman Finkelstein published his blockbuster *Beyond Chutzpah: On the Misuse of Anti-Semitism and the Abuse of History* in 2005.

The decline in informed critical commentary has contributed, in turn, to the structural/institutional changes we are seeing in universities. In a rare piece on "Intellectuals, the Media and the Gulf War," Patrick Wilcken, an anthropologist at Goldsmiths College, University of London, began by noting, "One of the notable features of the reporting of the Gulf War in the mainstream US press was the near total unconcern with Iraqi casualties (Herman, 1991: 5)... a complete blindness to the devastating consequences of such one-sided military action" (Wilcken, 1995: 37). "Where were the dissenting voices?" Wilcken asks. He argues that the silence is due to structural changes, institutional changes, that are causing a decline in informed critical commentary. For him, the massive expansion of the universities means that intellectuals have been absorbed into the state, to wit, there has been an institutionalization of intellectuals, increasing specialization and the disappearance of generalists, and the inability of public intellectuals, highly visible intellectuals, to critically assess a major political event like the Gulf War, (or the September 11 happenings). *Audit Cultures* (Strathern, 2000) provides ethnographic accounts of such changes in the academy, contextualizing Wilcken's observations.

Wilcken gives examples of three public intellectuals who spoke more generally without dissenting or presenting information useful to dissenters. The first described the Gulf War as "virtual reality," a form of war in which one never has to face up to war. The second saw war as inevitable because of the impossibility of adjudicating the conflict, and the third wrote that war reflected the predisposition of a warrior cult in the United States. Hardly critical assessments, it is true. Dissent in the press by academics was virtually nonexistent with the exceptions of two university professors – both non-anthropologists, Noam Chomsky and Edward Said, followed by Norman Finkelstein then of DePaul University where in 2007 he was denied tenure although DePaul praised him as a prolific scholar and outstanding teacher.

In his section on anthropology's silence, Wilcken's question, "Where are the anthropological voices to counter the ethnocentric claims (or racist claims)?" indicates they are largely mute in the United States and inert in Great Britain, both countries involved in the Gulf War bombing and in the passive violence of sanctions on Iraq that has resulted in greater loss of civilian life than the nuclear bombing of Nagasaki/Hiroshima.

Wilcken concedes a conference on the Gulf War was held at the London School of Economics during which the war was intellectualized and metaphorized by anthropologists: the Kurdish and Shi'ite kinship systems were segmentary, the Iraqis were caught up in patriarchy, their leader was a psychopath, and Arabic/Islamic codes were part of the problem. He also reports comments attributed to Ernest Gellner to the effect that, "Only the developing world with its devotion to economic development could be trusted with high-tech weaponry since the West no longer valued aggression and had no interest in acquiring land. Saddam, on the other hand, had proven untrustworthy" (Wilcken, 1995: 59). One observer determined (Mir-Hosseini, 1991: 6) that anthropology has very little to contribute "in a world in which realpolitik rules," that is, a world in which self-interest rules. Wilcken concluded that anthropologists have been institutionalized into what C. Wright Mills (2008: 18) called "organized irresponsibility." The media expect people who can comment on the larger picture, whereas the anthropologist, he bemoans, prefers to focus on "fine-grained ethnography" and internalist analyses. We might put it differently and expect the media to want the greater depth that anthropology might offer.

The problem of Iraq, and Afghanistan, was not cultural misunderstanding or ineptitude but propaganda shrouding the mass destruction of the war. That a ruthless regime that had been receiving military and economic support from the West for almost a decade could be toppled by segmentary opposition or a war against patriarchy was not only absurd but reminiscent of *Orientalism* or the "filtered western scholarship" that Edward Said had long written about. The lack of information or the flood of misinformation contributes to desensitization. Musicologist, Dwight Reynolds (1991: 20) wrote about cultural translation noting, for example, how Thomas Friedman of *The New York Times* serves as the "tolerant-to-Arabs" foil by describing the region as "a culturally unique phenomenon, a land where no one means or understands anything."

As noted in Chapter 7, one attempt to break the silence was a project titled *Forces of Change: Artists in the Arab World* (1994), an art exhibit of modern Arab women artists. The International Council for Women in the Arts found talented Arab women artists whose voices of dissent often endangered their lives because they painted scenes of violence and torture, war, revolution, and resistance. The effort aimed at humanizing the present Arab world using a venue comprehensible to Western elites, and called attention to the silences by visual means. This exhibit opened at the National Museum of Women in the Arts (1994) in Washington DC and traveled to ten major cities around the country – the first major contemporary Arab cultural exhibit ever. The common reaction of viewers was: Arab *artists*? Arab *women* artists? Arab women artists *speaking up*? They could not imagine Arab artists, let alone Arab women artists, speaking up. Such is the power of repetition of misinformation.

Although little has changed since September 11, it may be too early to tell. Anthropologist William Beeman was initially the sole voice. In his op-ed pieces for *The Milwaukee Journal Sentinel, The Baltimore Sun, The Columbia Dispatch*, he speaks about root causes, such as the relationship between the United States and the Islamic world, for which he is being excoriated for seemingly justifying rather than explaining September 11. In an earlier piece Beeman (1989) ended with a section on the United States arms race and the potential for a war in the Gulf. Who listened then?

September 11 did inspire a few anthropologists; Arthur Kleinman and others spoke of the shock to American emotional stability; Diane France, forensic anthropologist, from Colorado State University, and archaeologists from Columbia University and else-where offered their services at ground zero. Anthropologist Nabeel Abraham, who studied Arab-American communities as in Deerborn, Michigan, spoke about their anxieties and the racist anger following the terrorist attacks as it impacted them. Catherine Lutz once again tried to contextualize and respond to Americans who asked, "Why do they hate us?" Ali Quiebo of Jerusalem spoke about the tolerance of Islam. But it was the anthropologists from the areas concerned who came forward to inform and recommend how to reconstruct an independent Afghanistan after decades of external meddling. Although there are eloquent others, such as David Edwards (see pages 179–186 in the Winter 2002 issue of the *Anthropological Quarterly*), Ashraf Ghani (2001) has been the most ubiquitous presence on the "Lehrer News Hour," the ABC Nightly News, PBS, CBC, and the Financial Times, carefully outlining the catastrophe that is Afghanistan today, using his knowledge of economics and political alliance to recommend forward movement. On the other hand, Robert and B. J. Fernea, who had published bestsellers after years of anthropological research on Iraq, Egypt, and Morocco, were largely ignored by the media and government (Fernea and Fernea,

1997). Even at the 2003 American Anthropology Meetings, in which archaeology looting in Iraq topped the professional agenda over and above the death of innocent civilians, the Ferneas were not invited to speak, although they were in attendance.

Desensitization

Anthropology is not only an unfolding of ideas inside the discipline, it is also shaped by a wider sociopolitical environment (Wolf, 1999). The first step to avoiding having our agenda set by broader, mainstream ideologies is to recognize how they work on the discipline. If we ignore external influences in favor of internal dimensions, a significant part of the power dimension is neglected. This is what Beeman and Lutz point out. The Arab and Islamic worlds are probably the only region of the world suffering from the absence of multi-sited ethnographies that make the connections. Eric Wolf (1999: 132) remained hopeful: "We are one of the very few remaining observational sciences [and] . . . we are able to entertain the possibility of multiple causation."

During the Gulf War the overall silence had multiple causes, none of which are emphasized, and are seldom even mentioned in anthropological contributions: (i) religious zeal – Christianity vs Islam and the possibility that the Crusades had never ended (at least since Pope Urban II, in a rousing speech in 1095, had challenged Christian Europe to meet Islam on its own doorsteps); (ii) militarism – the military-industrial complex that President Eisenhower warned us about that at times operates independent of democratic governance; (iii) racism – the need for weaponry (and the people who run it) to be tested to see if it works, and where better than on the barbarians or "inferior races"; (iv) ideology – the powerful and pervasive impact on Western intellectuals of Zionist ideology; and, most important, (v) desensitization to the forms of war, which means we never have to face up to war or to the passive violence that follows, justifying wars through double-talk. Ideology, both religious and political, racism, self-interest, and pragmatism were then and now at work in silencing dissent. After September 11, the silence was less deafening; Americans asked, "Why do they hate us?" and anthropologists and others tried to answer these and other questions about Islam and the region. But if the vituperative responses to Catherine Lutz or William Beeman's nonconforming pieces are any indication, we may all be facing more difficulties ahead.

The overall issue that I think we need to think deeply about is the issue of desensitization. Desensitization is what occurred in Nazi Germany and allowed genocide to proceed unnoticed. Desensitization is trained into those fueling the various genocides in the contemporary scene. Genocide is not solely part of national fabrics and internal happenings in nations, it is also embedded in war. The total unconcern with the consequences of one-sided military action whether by the Unites States or its allies in Iraq, or the United States in Libya or Sudan, or the Israelis in Lebanon, or the "allied" forces in Afghanistan or by NATO in Libya in 2011 – is fed by silences that, at bottom, may be about deeply embedded racism about Arabs and Islamic countries more generally, a cultural racism in the guise of orientalism about which most anthropologists have had little to say, contrary to the enlightened positions they have taken elsewhere.

There cannot be serious knowledge about a region of the world where there are so many taboo subjects and myths. Think of them. Where in the anthropology of the Arab world do we write about the impact of Western economic interests on the Gulf, a region of strategic importance? Where do we write about relations between oil-supply nations and Western support of dictatorial regimes? Where are the studies of the myth that Israel is the only "democracy" in the Middle East, when it practices apartheid? One might think that a study of Israel's syphoning water and top soil from south Lebanon into Israel punctuated by sporadically bombing power stations in Beirut would make a contribution to the anthropology of imperialism. What anthropologist speaks to the fact that Israel is a military force of such technological power that it could wipe out the Arab world in one day? What anthropologist writes about normalized racism, about the double standard? It is possible to still say things about Islam that would be unacceptable if said of Christianity or Judaism, and we too often, and too easily, work within these strictures. One source on sanctions reports the loss of 4000 Iraqi children a month. Imagine the effect of a comparable loss of children's lives from the United States or Israel. How many anthropologists who document war zones elsewhere include the Arab world? Anthropologists, of all people, should be the most sensitive to being caught by cultural hegemonies. Our work suffers, and so do the people we study, and so does our country.

If one considers the cultural misinformation emanating about the Islamic world and between the Islamic world and the West, it is a cultural parallel to the biological misinformation the Nazis promulgated about Jews, gypsies, gays, handicapped people, and others. If biological misinformation is so horrific, why not make the same critique on the cultural front? And if anti-semitism is not acceptable, why not apply the same reasoning to anti-Arab Semitism, sometimes cloaked as Islamophobia (Ali *et al.*, 2011), which goes unnoticed as anti-Semitism? When the obvious is ignored, self-censored questions of policy can easily go awry. Surely we should have learned from Pierre Bourdieu's *Outline of a Theory of Practice* (1977) that what's not mentioned publicly may be consciously working to serve the interests of powerful groups. Prior to the Iraq war initiated by President George W. Bush, the silences were broken only by a few.

Mistakes Repeated in the Iraq Invasion

An anthropologist and a Vietnam veteran put it bluntly after the 2000 American elections: "We've lost all three branches of government – the judiciary when they selected the President, the Congress when they abdicated to the Executive Branch, the Executive Branch when they refused to listen to dissenting Americans."

The founding fathers of the United States placed war-making power in the hands of Congress where decisions could be openly debated. Yet a dozen unelected men and one woman make decisions that compromise the lives of American fighting forces, the lives of Iraqis, the future of American schools, health care, our relations with old allies. The costs of war are unfathomable. Senator Byrd's "we stand passively mute" speech objected to Congressional abdication (Byrd, 2003). Three branches of government are now one; objections by high-ranking military officers are muted – all of this justified by *unsubstantiated presuppositions* fed to the public *ad nauseam*: (i) that Iraq has weapons of mass destruction and that they are linked up with al Qaeda; (ii) that the rest of the world, including NATO allies, are wrong; (iii) that the Iraqis would welcome us as liberators – in spite of 12 years of sanctions and thousands of child deaths, in spite of daily bombing missions since 1991, in spite of an illegal invasion. Such prognostication is indicative of poor intelligence, an example of what happens when a president is isolated by a band of self-serving advisors. Silences and self-censorship dominate.

How little we know about the Arab world – do we really think there is no consequence of our *double standard foreign policy*? One for Saddam Hussein and one for Ariel Sharon – both brutal men responsible for the death and destruction of innocent civilians. Hussein gassed the Kurds, Sharon was responsible for the death of 17 000 Lebanese civilians before he got to Sabra and Shatilla, leaving aside his provocation of the present intifada – both were fed by arms from the United States. Double standard – the attack on the USS Cole by Muslim terrorists was rightly condemned, but the bombing of the USS Liberty in 1967 by Israeli war planes was covered up by the Pentagon (Ennes, 1979). American lives were lost in that Israeli bombing. Israel is the sole country in the region with weapons of mass destruction. The focus on Iran having nuclear capability clouds the need for nuclear disarmament worldwide.

I've taught about the peoples and cultures of the Arab world at the University of California, Berkeley since 1960. In teaching I have been struck by the depth of ignorance about this large expanse of the world and in my research I have noticed mirrored images. The Arab historians of the Crusades thought the Crusaders were barbaric savages, ignorant of medicine, without culture or civilization, although they had technology. Gandhi said the same about the British – brute force. In *Leap of Faith* (2003: 310) Queen Noor of Jordan quotes George Bush Sr. as saying to her husband, "I will not allow this little dictator [Saddam Hussein] to control 25% of the civilized world's oil." Of course the key words here are "the civilized world." By their very nature, fundamentalists of all stripes consider their doctrines to be the truest, superior to all others, who fall into the category of the uncivilized.

At the time of the first Gulf War, I was told by a distinguished Kuwaiti woman that the invasion of Kuwait was a family quarrel that should be settled by Arabs. Queen Noor tells us that King Hussein thought his peace effort was sabotaged; his mission was to avoid bringing Western troops into the region, which would trigger radical Islamists. Why didn't we let the King of Jordan deal with the problem? If we had a Senator Fulbright today, he would answer, "the arrogance of power." How is such arrogance expressed? In religious zeal – perhaps the Crusades have never ended; in militarism – the military-industrial complex that President Eisenhower warned about, independent of democratic decision-making; in racism – the need for weaponry to be tested on somebody; and finally the powerful impact of intertwining domestic fundamentalist Zionist ideology with American foreign policy, a position which, under the Truman administration, Secretary of Defense Forrestal passionately warned against as dangerous to the security of the United States.

Today we face the consequences of unilateral invasion of a sovereign country, which at the time of invasion posed no threat to the United States. It is, as my neighbor said, like taking a baseball bat to a bee's nest, playing free and easy with American lives. The double-talk is extraordinary. On the one hand, we are bringing democracy to Iraq, by means of war not democratically declared. As is common, democracy promoters ignore the traditions of those they seek to assist, and lack a grounded understanding of their own political democracy. Although it has been repeated *ad nauseam* that there is only one democracy in the Middle East, a recent study of Muslim and non-Muslim nations concluded that, while few citizens of Muslim states enjoy democratic rights, there is roughly equal respect for democratic principles in Muslim and Western societies. Representatives are amplified and coarsened by the mass media. The current US invasions of Afghanistan and then Iraq can only exacerbate the vicious circle of anti-American and anti-Muslim or Arab stereotyping.

There are times when events compel nations to bring their actions to the test of principles. At such times the truly patriotic citizen is forced to compare national ideals with immediate national purposes and policies. Decisions made at these crisis points determine the fate of the nation – whether it rises farther towards its ideals or moves away from them. Under the leadership of George W. Bush and Tony Blair, we moved to massive assaults in Iraq in the midst of civilian populations that eclipsed the bombing of Hanoi during the Vietnam War. The actions taken under the cover of the Patriot Act make the Palmer raids of the 1920s and the McCarthyite tragedies of the 1950s minor by comparison. A silver lining in all this is the worldwide objection to unilateral war. The worldwide peace movement is a movement for global survival. Democracy has made great strides – people want to decide the fate of the world, sometimes in direct opposition to their governments and against talk of nuclear strikes. As is often said, "governments make war, people make peace."

Before the Iraq war, the peace protests were our best citizen efforts at homeland security – not all Americans agree with the actions of their government. It is also true that peace protesters, often harassed, have been unsuccessful thus far in communicating with our own government. We need to be more *politic* on the international scene. There is nothing inevitable about the military-industrial complex. Even free marketeers should find compelling the comment of a Chinese observer of American imperialism: "In China we think buying oil is cheaper than going to war to steal it."

Before the 1990 Gulf War, the invasion of Afghanistan, and the wholesale invasion of Iraq in 2003, Iraq had a stable middle class, the largest in the Arab world, education and health care were almost universal, women had achieved in the professions and elsewhere. For a post-conflict Iraq, there is no culturally sensitive plan of the kind that General McArthur had before he entered Japan, where the first rule was "Do not humiliate the enemy."

Note

1 Earlier versions of this chapter come from essays published in *Anthropological Quarterly*, "Breaking the Silence – Politics and Professional Autonomy" appeared in December 2001, pp. 479–483, "Iraq and Democracy" Summer 2003, pp. 479–483, and the latter was part of UC Berkeley Chancellor's colloquium the week before the invasion of Iraq and aired on national television in the United States.

References

Ali, Wajahat, Eli Clifton, Matthew Duss, Lee Fang, Scott Keyes, and Faiz Shakir (2011) *Fear Inc.: The Roots of the Islamophobia Network in America*. Center for American Progress. Available at http://www.americanprogress.org/issues/2011/08/pdf/islamophobia.pdf (accessed April 16, 2012).

Bourdieu, Pierre (1977) *Outline of a Theory of Practice*. Cambridge: Cambridge University Press.

Beeman, William (1989) Anthropology and the Myths of American Foreign Policy. In *The Anthropology of War and Peace*. P. R. Turner and David Pitt, eds. South Hadley, MA: Bergin and Garvey Publisher, Inc.

Byrd, Robert (2003) We Stand Passively Mute. Extract from a speech to the US Senate on February 12. Available at http://www.guardian.co.uk/world/2003/feb/18/usa.iraq (accessed 25 April 2012).

Coon, Carleton (1951) *Caravan*. New York: Holt, Rinehart and Winston.

Coughlin, E. K. (1992) As Perceptions of the Palestinian People Change, Study of Their History and Society Grows. *The Chronicle of Higher Education*. Feb. 19, A8–9, A12.

Edwards, David (2002) Bin Laden's Last Stand. *Anthropological Quarterly*, 75, no. 1, pp. 179–186.

Ennes, James N. (1979) *Assault on the Liberty: The True Story of the Israeli Attack on an American Intelligence Ship*. New York: Random House.

Fernea, Elizabeth Warnock, and Robert A. Fernea (1997) *The Arab World: Forty Years of Change*. New York: Doubleday.

Findley, Paul (1985) *They Dare to Speak Out: People and Institutions Confront Israel's Lobby*. Westport, CT: Lawrence Hill and Company.

Findley, Paul (2001) *Silent No More: Confronting America's False Images of Islam*. Beltsville, MD: Amana Publications.

Finkelstein, Norman (2005) *Beyond Chutzpah: On the Misuse of Anti-Semitism and the Abuse of History*. Berkeley: University of California Press.

Ghani, Ashraf (2001) The Folly of Quick Action in Afghanistan. *Financial Times*, September 27.

Herman, Edward E. (1991) Mere Iraqis. *Lies of Our Times*, February, p. 5.

Mills, C. Wright (2008) *The Politics of Truth: Selected Writings of C. Wright Mills*, ed. John H. Summers. New York: Oxford University Press.

Mir-Hosseini, Z. (1991) RAI Public Seminar on the Cultural Aspects of the Gulf War. *Anthropology in Action*, Autumn.

Nashashibi, Selma, Laura Nader, and Etel Adnan (1994) *Forces of Change*. National Museum of Women in the Arts, Washington, DC.

Peteet, Julie (1991) *Gender in Crisis: Women and the Palestinian Resistance Movement*. New York: Columbia University Press.

Peteet, Julie (n.d.) Violence, Borders, and Crossings: The Potential for Recovery and Reconciliation. Unpublished manuscript.

Pollock, S. and Catherine Lutz (1994) Archaeology Deployed for the Gulf War. *Critique of Anthropology*, 14, no. 3, 263–284.

Queen Noor of Jordan (2003) *Leap of Faith: Memoirs of an Unexpected Life*. New York: Miramax Books.

Reynolds, Dwight (1991) Language, Translation, Culture, Conflict. *Prism*, IV, no. 3, pp. 18–21.

Strathern, Marilyn (ed.) (2000) *Audit Cultures – Anthropological Studies in Accountability, Ethics and the Academy*. London and New York: Routledge.

Swedenburg, Ted (1995) With Genet in the Palestinian Field. In *Fieldwork under Fire – Contemporary Studies of Violence and Survival*. C. Nordstrom and A.R. Robben, eds. Berkeley: University of California Press, pp. 25–60.

Wilcken, P. (1995) The Intellectuals, the Media and the Gulf War. *Critique of Anthropology*, 15, no. 1, 37–69.

Wolf, Eric (1999) Anthropology among the Powers. *Social Anthropology*, 7, no. 2, 121–134.

Young, William (1999) Anthropologists and the Problematic of Human Rights Activism in the Middle East. *Human Peace and Human Rights*, 12, no. 1, pp. 3–9.

Zolberg A. R., A. Suhrke, and S. Aguayo (1989) *Escape from Violence*. New York: Oxford University Press.

9

Lessons

We cannot continue accepting . . . Western civilization's claim to universality. Its universalization owes much to the argument of force rather than the force of argument. We have to rediscover other civilizations and weave together a new tapestry borrowing from different cultures and peoples.

(Shivji, 2003)

Lessons Learned

Lessons in culture and dignity stemming from each of the preceding chapters may perhaps seem obvious, no matter how interesting the specific content of each topic may have been. The collection of topics ranges from nineteenth-century travelers coming from the East to the West, to hegemonies in anthropological scholarship that effectively silence the observer, to disharmonic fundamentalisms, to the seeds of

Culture and Dignity: Dialogues between the Middle East and the West,
First Edition. Laura Nader.
© 2013 John Wiley & Sons, Inc. Published 2013 by John Wiley & Sons, Inc.

nonviolence that are found regionally from nomadic and settled to urban life in the Arab world. In this last chapter my challenge is to further explain how these seemingly disconnected settings interrelate in the present and how they may connect to human traditions that sustain us no matter where we come from.

The quote above is taken from an impassioned piece that Professor Issa Shivji wrote just after the USA invaded Iraq in 2003. In 2003 the "enlightened" were still acting like the barbarians of the past. How could that be? And is there any possibility of a planetary civilization that takes the best that humans have been capable of worldwide? The alternatives of empire and imperialism are unacceptable, given the ease with which those wielding military technologies can wipe out innocent peoples, devastate the environment, and destroy millennia of human achievements. We live in a time of unprecedented speed of change. But it is the demonstrated potential for technological destruction that creates a general unease. The chances that politicians might learn any lessons from the experiences of the ages, or even from contemporary observation, are probably minimal. The arrogance of power is blinding. But perhaps there are lessons that can at least show the way for those publics open to learning.

The travelers from the East opened windows as they shared a certain wonderment at first contact in the West. They came from a tradition of recording observations about the Other while at the same time looking in the mirror. Theirs is a tradition of explicit and forthright comparison. The early scholar-travelers did not withhold judgment, nor did they withhold praise. They wrote "we can learn from these others," but they did so with dignity and self-confidence in their own traditions. They had no sense of being subordinate, or underdeveloped in the contemporary usage of that term. For them, observations became true or false in relation to their impact on the world. They were pragmatists. They were not objective and detached. They searched for common points of reference and the possibilities for the co-existence of separate traditions. "Remember the precursor as well as the innovator" – lessons in culture and dignity involve both.

Anthropologists are also traveler-scholars, if more specialized than their precursors. The best anthropologists use both loose and strict thinking in their writings about encounters, originally first contact with native peoples. They, too, are recording their observations using ethnography, something that can be read as a theory of description. Anglo–American anthropologists are not monolithic, but only the most sensitive are doubters who critically engage as critics of Western exceptionalism. "We are all human," might be the simplest creed; it applies to the best who violate the unstated rules of their profession when rules cripple their abilities to understand. They, too, compare both implicitly and explicitly, shaking notions of a "primitive mentality" as they work. They explore the very nature of explanation, and take a global view. The idea that "we are all rational," challenges Euro–American notions of what constitutes rational behavior and accords dignity to those we study. These anthropologists challenge those who would divide the human species while under the delusion of "civilizing others."

The analysis of fundamentalisms covers a world characterized by multiple face-to-faceless contacts by means of global commercialisms. There are no longer first contacts. Three fundamentalisms are intertwined – corporate, evangelical, and Islamic; the first is a conflation of democracy with commercial markets, while the mosques and the churches desire tradition, stability, and dignity for families and children. The linkages are worldwide and parents feel powerless in the face of a commercialism that participates in the construction of childhood by means of values originating in the United States, one that equates common taste or mass consumption with a universal good – the manufacturing of a lifestyle in which family loyalties become brand loyalties. Under domino effects families are generation-gapped while a reverse response causes generations of parents and children to come together in politics as well as in religion. Some call this disharmonic Westernization.

Thus, although early discussion of the seeds of nonviolence in the Middle East must attend to culture, society, international media, and history, the seeds can be used as an antidote to stereotyping Arab Semites as violent. No world area is born violent or nonviolent.

Circumstances create possibilities. Hi-tech arms dealers make large-scale violence possible, while history and tradition (religious or other) make nonviolence possible, especially when violence results in repeated failure, when it is not an option (no arms), or when fear no longer controls a population. All this is uncovered as we examine the dynamics of violence and nonviolence.

In the Middle East there is a plethora of controls that limit violence, or at least its escalation: self-regulation, a law culture, honor and shame, mediation (*wasta*), a questioning of who stands to gain from violence or its opposite. Although these questions are not easy, it becomes clear that humiliation of an enemy is a bad idea in both the short and the long run. The Koran urges patience, but hurt to dignity, loss of civil rights eventually erupt in public view, and this is true through the ages. Some view the Arab Spring as a mass movement to restore dignity.

These lessons from centuries on the ground may go unnoticed and unused. So, is it possible to spread enlightenment by combating falsities? Can publics learn? One observation seems clear. When life is bounded and to some extent predictable, solutions are invented over time and used for group survival if for no other reason. The thought that solutions can be legislated to deal with the complexities and uncertainties of the contemporary world is probably naive in and of itself. But sometimes ideas spread incrementally, as with the spread of civil rights and democracy. And then there is the breaking point. The Arab Spring was a breaking point and as such not predictable as noted in Mondher Kilani's "What are 'Arab Revolutions' expressions of?" (Kilani, 2011).

Thus there is no rousing how-to-do-it conclusion to this book, only the optimism based on humans historically surviving because they sometimes learned survival. But now we are an entire planet learning to survive, and that is a challenge unlike any that came before. Worldwide we have been experiencing Occupy events, from Tahrir Square to Wall Street, expressing sentiments relating to planetary survival and transformation. Progress will take on new meanings requiring new strategies, to wit, strategies of subordination in reverse.

Strategies of Subordination – In Reverse

Anthropological texts are littered with strategies of subordination, traditionally part of the dominance strategy that Euro–Americans powers used in dealing with others. Most conspicuously, these strategies are associated with the concept of progress, a recent notion that first appeared with the early industrializations in Europe. People were, and still are, classified in social evolutionary categories. In spite of early twentieth-century Euro–American anthropological efforts to critique unilineal evolution, the profession has been complicit with the strategies of subordination that followed: *modernization*, implying that some people, although contemporary, were not modern; *underdeveloped* to describe those who did not fit the criteria of development; other terms like *ethnicity*, something that only some people possessed; or the use of hyphens – African-American, Mexican-American or Arab-American – when Anglo-American, French-American, or Israeli-American are rarely in common usage.

Such strategies of subordination were distilled by Western thinkers through the concept of lack (Nader, 2005). Some say that Islamic societies lack a law based on rationality – Weber's contribution, which is still used today to justify subordinating Iraqi peoples who "need" a more rational rule of law. The Chinese are said to lack a jurisprudence, if it can be said that they even have law at all. The concept of human rights presumably applies to non-Western cultures primarily, places where, for example, it is argued that Islamic women need our protection from their patriliny. And other terms are used by powerful economic institutions such as the World Bank to indicate subordinate positions, as in the classifications First World, Second World, Third World, and even Fourth World. Unilineal evolution is still with us.

I lived in a Connecticut mill town of hyphenated peoples – Italian-American, Polish-American, Irish-American, and Lebanese- or Syrian-American – as contrasted to those whose ancestors presumably came over on the Mayflower and who therefore had no "ethnicity." At any rate I felt impelled, though not self-consciously, to *subordinate in reverse* as early as 1969 in my work on "Up the Anthropologist," which appeared in Dell Hymes's volume *Reinventing Anthropology* (1969). Calling for anthropology to study up, down, and sideways – to include banks that redline in our study of poor Americans who live in ghettos, to include the colonizers when writing ethnographies of African peoples, to study elites along with the poor, the down-trodden, and the colonized, in order to create a more adequate, maybe even a more scientific anthropology. For how could one understand Africa, for example, without understanding colonialism and its continuance in an era of supposed post-coloniality? The British still own the diamond mines in Sierra Leone. Iraq's oil is up to the foreign bidders who think they know best what to do with this precious resource, and some Iraqi leaders want these companies as well.

Following the civil rights movement in the United States we were inundated by difference or by the *diversity* movements. Teachers of diversity sprang from nowhere and seem to have difficulty acknowl-edging the proposition that any differences may be superficial com-pared with an appreciation of what all humans have in common. The subordination of race gets reified and perpetuated by means of expertise deeply invested in social and cultural engineering, and deeply invested in difference as a "problem." One might ask: When is difference an issue at all? When Americans do not have access to the voting booth? When is bridging equality and difference a major preoccupation? And when is it not?

Emphasizing difference to facilitate exclusion has long operated as a feature of colonial control and domination. The ideology of deriving homogeneity out of diversity underlies the cultural engi-neering of minorities in the United States and risks the emergence of something akin to cultural fascism! For example, ideologies of homogeneity ensure that we all drink Coke and have similar con-sumerist tastes. The question is, who benefits from difference or homogeneity? And where does co-existence or mutual respect appear? Europeans are terrified by Islamic immigrants and the habits and religion they bring with them. Were Egyptians terrified that Alexandria was being overrun by Europeans, traders? We need to relocate our questions in history. In 1996 *Naked Science:*

Anthropological Inquiries into Boundaries, Power, and Knowledge (Nader, 1996) appeared. It was partly about the consequences of having one science tradition subordinating other science traditions. Even in Europe there are multiple science traditions. We were revealing why science in the plural is something important to cherish.

The national security state has been and is attentive to uses that may be made of anthropology. My essay "The Phantom Factor: Impact of the Cold War on Anthropology" (Nader, 1997) and anthropologists such as David Price have made good use of the Freedom of Information Act to enlarge our scope about *Anthropological Intelligence* (2008) in the service of power. As regards constructing the Middle East, anthropologists' participation is not new, but has been increasing since the early twentieth century. After World War II, Franklin Delano Roosevelt called in Middle Eastern archaeologist Henry Field. He wanted to know where the unpopulated areas were in the Middle East. The Euro–Americans have always known how to make use of "empty places," and Roosevelt was no exception at a time when oil deposits were seen as a crucial resource, and relocating World War II refugees as a Western foothold was at issue. The discovery of, and growing appetite for, oil has from the beginning functioned to destabilize parts of the Middle East and Africa, and sparsely populated areas in North America.

For every anthropologist who is open for hire (as in the Human Terrain Project, initiated under the presidency of George W. Bush), there are those who concern themselves with issues of collective well-being and contemporary debates over the militarization of anthropology (Gonzalez, 2009). Mostly, however, people are apathetic, anthropologists included. Margaret Mead would remark that it only takes a few people to change the world – and if we don't believe that, first look at the past ten years before and after George W. Bush's Washington, DC, and the impact of neoliberalism in the service of empire.

One of these days we might have book fairs featuring good public anthropology. I'd be sure to include *Swimming up the Tigris* (2007) by Barbara Nimri Aziz, an anthropologist/journalist who documents the genocidal impact of 12 years of economic sanctions by the United

States, the United Kingdom, and the United Nations during the period *prior* to the 2003 invasion of Iraq – a loss estimated at 1.5 million people, while we looked the other way. Good researchers do not simply look at communities in distress; they indicate how they came to be distressed, linking the local with national transformations (Doukas, 2003; Scheper-Hughes and Wacquant, 2003).

Strategies of subordination in reverse, to complete the picture, are the opposite of studies that focus on victims and differ from social welfare approaches. Rather, strategies of subordination in reverse link their subjects to larger processes of change. That's what anthropologists are good at – looking at *Homo sapiens* over thousands of years, and, after enough surplus was developed to have centralized-states, seeing where the human animal may be heading. Maybe we can gain some perspective from history.

Mirza Abu Taleb Khan (1814) went to England from India in the eighteenth century, and Al-Jabarti (1798), the greatest of Arab historians, wrote about Napoleon in Egypt, Napoleon who preached freedom and liberty while practicing the opposite. These elites traveled when the East *was* the World, before Western notions of superiority took hold, and they have a good deal to teach us about ourselves, both good and bad. Their critiques were not unidirectional. After discussing the punitive "terrors" of the British legal system in India, Abu Taleb draws a comparison with Calcutta courts by invoking familiar Indian procedures in which witnesses accused of being liars are sent home without remuneration. He looked in the mirror. His critique is ultimately constructive: he suggests that lawyers, like judges, be paid by public funds in order to eliminate any incentive for financially interested delays. In addition to his critique of English legal liberties, he draws comparisons between the liberties of Indian and British women in an attempt to vindicate perceptions of Asian women. Not only does he refute notions of an oppressed Asiatic (elite) woman, he proposes a bolder claim – that she actually has more liberties compared to European women: she has separate quarters, which she can run without interference from her menfolk.

Similarly, in discussions about energy, unscientific beliefs are prevalent among some energy scientists, politicians, and economists:

nuclear is "too cheap to meter," change means maintaining the *status quo*, progress is equal to growth, GNP is equal to increased human welfare, energy growth means more economic growth, more energy expenditure does not change lifestyle while less does, technical fixes can solve human problems and forestall crises, solving a problem on paper is equal to solving one in real life, numbers are real, the future can be planned, conservation and efficiency are oppressive, bigger is better – grow or die (Nader, 2010). These are just a few beliefs, for starters. There is data to disprove almost all such beliefs, which are guiding us into wars over resources and unnecessary health tragedies. How few scientists and medical doctors there are who recognize the illusions and delusions built into their paradigms!

Plunder: When the Rule of Law is Illegal (Mattei and Nader, 2008) is a synthesis of 500 years of Euro–American expansion and the illusions and delusions associated with Euro–American colonialism. Ugo Mattei and I wanted to document the use of rule of law ideology in imperial adventures from the time that Columbus took a notary, Rodrigo Escobeda, along on the Santa Maria when he came to the New World.

John Locke in England (1698) and Emerich de Vattel in Switzerland (1797) articulated plunder by means of law: "As much land as man tills, plants, improves, cultivates and can use" and the idea of "terra nullius" – empty lands (Mattei and Nader, 2008: 67) that then can be allocated to the powers that be. In 2003 President Bush sent Paul Bremer to Iraq on the pretext of taking rule of law to a place that presumably had none because it was a dictatorship. Bremer printed 100 edicts to justify the plunder of Iraq. Bremer, as head of the then Coalition Provisional Authority, gave preference to US corporations (Mattei and Nader, 2008: 118), a recipe for plunder at least 500 years old, and extended Saddam's ban on trade union organizing. Order no. 39 allowed for the corporatization of Iraq's 200 state-owned enterprises, allowing 100% foreign ownership of Iraqi business, "national treatment" of foreign firms, unrestricted tax-free remittance of all profits and other funds, and 40-year ownership licenses. Order no. 17 granted foreign contractors full immunity from Iraq's laws. In everyday terms, the Bremer orders deny Iraq the ability to give preference to Iraqi companies or employees in reconstruction. Foreign products are allowed to flood the Iraqi market, forcing local producers out of business. US Executive Order no. 13303 of May 2003 also granted blanket immunity to US corporations that gain possession or control of Iraqi oil or products. Bremer's Orders were illegal according to international law, under which an occupying nation cannot transform a defeated society into its own likeness. It is yet to be seen whether these orders have a lasting effect.

Rule of law has a long pedigree of being portrayed as a "good thing." As part of a strategy focused on the public good, it is crucial to interrupt the use of rule of law as a vague-enough notion to fit the needs of every side of the political spectrum as an icon, a raison d'être – when occupying Iraq, or any other country, for example. The rule of law should be considered illegal when it is used as a key tenet in American discourse on foreign policy – a major part of the "white man's burden" – that is, when it is used to justify imperialism whether in Iraq or elsewhere. The rule of law can be deemed illegal when it is applied criminally, arbitrarily, and capriciously, victimizing weaker subjects, or where it violates the spirit and the letter of treaties such as the Geneva Convention, aimed at limiting war related to plunder, or when those in power purposefully and systematically do not enforce the law or enforce it based on double standards or discrimination. Subordination in reverse does not allow violations to hide behind rule of law ideologies. It also reflects on what naming means in relation to geographic areas. It was Alfred Thayer Mahan, a leading proponent of American naval power, who in 1907 named the "Middle East," a term that was adopted and continues in use, not without controversy, as in the middle of what and east of where (Koppes, 1976).

Macro-histories

The essays collected here are an outline of new and old connections between the past and the present, between geographic areas, between individual ethnographers, their professions, and the wider public. We need more work that is connective in a worldly manner.

For example, water is a substance needed by all living species. When examining international river disputes critically, it is not possible to think creatively in a bounded manner (Nader, 1995). The Danube River Basin is international, crossing eight countries. Similarly the Jordan River crosses borders. The Dan River originates in pre-1967 Israel and discharges into the upper Jordan; the Hasbani River, originates in south Lebanon and discharges into the upper Jordan; the Banias River, which originates in the Syrian Golan Heights, discharges into the upper Jordan; the Yarmouk river forms the border between Syria and Jordan and discharges into the lower Jordan. Understanding water knows no borders.

To unleash the anthropological imagination, a broader compass must *simultaneously* include history, ethnography, and comparison. If Saddam Hussein modernized Iraqi educational institutions, the Iraq war "de-modernized" Iraqi universities, and targeted professors and scholars. We might ask what the fate of American universities was during the period – further militarization (Gusterson, 2011)? If under Saddam Hussein's dictatorship Iraqi women were liberated, why under Western intervention are Iraqi women increasingly wearing the "hijab" for public dress? And are such happenings related to the increasingly high rape rate and unresolved problems for women in the American military? Juxtaposing such observations liberates the imagination. We begin to make connections that may stimulate an examination of competition between two patriarchies – Arab and American.

Margaret Mead used cross-cultural juxtaposition of Samoan and American patterns of adolescence as defamiliarization, a technique that forced Americans to "see" the familiar. Placing the familiar in unfamiliar contexts enables the reader to contemplate consequences or alternative possibilities. Observing Tahrir Square and Wall Street occupiers brings to the foreground not only the defiance of the young, but an awareness of a generation who upon completion of their education see no future. The ultimate failure is that of the imagination. Markets are not people, yet we are told markets do this or that. Corporations also "act" and are allocated personal rights in the United States, but are not human beings. Governments say one thing and do another. The defiant may be seeing what the entrenched generation is refusing to see – the need for reality testing.

Although anthropology traditionally focused attention on the exotic, with the contemporary technologies of the internet and television nothing might be considered strange anymore. Yet the composition of the world today is indeed strange – even bizarre. Nothing like this has ever been known in human history. Thus the present may look quite different through the prism of the *longue durée*, offering new insights that might be too close to notice. There is a difference between word and deed, democracy and democratic practice, progress as ideal for human happiness and a definition of progress that leads to underdevelopment or "de-modernization." The moral imperative in scholarship means a reassessment of who we are, where we have been, and where we are heading – an integrative macro-history with purpose.

Macro-history means we can use knowledge of culture and environment to learn something of value to ourselves. The Middle East probably has the longest recorded history of any geographic area – it is a place where cereals were first domesticated, and has a history of progressively deteriorating environment. Out of the world's 15 most water-scarce countries, 12 are in the Middle East (Ahmed, 2011). How have people learned to cope over the centuries? How did they adjust to soil erosion, deforestation, lowered water registers? Having the first cities accompanied by specialization and centralization, how did they manage inequalities? Natives tell us that urban inequalities were mitigated by levelers, as with the urban use of veiling, or in places like the Sudan, the ubiquitous wearing of all-white garments by rich and poor. There were rules against boastful behavior, rules embedded in evil-eye beliefs. Peace between religious groups nourished philosophies of co-existence. Automatic controls such as shame may be survival techniques. In other words, collective attempts emerge to deal with collective problems. All peoples can benefit from the study of others, especially as all peoples address planetary problems of climate change, violence, wars over resources, population displacements. There is no Us and Them in the long run.

References

Ahmed, Nafeez Mosaddeq (2011) Freedom Will Not Chase Away the Arab World's Triple Crisis. *Beirut Daily Star*, February 19. Available at http://www.dailystar.com.lb/Opinion/Commentary/Feb/19/Freedom-will-not-chase-away-the-Arab-worlds-triple-crisis.ashx#axzz1stlaWmk2 (accessed April 23, 2012).

Aziz, Barbara Nimri (2007) *Swimming Up the Tigris: Real Life Encounters with Iraq*. Gainesville: University of Florida Press.

Doukas, Dimitra (2003) *Worked Over: The Corporate Sabotage of an American Community*. Ithaca, NY: Cornell University Press.

Gonzalez, Roberto (2009) *American Counterinsurgency: Human Science and the Human Terrain*. Chicago: Prickly Paradigm Press.

Gusterson, Hugh (2011) Universities and the Costs of the Iraq War. *The Brussels Tribunal*. Available at http://www.brussellstribunal.org/University_At_War.htm (accessed April 17, 2012).

Khan, Mirza Abu Taleb (2008 [1814]) *The Travels of Mirza Abu Taleb Khan*. Ontario, Canada: Broadview Press.

Kilani, Mondher (2011) What are "Arab Revolutions" Expressions Of? An Anthropological Perspective. Unpublished paper presented at American Anthropological Association Annual Meeting, Montreal, November 19, 2011.

Koppes, Clayton R. (1976) Captain Mahan, General Gordon, and the Origins of the Term "Middle East." *Middle Eastern Studies*, 12, January, pp. 95–98.

Mattei, Ugo and Laura Nader (2008) *Plunder: When the Rule of Law is Illegal*. New York: Blackwell.

Nader, Laura (1969) Up the Anthropologist: Perspectives Gained from Studying Up. In *Reinventing Anthropology*. Dell Hymes, ed. New York: Pantheon Books, pp. 284–311.

Nader, Laura (1996) *Naked Science: Anthropological Inquiry into Boundaries, Power, and Knowledge*. New York: Routledge.

Nader, Laura (1997) The Phantom Factor: Impact of the Cold War on Anthropology. In *The Cold War and the University*. Noam Chomsky, ed. New York: New Press, pp. 107–146.

Nader, Laura (2005) Law and the Theory of Lack. *Hastings International and Comparative Law Review*, 28, no. 2, pp. 191–204.

Nader, Laura (2010) *The Energy Reader*. Oxford: Wiley-Blackwell.

Price, David (2008) *Anthropological Intelligence: The Deployment and Neglect of American Anthropology in the Second World War*. Durham: Duke University Press.

Scheper-Hughes, Nancy and Loic Wacquant (2003) *Commodifying Bodies*. London: Sage.

Shivji, Issa G. (2003) Law's Empire and Empire's Lawlessness: Beyond Anglo-American Law, *Journal of Law, Social Justice and Global Development*, no. 1. Available at http://elj.warwick.ac.uk/global/issue/2003-1/shivji .html (accessed April 17, 2012).

Appendix

Laura Nader
*Selected Publications Relating
to the Middle East*

1962 A Note on Attitudes and the Use of Language. *Anthropological Linguistics*, 4, no. 6, pp. 24–25. (Reprinted in *Readings in the Sociology of Language*, Joshua A. Fishman, ed. The Hague: Mouton 1968).

1965 Choices in Legal Procedure: Shia Moslem and Mexican Zapotec. *American Anthropologist*, 67, no. 2, pp. 394–399. (Reprinted in *The Social Organization of Law*, Donald Black and Maureen Mileski eds. New York: Seminar Press, 1973).

1965 Communication between Village and City in the Modern Middle East. *Human Organization, Special Issue: Dimensions of Cultural Change in the Middle East*, John Gulick, ed., pp. 18–24. (Reprinted, Institute for International Studies, Berkeley).

1967 Review of *Turkistan*, by Eugene Schuyler. *Science*, 156, no. 3776, pp. 791–792.

1970 From Anguish to Exultation in Mexico and Lebanon. In *Women in the Field*, P. Golde, ed. Chicago: Aldine Press, pp. 96–116.

Culture and Dignity: Dialogues between the Middle East and the West,
First Edition. Laura Nader.
© 2013 John Wiley & Sons, Inc. Published 2013 by John Wiley & Sons, Inc.

1971 Review of *Bedouin Justice*, by Austin Kennett, *American Anthropologist*, 73, no. 7, p. 349.

1972 Some notes on John Burton's Papers on "Resolution of Conflict." *International Studies Quarterly*, 16, no. 7, pp. 53–58. Reprinted in *The Theory and Practice of International Relations*, S. McLellan, William C. Olson, and Fred Sonderman, eds. Englewood Cliffs, NJ: Prentice-Hall, 1974.

1976 (with E. Combs-Schilling) Restitution in Cross-Cultural Perspective. In *Restitution in Criminal Justice, First International Symposium on Restitution*, Joe Hudson, ed., Minnesota Department of Corrections. (Reprinted in *Restitution in Criminal Justice*, Joe Hudson and Burt Galaway, eds. Lexington, MA: Heath Publishing Co., pp. 27–44.)

1976 (with Samuel Huntington, Mustafa Safwa, and Edward Said. Moderated by Edward Stewart.) "Can Cultures Communicate?" An AEI Round Table held on September 23. American Enterprise Institute for Public Policy Research, Washington, DC.

1979 Review of *Wasita in a Lebanese Context: Social Exchange among Villagers and Outsiders*, by Frederick Charles Huxley. *The Middle East Journal*, 33, no. 4, pp. 511–512.

1980 Review of *Changing Veils – Women and Modernization in North Yemen*, by Carla Makhlouf. *The Middle East Journal*, 34, no. 3, p. 511.

1983 A Comparative Perspective on Legal Evolution, Revolution, and Devolution. *Michigan Law Review*, 81, no. 4, pp. 993–1005.

1985 Review of *Aesthetics and Ritual in the United Arab Emirates: the Anthropology of Food and Personal Adornment among Arabian Women*, by Aida Sami Kanafani. *The Middle East Journal*, 39, no. 2, pp. 386–387.

1985 Property, Power and Law in Middle Eastern Societies. In *Property, Social Structure and Law in the Middle East*. A. Mayer, ed. Albany: State University of New York Press, pp. 1–24.

1985 Review of *Recognizing Islam – Religion and Society in the Modern Arab World*, by Michael Gilsenan. *International Journal of the Middle East*, 17, no. 4, pp. 391–393.

1987   The Subordination of Women in Comparative Perspective. In special issue *Women in the Americas: Relationships, Work and Power*, A.S. Barnes, ed. *Urban Anthropology*, 15, no. 3–4, pp. 377–397.

1988   Review of *Women without Men: Gender and Marginality in an Algerian Town* by Willy Jansen. *Middle East Journal*, 42, no. 2, pp. 329–30.

1988   Review of *The Persistence of Patriarchy: Class, Gender and Ideology in Twentieth Century Algeria* by Peter R. Knauss. *Middle East Journal*, 42, no. 3, pp. 519–520.

1989   Orientalism, Occidentalism and the Control of Women. *Cultural Dynamics*, II, 3, pp. 323–355. (Reprinted and translated as "Orientalisme, occidentalisme et contrôle des femmes." *Nouvelles Questions Feministes – Revue internationale francophone* op. 25, no. 1/2006, pp. 12–24.

1990   Review of *Muslim Preacher in the Modern World: A Jordanian Case Study in Comparative Perspective*, by Richard T. Antoun. *The Middle East Journal*, 44, no. 1, pp. 153–54.

1993   Review of *Gender in Crisis: Women and the Palestinian Movement* by M. Peteet. *American Ethnologist*, 20, no. 3, pp. 640–641.

1994   Arab Women Artists. In *Forces of Change – Artists of the Arab World*. Salwa Nashashibi, Laura Nader, and Etel Adnan, eds. Washington, DC: The National Museum of Women in the Arts, pp. 1–36.

1995   Civilization and Its Negotiators. In *Understanding Disputes: The Politics of Law*. Pat Kaplan, ed. Oxford: Berg Publishers, pp. 39–63.

1996   Review essay (with M. Ferme) on *Transplants, Innovation and Legal Tradition in the Horn of Africa*, E. Grande, ed. *American Journal of Comparative Law*, 45, December, pp. 209–213.

1998   Review of *Women of Lebanon – Interviews with Champions for Peace* by Nelda LaTeef. *Middle East Journal*, 52, no. 2, pp. 291–292.

1999   In a Woman's Looking Glass – Normative Blindness and Unresolved Human Rights Issues. Portuguese title: Em um espelho de mulher: cegieira normativa e questioes nâs – resolvidas de direitos humanos. *Horizontes Antropológicos*, no. 10, pp. 61–82. Special Issue on Cidadania e Diversidade Cultural.

2001 Breaking the Silence – Politics and Professional Autonomy. *Anthropological Quarterly* (Special Section: Social Thought and Commentary), 75, no. 1, pp. 161–169.

2003 Iraq and Democracy. *Anthropological Quarterly*, 76, no. 3, pp. 479–483.

2006 Naturalizing Difference and Models of Co-existence. In *Racism in Metropolitan Areas*. R. Pinxten and E. Preckler, eds. New York: Berghahn Publishers, pp. 173–182.

2006 Orientalisme, Occidentalisme et contrôle des femmes. In Revue internationale francophone du sexisme et racisme: le cas francais. *Nouvelles Questions Feministes* 25, no. 1, pp. 12–24.

2008 Review of *An Invitation to Laughter: A Lebanese Anthropologist in the Arab World* by Fuad I. Khouri. *American Anthropologist*, 110, no. 4, pp. 262–263.

2009 What the Rest Think of the West – Legal Dimensions. *Hastings International and Comparative Law Review*, 32. no. 2, pp. 765–777. Also available at *Global Jurist*: vol. 9. ISS.1 (Advances) Article 3, http://www.degruyter.com/view/j/ gj.2009.9.1/gj.2009.9.1.1289/gj.2009.9.1.1289.xml.

2009 Law and the Frontiers of Illegalities. In *Law, Power, and Control*, A. Griffiths, K and F. von Benda-Beckmann, eds. New York: Berghahn Press. pp. 54–73.

2010 Side by Side – The Other is Not Mute. In *Edward Said: A Legacy of Emancipation and Representation*. A. Iskander and H. Ruston, eds. Berkeley: University of California Press, pp. 72–86.

2012 Rethinking Salvation Mentality and Counter-Terrorism. Paper published in the volume *Ten Years after 9/11: Rethinking Counterterrorism. Transnational Law and Contemporary Problems*, Spring.

Index

Culture and Dignity: Dialogues between the Middle East and the West,
First Edition. Laura Nader.
© 2013 John Wiley & Sons, Inc. Published 2013 by John Wiley & Sons, Inc.